Immigrants and Poverty

ECPR Press

ECPR Press is an imprint of the European Consortium for Political Research. It publishes original research from leading political scientists and the best among early career researchers in the discipline. Its scope extends to all fields of political science, international relations and political thought, without restriction in either approach or regional focus. It is also open to interdisciplinary work with a predominant political dimension.

Immigrants and Poverty

The Role of Labour Market and Welfare State Access

Beatrice Eugster

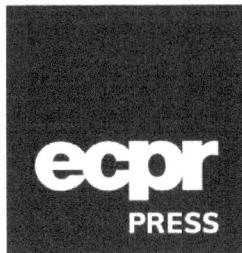

ecpr PRESS

Published by the European Consortium for Political Research, Harbour House, 6–8 Hythe Quay, Colchester, CO2 8JF, United Kingdom

British Library Cataloguing in Publication Data
A catalogue record for this book is available from the British Library

ISBN: HB 978-1-78552-293-2
ISBN: PB 978-1-78661-315-8

Library of Congress Cataloging-in-Publication Data

ISBN 978-1-78552-293-2 (cloth)
ISBN 978-1-78661-315-8 (paperback) ISBN
978-1-78552-294-9 (electronic)

ecpr.eu/shop

Contents

List of Figures and Tables

FIGURES

TABLES

APPENDIX

Tables

Figure

Acknowledgements

Without the support and encouragement of numerous people, I would have never finished this book, which is based on my dissertation thesis. My warmest thanks go to my friends Hanna Schwander and Oliver Strijbis, who unwittingly built the foundations of this book; Valeria Camia, Christine Scheidegger, Peter Platzgummer, Michael Bechtel, Patrick Emmenegger and my colleagues at the University of St. Gallen for time, ideas and motivation during my PhD; and Dominik Geering, Flavia Fossati, Nadja Mosimann, Bruno Wüest, Lena Zollinger, Daniel Oesch, Julian Garitzmann, Maureen Eger and other participants at conferences for helping me to bring my ideas and previous versions forward. I would also like to thank the two anonymous reviewers, Laura Sudulich from ECPR, and Dhara Snowden and her colleagues from Rowman & Littlefield International (RLI). Special thanks go to Jean-Paul, my piano-playing neighbour, who inspired me while writing down my thoughts, Jasmin and Gerhard Kerscher for the weekly indispensable distraction, my friend Neela Mühlemann for all the memorable coffee talks, my beloved parents and sister for their encouragement and being who they are, and Thomas Schneider for his incredible patience, infinite support and a sympathetic ear for my doubts and crude thoughts.

Furthermore, I greatly value the motivation, assistance and time that Silke Adam provided me with to finish this book. My gratitude also goes to Daniele Caramani for his experience and friendship, to Jonas Pontusson for his ideas and critical remarks and, last but not least, to Silja Häusermann who encouraged me from the beginning by challenging my work and providing invaluable ideas and comments at many times during the formation of this book.

Introduction

The European refugee crisis that started in the summer of 2015 has brought the issue of how refugees can be integrated into society to the forefront of public discourse. Even if immigration and ethnic diversity have become important characteristics of advanced industrialised countries over the past decades, the debate on how to integrate immigrants into society has continued to accelerate. At a time in which inequality has been rising in a majority of advanced industrialised countries, this debate has intensified (Atkinson 2015; OECD 2015a). This book explores the socio-economic integration of immigrants: first, in terms of *social rights of immigrants*, that is, what nation states do for immigrants; and, second, in terms of *poverty of immigrants* as socio-economic outcomes, that is, how these immigrants fare. In other words, the focus of this book is on how post-industrialised countries differ in granting welfare access to immigrants and whether, and if so how, these social rights influence marginalised immigrants living in those countries.

Although those questions centre upon the perspective of immigrants, the ability of receiving countries to integrate immigrants is relevant not only for immigrant minorities but also for the native majority. Through redistribution, nation states not only reduce poverty but also compensate for socio-economic disparities between different segments in the population. Since being introduced with the formation of the nation state (Wimmer 1998), the social welfare system has been built on the principles of democracy and thus equality among its citizens. It essentially relies on the ideal of enabling any citizen and member of the community a civilised life according to the prevailing standards in a society (Marshall 1950). Welfare efforts and public expectation that welfare states can deliver this ideal are what shape public attitudes towards redistribution and poverty and, in turn, create and foster the social solidarity needed to preserve a welfare system.

However, the viability of welfare states depends on not only public support but also public funds. Both can be linked to the 'liberal paradox' of immigration that nation states face (Hollifield 2004). In the context of austerity, welfare states have been confronted with various challenges such as retrenchment resulting from sluggish economic growth and population ageing accompanied by declining birth rates. The shrinking workforce and shortage of high-skilled personnel, in particular, have driven economic interests and demand in the labour market for additional foreign manpower, and thus for liberal labour migration. At the same time, other political forces have been pushing for stricter control of migration. These voices represent not only economic concerns of globalisation losers fearing the consequences of international competition regarding their job prospects (see Kriesi et al. 2006) but also worries related to security and their own culture. Immigration and ethnic diversity are seen as blurring a country's national identity by reducing the differences vis-à-vis other nations. As soon as the community, or part thereof, views its distinguishing markers, such as traditions and values, as endangered, this might give rise to political backlash. The emerging discontent with immigration is already visible in the rise of populist parties and media coverage.

One recurrent topic in public discourse is the framing of immigrants, primarily asylum seekers as welfare abusers who, in public perception, are considered to be less deserving when compared to other social groups in need (e.g. elderly, sick and disabled or unemployed persons; see Van Oorschot 2006). The related and resulting political demand to restrict welfare services to the native community, known in the welfare attitude literature as 'welfare chauvinism' (Andersen and Bjørklund 1990, 212), deals at its core with the social rights of immigrants. Accordingly, immigrants' full access to welfare benefits creates political resistance because immigrants are seen as illegitimate benefit receivers as they neither belong to the national community nor have they contributed to the welfare system (see also Kitschelt and McGann 1997, 22). But welfare attitudes among others not only depend on whether foreigners are perceived as legitimate welfare receivers. They also depend on how foreigners are treated, equally as citizens or as a distinct social group, and how they are doing in the host society in economic, social and cultural terms (e.g. Burgoon 2014). Therefore, the ability of receiving countries to integrate immigrant minorities has consequences for not only immigrants but also the native population (see also Myles and St-Arnaud 2006). Concerning the salience of immigration in Europe and North America, it is therefore important to understand whether and to what extent nation states reduce immigrants' poverty.

The empirical evidence so far indicates that differences between immigrants and non-immigrants in socio-economic outcomes prevail in advanced industrialised countries. Immigrants have a higher tendency to be unemployed or to earn lower wages compared to their native counterparts, even after controlling for individual characteristics such as country of origin, year of arrival and human capital (e.g. Van Tubergen, Maas and Flap 2004; Kesler 2006; Kahanec and Zaiceva 2009; Koopmans 2010; OECD 2015b). This is also the case when poverty rates of immigrants and non-immigrants are compared.

As evident in figure 0.1, immigrants' poverty is higher than that of non-immigrants across the countries (see also Morissens and Sainsbury 2005; Sainsbury 2012; Corrigan 2014; Kesler 2015).[1] In the majority of the countries, immigrants' poverty levels are twice as high as that of non-immigrants (below dotted line). In addition, cross-national variations in poverty differences between immigrants and non-immigrants can be observed. They are less pronounced in countries such as Australia, the Netherlands and Ireland, which are close to the solid line that represents countries where immigrants and non-immigrants have similar poverty levels. By contrast, the differences are considerably higher in countries such as Belgium, Denmark and France, where immigrants' poverty rates are more than four times as high. Finally, figure 0.1 further reveals that the classical welfare regime approach, which distinguishes different 'types' or 'regimes' or 'families' of welfare states (for

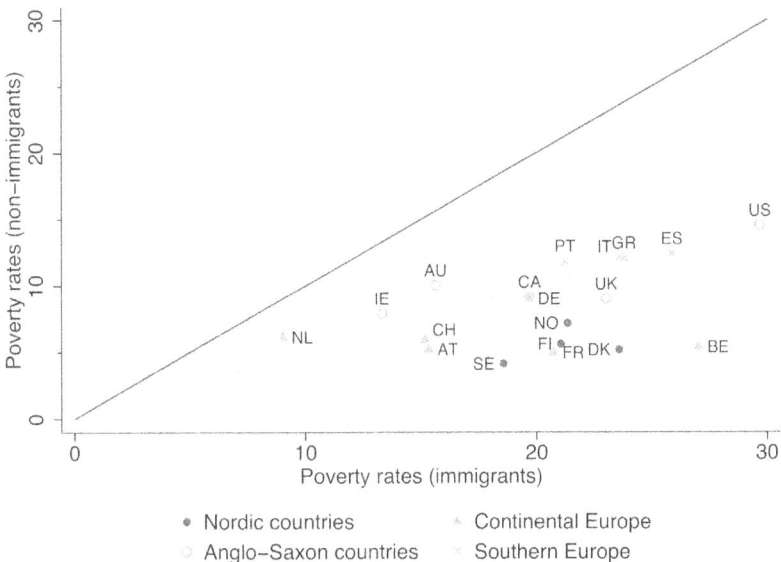

Figure 0.1 **Poverty rates of immigrants and non-immigrants based on disposable income (50 per cent of median income).** *Source*: **EU-SILC (European countries), HILDA (Australia), SLID (Canada) and CPS (United States).**

a summary, see Arts and Gelissen 2010) and is traditionally used to explain cross-national variations in poverty rates, falls short of explaining cross-national variations in immigrants' poverty rates. For example, in Anglo-Saxon countries characterised by means-tested programmes, immigrants' poverty rates are much higher in the United States (around 30 per cent) compared to Ireland and Australia (around 15 per cent). But intra-regime variations can also be observed in Continental European welfare states with mainly earnings-related social programmes, namely lower immigrant poverty levels in the Netherlands versus Belgium (9 per cent and 27 per cent). Summing up, the results show that traditional comparative welfare approaches fall short of explaining immigrants' poverty and thus have to be complemented by taking insights from the migration and citizenship field into account.

The main goal of this book is to explain this cross-national variation in immigrants' poverty. In order to do so, this book focuses on *social rights of citizenship*, understood broadly as access to social benefits and paid employment. A central assumption is that immigrants are not a homogenous group. Instead, different categories of immigration can be distinguished (e.g. labour migration and family reunification). The analytical framework proposed in this book embeds immigrants' social rights, on the one hand, in a country's prevailing *labour market and welfare system* – the major determinant of poverty – and, on the other hand, in the *immigration policies* regulating the admission, control and selection of immigrants into the country and thus the immigration category foreigners are given. In sum, this book aims to answer three research questions: What do poverty patterns of immigrants look like, across countries and compared to non-immigrants? How do nation states integrate immigrants, that is, how inclusive are social rights towards immigrants and how are they related to immigration policies and the labour market and welfare system? How do they jointly affect immigrants' poverty?

OUTLINE OF THE ARGUMENT

In brief, the argument is that immigrants' varying social rights condition the impact of a country's labour market and welfare system on immigrants' poverty. The comparative welfare state literature, which finds the welfare state to be the major determinant of poverty (for a detailed literature review, see Brady 2009), is used as a starting point for the framework. Indeed, the reduction of inequality and poverty has been one of the main goals that have driven the emergence of the welfare state.

A central characteristic of the welfare state is social rights that, in turn, give citizens access to social programmes. Therefore, more or less generous social policies targeting the unemployed, families and the poor welfare states directly affect poverty. In addition, welfare states can have an effect on employment chances and earnings through the labour market, and thus diminish individuals' poverty risks (Esping-Andersen 1990; Huber and Stephens 2001; Moller et al. 2003; Andress and Lohman 2008; Brady 2009). Wage-setting institutions and minimum wage laws ensure that decent wages are paid and thus influence poverty indirectly.

Whether the labour market and welfare system also affect immigrants' poverty depends on whether immigrants – in various immigration categories – are granted access to social programmes and paid employment. One major drawback of the comparative welfare state literature is that it has so far paid little attention to immigrants (but see Sainsbury 2006, 2012 and the welfare chauvinism literature). Moreover, it implicitly assumes that citizens and immigrants enjoy the same social rights regarding access to the labour market and social programmes, especially in studies explaining immigrant poverty (e.g. Hooijer and Picot 2015; Kesler 2015).

Indeed, immigrants' and citizens' social rights differ as the migration literature suggests (e.g. Brubaker 1989; Soysal 1994; Aleinikoff and Klusmeyer 2002; Römer 2017). This literature tradition has scrutinised the manner in which nation states integrate foreigners, and thus the rights they confer. Two central insights can be found in this literature: first, the differentiation between *immigration policies* that regulate the admission and selection of immigrants at a country's border and *integration policies* that concern immigrants once they are settled in the country (including immigrants' social rights, see Hammar 1985); and, second, the necessity to distinguish between various *immigration (or entry) categories* that are related to 'motives for migration' (e.g. labour migrants, family reunification, refugees and co-ethnics; see Brubaker 1989; Morris 2003; Helbling et al. 2017).[2]

Immigration categories are related to both types of immigration-related policies. *Immigration policies* specify the requirements that immigrants have to meet when they cross a country's border with the intention to settle permanently. These conditions differ depending on the immigration category and thus the residence permit an immigrant applies for. In addition to conditions, immigration policies might also impose specific quotas on the number of immigrants and immigration categories that are allowed to settle in the host country. Immigration policies thus steer the composition of immigrants living in the territory, though only to a certain extent.[3] Depending on the immigration category and residence permit, foreigners are entitled to miscellaneous rights ranging from social, economic, cultural and sometimes even political rights. For the purpose of this book, they are confined to social rights, including the right to paid employment. In other words, socio-economic integration policies regulate which social rights certain immigration categories are granted. Both immigration and socio-economic integration policies (i.e. social rights of immigrants) can range from being inclusive to exclusive (or restrictive) depending on the ease with which immigrant categories are allowed to settle in the country and the range of social rights that entitle access to the labour market and the welfare system.

Bringing the insights from both literatures together, the argument in brief is that the *inclusiveness of immigrants' social rights* conditions the impact of a country's labour market and welfare system on immigrants' poverty. In other words, immigrants' poverty levels should be lower in countries that combine highly regulated labour market policies and/or generous welfare programmes with inclusive social rights for immigrants than in countries with more restrictive social rights.

Turning to immigration policies, their impact is expected to affect immigrants' poverty indirectly: first, via immigrants' social rights, as immigrants are assigned specific immigration categories upon arrival and during settlement; and, second, via the composition of the immigrant population, that is, the outcomes of immigration policies. The idea behind this is that the extent of socio-economic integration, and consequently immigrants' poverty, varies between immigration categories. For example, immigrants moving for economic reasons are able to invest time in the transferability of their marketable skills while still in their country of origin, in contrast to individuals migrating for political reasons, such as refugees or asylum seekers (Bauer, Lofstrom and Zimmermann 2000).

Drawing on comparative welfare state literature, alternative explanations of poverty are controlled for, namely socio-demographic factors such as employment patterns and education levels at the micro-level and economic factors at the macro-level (Brady 2009; see also Moller et al. 2003; Brady, Fullerton and Cross 2009; Lohmann 2009; Kesler 2015). This has two advantages. On the one hand, it considers cross-national variations in exposure to the effects of economic and structural transformations that have put a strain on the welfare state and the labour market (Bonoli 2005). On the other hand, the inclusion of structural, that is, socio-demographic, factors at the micro-level allows for the accounting of heterogeneity regarding socio-demographic characteristics within immigrant groups between countries (e.g. that immigrants' poverty is lower in a country where immigrants are in general highly skilled than in a country with less-skilled immigrants).

CONTRIBUTION OF THE BOOK

By drawing specific attention to immigrants' social rights, this book contributes to comparative welfare and migration literature in three ways. The first is to provide an extended framework that focuses on immigrants and links their social rights to the labour market and welfare system as well as immigration policies in order to explain cross-national variations in immigrants' poverty. Thereby, particular attention is drawn to immigrants' work and the social rights of different immigration categories. This approach addresses the weaknesses of the comparative welfare state literature, which, despite the prominent role of social rights, neglects the fact that immigrants' and non-immigrants' rights differ. This aspect, however, is central to explaining why immigrants and non-immigrants have different poverty outcomes and thus why traditional approaches cannot explain cross-national variations. In addition, it also contributes to the recently growing literature that focuses on the perspective of immigrants and how immigrants are affected by labour market regulations and welfare state arrangements (Morissens and Sainsbury 2005; Sainsbury 2012; Corrigan 2014).

The second contribution is to provide a methodological understanding of poverty as a concept that affects entire households rather than just individuals and thus considers mixed categories related to socio-demographic characteristics as well as immigrant background. Poverty is a 'family-level concept' that, in contrast to labour market outcomes, cannot be studied without considering the socio-demographic characteristics of other family members (Kesler 2015, 40). Recent research points to the importance of socio-demographic and immigration-related characteristics such as human capital and employment patterns, country of origin and language proficiency as well as, or even in combination with, the prevailing institutional setting in explaining socio-economic outcomes such as labour market participation and poverty (e.g. Kesler 2006; Kogan 2006; Misra, Moller and Budig 2007; Brady, Fullerton and Cross 2009; Corrigan 2014). However, the majority of these studies choose the head of the household, who is usually the highest earner, and assign his or her socio-demographic characteristics to the whole household (see Obućina 2014; Kesler 2015). By doing this, they neglect the existing diversity of lifestyles and household types alongside the traditional male breadwinner family of an average production worker, such as households with dual-earners and atypically employed persons pursuing part-time or fixed-term employment (e.g. Häusermann and Schwander 2012). The drawback of this becomes even more evident when deciding whether a household has an immigrant background or not. Depending solely on the information about one household member hides the fact that native/immigrant households face different opportunities to households where all members were born either abroad or in the country of residence (see also Obućina 2014). Consequently, the book not only takes several combinations of socio-demographic characteristics as well as immigration-related factors into account, but also uses multilevel analysis to model the effects of socio-demographic characteristics on poverty.

Finally, the book contributes empirically to the comparative welfare state literature by using a newly collected dataset on immigrants' social rights in nineteen advanced industrialised countries. The dataset provides a comprehensive overview of immigrants' access to the labour market and several social programmes including unemployment protection, family-related programmes, such as traditional child benefits and dual-earner support, and social assistance. Following the migration contributions, the book differentiates between the following immigration categories: nationals, immigrants with permanent residence permits (denizens), immigrants with limited residence permits (mainly labour migrants) as well as their family members. It should be noted that the data have not been collected for immigrants staying for purposes other than work (e.g. students and pensioners), asylum seekers and co-ethnics (e.g. German Aussiedler). Furthermore, the dataset and this book in general do not cover the formal rights of irregular immigrants, although this topic has become a priority in most advanced industrialised countries (see Vollmer 2009). Nevertheless, the dataset complements major comparative projects on integration policies and immigrants' rights by paying closer attention to immigrants' access to a range of social programmes (e.g. the MIPEX project, Niessen et al. 2007; Koopmans, Michalowski and Waibel 2012) and extending the number of countries for which a detailed overview of immigrants' rights exists (e.g. Soysal 1994; Aleinikoff and Klusmeyer 2002; Sainsbury 2012).

In addition, based on this detailed dataset, the internal exclusion form of welfare chauvinism at the macro-level – where basic welfare states narrow access down to citizens, while more encompassing welfare states are open to all residents regardless of their nationality (see Banting 2000) – is empirically tested for a broader range of countries and various social programmes. Although relevant for contemporary politics, a systematic and comprehensive analysis of the internal exclusion form of welfare chauvinism thesis is missing. Existing studies are either based only on descriptive comparisons of a limited number of countries (e.g. Faist 1995; Banting 2000; Sainsbury 2006, 2012) or focus on specific social programmes (e.g. social assistance, see Römer 2017). This is mainly due to a lack of data. The lengthy empirical welfare state research tradition on social rights of average production workers (Esping-Anderson 1990) has only recently been matched in the migration literature. Over the past decade, scholars have started to empirically measure immigration policies and have proposed new indicators related to economic and social rights (for labour migrants, see Ruhs 2013; Helbling et al. 2017). But in general, too little still is known about immigrants' social incorporation[4] and their social rights (see also Sainsbury 2012). Therefore, this book systematically reviews whether and how immigrants' social rights – that is, whether they are inclusive or exclusive – are related to the type of welfare regime and its principle of entitlement based on citizenship/residence, need or work.

STRUCTURE OF THE BOOK

Chapter 1 starts with Sainsbury's (2012) central contribution underlining the close relations between immigrants' social rights, welfare states and incorporation regimes. The chapter then reviews the conceptualisation of social rights in the comparative welfare state literature and links them to insights from the migration and citizenship literature, which explores immigrants' rights of citizenship in more detail. Drawing on both literature strands, the chapter develops an analytical framework for explaining cross-national variations in immigrants' poverty in advanced industrialised countries. Besides clarifying the main concepts used in this book, the chapter also discusses the limitations of the analytical framework.

Chapters 2 and 3 present the descriptive results in detail. Chapter 2 depicts national variations in immigrants' poverty before and after taxes and transfers. The analysis is complemented by alternative measures of poverty, such as income gaps and intensity, which account for the financial situations of poor households. Chapter 3 starts with an overview of the immigrant population prevalent in each country. The major part of this chapter is devoted to the detailed description of immigrants' social rights, entitling access to paid employment and social programmes, in nineteen advanced industrialised countries. The last section analyses whether certain patterns regarding welfare regimes and access for immigrants can be identified, namely if Nordic and Continental European countries rely on rather inclusive social rights for immigrants compared to Anglo-Saxon countries, which opt for exclusive social rights, as the internal exclusion form of welfare chauvinism would expect. Chapter 4 assesses the explanatory potential of the analytical framework. Using multilevel analysis, it tests whether the effect of the labour market and welfare system on immigrants' poverty depends on immigrants' social rights concerning their access to paid employment and social programmes. The results suggest that the analytical framework can only partly explain cross-national variations in immigrants' poverty. The remainder of this chapter discusses alternative explanations. The final chapter presents concluding arguments and brings the major findings and implications of this book together. Drawing on the empirical analysis, three different strategies are identified that countries could pursue to reduce immigrants' poverty.

Chapter 1

An Approach to Explain Immigrants' Poverty

This chapter develops an analytical framework to analyse immigrants' socio-economic integration in advanced industrialised countries. The argument in brief is that the impact of a country's labour market and welfare system on immigrants' poverty is not direct but conditional on immigrants' social rights, here broadly understood to include work rights as a right to paid employment.

The analytical framework builds on two strands of literature. The first strand is comparative welfare state literature, which argues that the generosity of the welfare state, understood as a combination of labour market and social policies that redistribute economic resources, is an important determinant of cross-national variations in poverty (see Brady 2009). A central element of the welfare state is the social rights of citizenship it confers to its members. Thus, this chapter starts with a discussion of the prevailing conceptions of social citizenship. It will be argued that social rights such as rights to welfare benefits and thus access to social programmes are closely related to the right (and access) to paid employment. However, since comparative welfare state literature has paid scant attention to immigrants and thus the social rights of immigrants, especially research on immigrant poverty (but see Sainsbury 2006, 2012 and welfare chauvinism literature), the framework also draws on insights from citizenship and international migration literature. This second strand of literature has intensively studied how immigrants are incorporated into host countries. It deals with the requirements immigrants have to fulfil to formally become members of a society as well as the rights they are granted. Although citizenship is understood more broadly as going far beyond immigrants' social rights, these contributions provide two important insights into the conceptualisation of immigrants' social and work rights. On the one hand, immigrants are not a homogenous group that can be contrasted to citizens. Instead, different forms of immigration that relate to motives of immigration have to be distinguished. On the other hand, forms of immigration, more specifically immigration (or entry) categories, not only confer certain social rights to immigrant groups but also depend on immigration policies that regulate the admission of immigrants into the country. Building on both literature strands, the analytical framework to explain immigrants' poverty is presented in the last section.

SOCIAL CITIZENSHIP – THE LINK BETWEEN WELFARE STATES AND IMMIGRATION

The idea that social rights of citizenship can bridge welfare state and migration literature is not novel. Several contributions, though mainly from citizenship and migration literature, emphasise this connection (e.g. Faist 1995; Banting 2000; Aleinikoff and Klusmeyer 2002; Freeman 2004; Geddes and Wunderlich 2009; Ruhs 2009, 2013). Nevertheless, so far mainstream comparative welfare state literature has paid little attention to immigrants and their social rights, with two exceptions.

One notable exception is Sainsbury's (2006, 2012) recent contribution linking the welfare state and immigration regimes. Her main argument is that the type of welfare regime affects immigrants' social rights, but that, in addition, immigration (or entry) categories (e.g. labour migrants, family reunification and refugees) and incorporation regimes have to be taken into account. The latter is defined as containing the 'rules and norms that govern immigrants' possibilities to become citizens, to acquire the right of permanent residence, and to participate in economic, cultural and political life' (Sainsbury 2012, 16). Her book not only compares immigrants' social rights and their changes along the earlier mentioned three dimensions but also focuses on the politics of inclusion and exclusion related to immigrants' rights.

This book builds on Sainsbury's assumption that immigrants' social rights depend on not only the type of welfare state but also immigration categories as well as a country's prevailing incorporation regime. However, the scope is narrower; specifically, this book confines incorporation regimes and policies to a specific domain, namely the socio-economic incorporation of immigrants within the labour market and welfare system and the related social rights. The main reason to exclude other forms of immigrant incorporation (cultural, political or legal forms; see Entzinger and Biezeveld 2003; Freeman 2004) is that the primary aim, and most important difference compared to Sainsbury (2006, 2012), is to explain how immigrants' formal, that is, legal, social rights affect immigrants' substantive social rights, here poverty outcomes. In order to do so, her approach is extended in three ways. First, by taking the central role of the labour market in addition to the welfare state into account, as comparative welfare state literature finds both welfare states and labour markets have an impact on poverty outcomes (Esping-Andersen 1990; Huber and Stephens 2001; Moller et al. 2003). The classic definition of social rights as rights to welfare benefits is widened to include immigrants' right to paid employment. Second, the framework also considers immigration policies regulating the admission of immigrants into a country. As will be subsequently discussed, they determine immigration categories to which immigrants are assigned. Finally, a cross-national comparison and how countries combine welfare and social incorporation regimes are explored. As a result, Sainsbury's six-country analysis is extended to include a broader range of countries, which is admittedly at the cost of excluding alternative forms of immigrant incorporation. In sum, the analytical framework addresses the interplay between configurations of welfare regimes and immigrants' social rights as well as immigration policies and how this affects immigrants' poverty.

A second exception is welfare chauvinism literature. For the purposes of this book, the work focusing on a differentiated version of welfare chauvinism at the country level is especially relevant. Broadly speaking, this research investigates how welfare states can be preserved in times of austerity when confronted with increasing immigration inflows.[1] In brief, this version of welfare chauvinism distinguishes two distinct forms (or policy options). Accordingly, the viability of encompassing welfare states can only be maintained either through restrictive immigration policies that reduce the influx of low-skilled immigrants from outside advanced industrialised countries (external exclusion) or by limiting the access of immigrants to social programmes (internal exclusion). Whether nation states choose one option over the other depends on the design and structure of the welfare state (see Faist 1995; Banting 2000). Encompassing welfare states, that is, social democratic and corporatist welfare regimes, tend to opt for external exclusion, employing restrictive immigration policies that allow only labour migrants or 'desired' newcomers to cross the border. At the same time, these countries integrate immigrants across immigration categories into the welfare state by granting them full access to social benefits. In contrast, liberal welfare regimes tend to choose internal exclusion by combining open border policies with the banning of migrants from receiving welfare state benefits.[2] In other words, these authors argue that the nature of the welfare regimes, that is, the basis of entitlement and the main targeted beneficiaries, affects immigration regimes, understood as the institutional arrangements that regulate the admission of as well as the integration of newcomers (e.g. Faist 1995; Banting 2000; Geddes 2003).[3]

This differentiated version of welfare chauvinism has not yet been rigorously tested. Empirical studies on external exclusion are scarce and the results are often contrary to expectation. Boräng's (2015) research, for example, shows that comprehensive welfare states admit even higher numbers of forced migrants. This is explained by the effect of universal welfare institutions on norms and values. On the other hand, studies confirm the hypothesis concerning the internal exclusion form of welfare chauvinism, though only for a limited number of countries (e.g. Sainsbury 2012) or specific social programmes (e.g. social assistance in Römer 2017). This book contributes to the literature by providing further evidence for the internal exclusion hypothesis, yet for a broader range of countries and social programmes.

Social Rights in Comparative Welfare State Literature

The conceptualisation of social rights of citizenship as a cornerstone of welfare states in the comparative welfare state literature has been strongly influenced by Marshall (1950; for a comprehensive overview on the social rights of citizenship, see Stephens 2010). His seminal contribution starts with defining citizenship as 'a claim to be accepted as full members of the society' (Marshall 1950, 8). He elaborates how the emergence of modern nation states, together with economic changes, led to a steady expansion of citizenship rights over time to include civil, political and, finally, social rights.[4] An essential characteristic of his elaboration on citizenship is equality. In terms of a basic human equality of citizenship membership, everyone considered a full member of the community is equal with regard to respective rights and duties.[5]

According to Marshall (1950, 11), social rights can be understood as 'the whole range from the right to a modicum of economic welfare and security to the right to share to the full in the social heritage and to live the life of a civilised being according to the standards prevailing the society'. This conceptualisation entails two aspects that have been central to welfare state literature. The first part refers to the right to income security and social services and thus the responsibility of the state to distribute goods and services that have previously been safeguarded and allocated by the market and local entities. The second part goes beyond the mere provision of social services and emphasises the right to participate in society, that is, the right to self-development and self-fulfilment as a citizen. Marshall (1950, 26) refers, for example, to the role of states to provide elementary education that enables citizens to exercise their rights as an educated electorate and educated workers. This example also illustrates the importance of duties attached to citizenship alongside rights, namely the duty to participate in the political system, the duty to work as well as the duty to pay taxes and insurance contributions that are 'obviously and immediately necessary for the fulfilment of the right' (Marshall 1950, 78). By guaranteeing these social rights of citizenship and demanding the earlier mentioned duties, following Marshall (1950), welfare states not only prevent social and economic exclusion of citizens, albeit only those accepted as full members, but also promote social cohesion and solidarity as well as the productivity of the economy, which in the end benefits the whole of society (see also Soysal 2012, 2).

The relative emphasis on these two aspects of social rights in welfare state literature has changed over the past decades. Nevertheless, the redistributive capacity of welfare states as the common denominator remained the cornerstone. In fact, several welfare state scholars have aimed to capture and explain the development as well as to classify welfare states and social rights (Titmus 1974; Wilensky 1975; Flora and Alber 1981; Korpi 1983; Esping-Andersen 1990; Ferrera 1996; Sainsbury 1996; Huber and Stephens 2001).

The first generation of comparative welfare studies, mainly quantitative cross-sectional studies, assessed the extent of social rights more broadly as the general welfare effort, using social expenditure as a percentage of GDP as a proxy for social rights (Stephens 1979; Korpi 1983; Hicks and Swank 1984; Huber and Stephens 2001). Recognising the limits of using social expenditure, these studies tried to account for critiques by controlling for the proportions of recipients such as the elderly population or the unemployed and by using more fine-grained categories of social expenditures (e.g. for criticisms, see, Esping-Andersen 1990; Starke 2006). The second generation of comparative welfare studies, therefore, attempted to grasp social rights more directly. The analysis of specific social programmes such as unemployment insurance, sickness benefits and old-age pension gained momentum and with it the focus on particular characteristics such as net replacement rates, coverage, conditions for entitlement and duration of benefits (Myles 1984; Esping-Andersen 1990; Korpi and Palme 1998; Scruggs 2006). Without neglecting Marshall's conceptualisation of social rights as active participation, the focus of these contributions remained mainly on the first aspect of social rights, the socially accepted standard of economic welfare and security.

Among one of the most influential works on social rights is Esping-Andersen's (1990) welfare regime typology, which builds on three principles: de-commodification, stratification[6] and the interconnection between the role of the state, market and the family in social provision. Esping-Andersen's first principle of 'de-commodification' draws on Marshall's (1950) conceptualisation of social rights. He argues that a 'minimal definition [of de-commodification] must entail that citizens can freely and without potential loss of job, income or general welfare, opt out of work when they themselves consider it necessary' (Esping-Andersen 1990, 23). This definition stresses the importance of but also the different degrees to which social rights allow citizens to maintain their prevailing living standards in deliberately chosen and precarious situations for reasons beyond individual control. De-commodification as defined earlier, however, rests on two implicit assumptions. First, it takes as a given that individuals are already commodified, that is, fully integrated into the labour market through employment. The principle of de-commodification thus comes into play only once workers opt out of the labour market for any reason. Second, the ideal-typical worker is implicitly supposed to be an average male production worker employed full-time and with a continuous work record, an insider, living with a dependent wife and two children (Esping-Andersen 1990, 58; see also Orloff 1993, 308).[7]

The third generation of welfare state research consists of contributions from feminist scholars, and more recently the new social risks and dualisation literature has questioned these implicit assumptions (e.g. Lewis 1992; O'Connor 1993; Orloff 1993; Sainsbury 1994; Esping-Andersen 1999; Bonoli 2005; Davidsson and Naczyk 2009; Emmenegger et al. 2012). By doing this, it brought Marshall's aspect of social rights as 'a right to share to the full in the social heritage' to the fore.

Orloff (1993), among other feminist scholars, criticised that de-commodification as a right to (satisfying) work disregards gender differences related to 'commodification' as a precondition thereof, in other words the extent to which women are integrated into or excluded from the labour market. Although women are formally granted full access to the labour market and paid employment, their responsibilities related to domestic and caring work hinder them from participating in the labour market in the same way as male workers. Indeed, full-time employment is a precondition to obtaining comprehensive social citizenship rights on an individual basis and thus the possibility of economic independence to maintain an autonomous household, at least in employment-based welfare systems. Women's domestic and caring responsibilities thus affect their social rights, and their career chances, via the type of employment they are able to take up, that is, work that is compatible with their care responsibilities, which results in a segmented labour market. Depending on women's roles as carers or workers, they are entitled to social provisions via their husbands as wives or widows or independently as workers (O'Connor 1993; Sainsbury 1994; Lewis 1997). Therefore, a central feminist claim has been to consider, on the one hand, the extent to which the welfare state promotes women's opportunities to engage in paid work and thus their right to be commodified and, on the other hand, the services it provides to take over the caring functions from families and thus public policies that promote the reconciliation of work and family (see also Esping-Andersen's 1999 concept of de-familialisation).

This argument concerning the rights to commodification and (satisfying) work is also relevant for immigrants. In contrast to female citizens, the question is not primarily about whether immigrants and specific immigration categories can practice their rights, but initially, about whether they are granted these rights. Certain immigrant groups simply lack the formal right to paid employment such as family members of labour migrants (see chapter 3). Furthermore, immigrants' right to work cannot be equated with no or full access to the labour market. The reason is that the right to work can be further limited with regard to the type of employment (e.g. self-employment), to certain employers and industry sectors, or the public sector (see Koopmans, Michalowski and Waibel 2012). However, since commodification as the right to employment is intrinsically linked to social entitlements, it has to be considered when analysing the socio-economic outcomes of immigrants.

The obstacles to pursue satisfying work and be economically independent are not only confined to women and immigrants. Young and low-skilled individuals also face increasing difficulties in entering and remaining in the labour market due to different factors such as insufficient and obsolete educational credentials or labour demand. Several contributions point to the intersection between gender, age, skills and migration background, which, in turn, affects the chances of these social groups to enter the labour market and find stable employment relationships (O'Connor 1993; Orloff 1993; Bonoli 2005; Emmenegger et al. 2012).

In this regard, the second assumption concerning the ideal-typical worker, the average production worker, has been challenged in the literature. This breadwinner approach was attractive not only 'because the link to welfare attributes is easy to trace' and employment-based welfare systems implicitly favour the male breadwinner but also probably because it was dominant in the post-war period (Esping-Andersen 1999, 50–51). However, structural transformations such as changes in family structure and the labour market (e.g. increased female employment and divorce rates, deindustrialisation and immigration; see also Bonoli 2005) have changed the risk structure and undermined this once-prevalent family type. In the majority of OECD countries, with the exception of Southern Europe, the dual-earner pattern in families has become the new norm (OECD 2007a, 15). The emergence of dual-worker families has been accompanied by new individual work bibliographies and life courses that deviate from ideal-typical average production workers, that is, the insiders with stable, full-time and fully insured employment. Instead, new types of non-average production workers related to gender, age, skills and migration background have emerged. These outsiders share higher exposure to certain risks, such as ending up in discontinuous employment, including (involuntary) part-time employment or fixed-term contracts, or unemployment (Häusermann and Schwander 2012). Because welfare states and labour market regulations have struggled and been slow to adapt to these new social risks, non-average production workers face insufficient social coverage from traditional male-breadwinner social programmes, resulting in a higher risk of poverty. However, one central insight from this literature is that non-average production workers do not have to be worse off per se compared to the average production worker.[8] Moreover, exposure to the earlier mentioned risks depends on the welfare regime, that is, the combination of social protection and labour market institutions, and its interplay with other factors such as structural developments and political mobilisation (e.g. Emmenegger et al. 2012).

This book draws on these contributions in two ways. First, related to the critique of the average production worker, it focuses on social programmes that do not merely provide income replacement to insiders but those at the margins of society. This includes three social programmes that have been more or less explicitly designed to alleviate poverty, namely social assistance, unemployment programmes and family-related schemes (Huber and Stephens 2001, 108). Second, following the criticism of neglecting the precondition of being 'commodified', it takes into account immigrants' right to paid employment alongside the more traditional social rights. Indeed, in line with the feminist critique, one might argue that immigrants' formal right to paid employment does not go far enough to guarantee their labour market integration but that further migrant-specific services, which are comparable to social programmes reconciling work and family, should be considered. This is a legitimate claim and should be considered in future research. However, the comparative welfare state literature, with the exceptions mentioned in the beginning of this chapter, has only just started to take into account that differences exist between immigrants' and citizens' social rights but has not yet systematically identified the dimensions along which they vary. As the citizenship and migration literature in the next section shows, the immigration category plays a central role.

Social Rights in Citizenship and Migration Literature

A major subject in the citizenship literature is the incorporation of immigrants into a country. As different scholars have argued, the way in which members of a society perceive themselves, reflected in citizenship policies rooted and shaped by conceptions of nationhood or national identity, allows foresight into how newcomers will be integrated into the receiving country (e.g. Brubaker 1992; Ireland 1994; Koopmans and Statham 2000; Heckmann and Schnapper 2003).[9] This research tradition conceives citizenship, in line with Marshall (1950), as a 'form of membership in a political and geographic community', to which rights and obligations are attached on the basis of equality, which are usually granted and safeguarded by a state (Bloemraad, Korteweg and Yurdakul 2008, 154). However, research explicitly states that this inclusive and egalitarian conception of citizenship is limited to full members, who are usually legal citizens, with the result being the exclusion of noncitizens or foreigners. Nevertheless, most scholars agree that this dichotomy between citizens and non-citizens is too simple and that the correspondence between nationality and certain citizenship rights is blurred. Instead, whether immigrants are granted citizenship rights depends on their immigration status, that is, the immigration (or entry) category given by the state.

Citizenship literature has traditionally focused on nationality acquisition, which as mentioned earlier gives some insights into how foreigners will be integrated into the host society. One of the most influential contributions is Brubaker's (1992) historical analysis of Germany and France, which distinguishes between an ethnic-cultural and a civic-territorial model of citizenship and the related 'ius sanguinis' and 'ius solis' naturalisation practices, making it more or less difficult to be legally acknowledged as a full member.[10] This dichotomous typology has been criticised for several reasons.[11] Relevant for this book is the critique that the mere focus on nationality acquisition ignores alternative forms of immigrant incorporation without being a formal member of the state (see Soysal 1994; Bommes and Geddes 2000; Freeman 2004; Myles and St-Arnaud 2006).

Subsequent citizenship research moved its focus from naturalisation to the incorporation of settled immigrants. One general finding is that entitlement to classical citizenship rights does not depend on being a national and having established close ties to the receiving country. Consequently, the main division is not between nationals and non-nationals, but between different types of immigration categories, in particular between permanent and temporary residents (Brubaker 1989, 156; Hammar 1990; Sainsbury 2006). As these scholars argue, the rights of citizens and permanent and legal residents hardly differ. Moreover, permanent residence is accompanied by almost unrestricted access to the labour market, education, business, social programmes and civil rights, though not necessarily political rights (Hammar 1990; Layton-Henry 1990, 189; Soysal 1994; Guiraudon 1998; Joppke 1999). Hammar (1990) refers to these privileged immigrants as denizens who, in comparison to temporary residents, enjoy almost all citizenship rights. However, more detailed research and the empirical analysis in the following chapters show that differences concerning social rights of immigrants and thus access to welfare services exist even between citizens and permanent residents (Gran and Clifford 2000; Aleinikoff and Klusmeyer 2002; Sainsbury 2006; van Hook, Brown and Bean 2006). Although differentiating between denizens who are granted full social and civil citizenship without political citizenship and aliens, or 'margizens', is helpful, it is an over-simplification that neglects the stratification by immigrant groups and thus forms of partial membership (see also Morris 2003).

It is striking that despite considerable interest in the extension of citizenship rights to non-citizens, the majority of studies have barely addressed immigrants' social rights. A number of indicators have been proposed and collected to capture alternative dimensions of citizenship's legal aspect, that is, naturalisation (e.g. Howard 2009), but also include, among other things, immigrants' political (collective) and cultural group rights (e.g. Koopmans et al. 2005; Banting and Kymlicka 2006; Niessen et al. 2007; Goodman 2010; Huddleston et al. 2011; for a discussion, see Helbling 2013). These studies generally assume that all immigrant groups qualify for welfare benefits with the exception of public benefits, such as social assistance, that are reserved for immigrants with permanent residence permits (e.g. Koopmans et al. 2005, 31–32). The Migrant Integration Policy Index (MIPEX) assesses immigrants' access to social programmes and the labour market but only through crude proxies (Niessen et al. 2007; Huddleston et al. 2011). The few existing studies that have analysed immigrants' social rights in more detail are either outdated (North, de Wenden and Taylor 1987 quoted in Soysal 1994, 123; Aleinikoff and Klusmeyer 2002) and available for only a few countries (Sainsbury 2012) or focus only on a particular type of immigrants (e.g. migrant workers; Ruhs 2011). This book aims to fill a gap in the social citizenship research by providing an overview of the access of a broader range of immigration categories to different types of social programmes.

There are two major reasons as to why the citizenship literature has paid less attention to immigrants' social rights. The first is due to practical reasons. Koopmans et al. (2005), for example, argue that cross-national variations in immigrants' citizenship rights and policies are expected to be greater with regard to political and civil rights, on the one hand, and cultural rights on the other hand. The second reason relates to explanations put forward regarding why citizenship rights have been extended to non-immigrants (for an overview, see Koopmans, Michalowski and Waibel 2012). The post-national citizenship approach points to the worldwide human rights discourse with its growing focus on personhood and individual rights and the role of supra-national institutions (Bauböck 1994; Soysal 1994). This transnational discourse puts pressure on national institutions that gave rise to an alternative form of citizenship entitling socially and financially contributing residents with civil and social rights. Alternative explanations for the extension of immigrants' social rights at the national level have also been related to the role of courts and bureaucracies to 'silently' implement equal rights for residents without having to amend constitutions as is the case with political rights (Guiraudon 1998; but see Sainsbury 2012), to welfare state enlargements in the 1970s (Ryner 2000) as well as the importance of political parties and immigrant organisations (Sainsbury 2012). Common to most of these approaches is that they expect a convergence of social citizenship rights across countries, that is, the expansion of rights to include non-citizens.[12] However, recent studies indicate that several nation states have started to curtail immigrants' rights, at least when it comes to specific immigration groups such as asylum seekers; but most often they indirectly attempt to regulate migration flows, thus retrenching universal social benefits that disproportionately benefit immigrants (Banting 2000; Emmenegger and Careja 2011; Sainsbury 2012).

Immigration Category – The Link between Immigration and Integration Policies

A central insight from citizenship literature discussed earlier is that citizenship rights are not restricted to full members, that is, nationals, but have been extended to immigrants. Nevertheless, not all immigrants are granted full citizenship rights; it depends on their immigration status, that is, the immigration (or entry) category given by the state. This close relation between immigration status and citizenship rights, here social rights, is central for the analytical framework aiming to explain immigrants' poverty.

Before discussing the major immigration categories, it is important to define immigration and immigrants. In line with previous studies, this book is concerned with forms of 'permanent immigration'. Accordingly, an immigrant is defined as 'a person who migrates to a country and then actually resides there longer than a short period of time, i.e. for more than three months' (Hammar 1985, 11). This definition excludes not only persons who intend to stay for only a short time, such as tourists, commuters, seasonal workers or individuals on business trips, but also students, au pairs, artists and others who are not allowed to or do not plan to stay permanently. It should be noted that temporary labour workers are also considered to be immigrants, although they often move from country to country and do not have a priori the right to settle permanently in a country (for a discussion, see Helbling et al. 2013).[13]

International migration literature distinguishes four broader immigration (or entry) categories that are related to different motives for migration and reasons regarding why states admit foreigners (see Bauer, Lofstrom and Zimmermann 2000, 25–26; Sainsbury 2006; Helbling et al. 2017): first, labour migration based on economic reasons (e.g. to fill empty positions in the labour market); second, family reunification based on social reasons (e.g. to join settled immigrants); third, refugees and asylum seekers based on humanitarian reasons (e.g. fleeing persecution); and finally, co-ethnics based on cultural and historical reasons.[14] Within each immigration category and depending on the country, various subgroups of immigrants can be distinguished. For example, various permits are granted to labour migrants depending on their skills (e.g. the EU Blue Card being an example for high-skilled third-country nationals [TCNs], Cerna 2008), type of employment (e.g. seasonal work programmes in agriculture and the tourism sector) and region (e.g.

the 'Australian Skilled-Nominated Visa (subclass 190)' for workers that are nominated by a state or territory; see Ruhs 2013 for an overview). Likewise, the family reunification category can comprise several subgroups which are mainly dependent on the residence status of the migrant sponsor, for example, citizens or TCNs and the family relationship of the applicant to the sponsor, for example, spouse and children, civil and registered partners, parents and other relatives (IOM 2009). Further differentiations can also be identified regarding humanitarian protection, for example, recognised refugee status as described in the 1951 Refugee Convention, humanitarian protection status for those who do not fulfil the criteria for refugee status but nonetheless are considered in need of protection and cannot be returned to the country of origin, and asylum seekers whose decision related to the asylum application is still pending (e.g. for the United Kingdom; see Da Lomba 2010).

But there are additional groups and types of immigrants. Permanent residents can be considered as an immigration category too as their status is not secured until they go through the naturalisation process and become citizens (see also Hammar 1990; Brochmann 1999). Moreover, traditional immigration countries such as the United States, Canada and Australia grant permanent residence permits from the beginning of the stay in the receiving country. In contrast, European countries mainly grant permanent residence permits dependent on immigrants' length of residence in the host country, specific residence permits as well as further conditions such as integration, for example, knowledge of a host country's language, political system and history and sufficient income (Huddleston et al. 2011).[15] Undocumented immigrants with unlawful status resulting from either overstaying or entering the country illegally[16] (Morris 2002, 2003) or citizens of specific countries that are granted preferential treatment based on bilateral or international agreements (e.g. EU member states or the Nordic Passport Union between Iceland, Denmark, Norway, Sweden and Finland) can also be identified as further immigration categories.

Immigration categories are closely related to policies affecting immigrants. According to international migration literature, three major types of policies related to different phases of immigration can be distinguished (Hammar 1985; Helbling 2013):[17] policies regulating immigrants' entry into the territory (immigration policies), their settlement in the host country (integration policies) and finally their acquisition of nationality (naturalisation policies). This classification of immigration-related policies allows moving from the rather abstract conceptions of citizenship discussed earlier to policies; for example, citizenship literature deals primarily with naturalisation and integration policies. Moreover, it makes it possible to relate social rights of specific immigration categories, on the one hand, to immigration policies and, on the other hand, to a country's prevailing welfare state and labour market arrangements, which are both central aspects of the analytical framework.

Immigration policies refer to regulations governing the admission and selection of foreigners to the country as well as control of aliens (see Hammar 1985, 7–11).[18] These policies regulate immigration inflows by imposing specific quotas or specifying conditions and requirements immigrants have to fulfil to enter and reside legally in the country. The admission criteria and conditions not only vary across countries but also depend on the immigration category. They can range from liberal to restrictive, making it more or less demanding for particular categories to immigrate. For example, several countries such as the Netherlands, Germany and the United Kingdom have introduced pre-admission integration policies demanding language proficiency and knowledge of the host country from newcomers (see Scholten et al. 2011; Goodman 2012). However, these conditions do not have to be met by all immigrants. While the main target groups in Germany and the Netherlands are family members of nationals and TCNs, the language assessment in the United Kingdom only applies to foreigners between eighteen and twenty-five, except highly skilled immigrants and those originating from English-speaking countries.[19] Thus, immigration policies vary depending on the immigration category.

Through immigration policies, nation states control the inflow of particular immigration categories and thus can select 'preferred' types of immigrants. However, the extent to which states can steer immigration in flows and outflows is confined. While nation states retain the greatest control over labour immigration, they are more restricted regarding other immigration categories due to the assertion of human rights, the rights of protection and family reunification. Nevertheless, a tightening in residence requirements for family members as well as more recently for refugees can be observed across countries (see Goodman 2012). An example is the tightening of conditions of family reunification for asylum seekers in force in Denmark since 2 February 2016, increasing the waiting period from one to three years (see Damon and Hume 2016).

Depending on the immigration category, or more precisely the residence permit immigrants are given upon their entry to the host country, different rights and obligations are attached. These relate to *integration (or immigrant) policies,* which affect immigrants once they are settled in the country.[20] Hammar (1985, 9–10) further distinguishes between direct immigrant policies that target only the migrant population. Examples of so-called cultural collective rights are funding of ethnic group activities, mother-tongue instruction or preferential hiring of immigrants in the public sector (e.g. Koopmans et al. 2005; Banting and Kymlicka 2006; Niessen et al. 2007; Goodman 2010, 2012; Huddleston et al. 2011). Indirect immigrant policies, on the other hand, refer to public policies that affect all residents living in a country, including both nationals and immigrants. The aforementioned classic citizenship rights that regulate access to the labour market, social services and programmes and the political system are an example of indirect immigrant policies. They just vary with regard to the extent to which they incorporate different types of immigrants and thus can be more or less inclusive/discriminatory. For example, EU citizens enjoy immediate free access to the labour market and can participate in local elections in any other member country and recognised refugees have privileged access to public assistance and social insurance programmes, in contrast to asylum seekers and undocumented immigrants (Sainsbury 2006, 230). Consequently, integration policies vary depending on the immigration category.

As different authors argue, it is important to highlight the close relation between immigration and integration policies (Helbling et al. 2017, 84). First, the distinction between immigration and integration policies is not always clear-cut. For example, family reunification falls into both categories. On the one hand, immigration policies regulate the conditions that have to be fulfilled by family members in order to cross the border and obtain their respective residence permits. On the other hand, family reunification can also fall into the category of an integration policy, namely the right of the sponsor to reunify his family after having settled in the receiving country. Second, immigration policies are connected to integration policies through the immigration category they assign to immigrants. The residence permit is linked to (or already includes) a work permit that grants access to employment.

Hammar's (1985, 9–10) conceptualisation of indirect immigrant policies is relevant for this book. Social rights and thus access to paid employment and welfare benefits, as conceptualised in comparative welfare state literature, fall into the category of indirect immigrant policies. Social policies were not originally designed with immigrants in mind but address the resident population in general, though with different levels of success as the discussion on de-commodification has shown. But Hammar's (1985) definition of indirect immigrant policies further takes into account that immigrants (or immigration categories) might differ with regard to their social rights. However, in order to avoid confusion between the former, that is, social policies addressing all residents, and the latter, that is, those referring to immigrants' social rights as access to the labour market and social programmes, I will confine the term (indirect) 'integration policies' to immigrants' social rights that regulate their access to paid employment and welfare benefits, namely socio-economic integration policies.

This book is primarily concerned with socio-economic integration policies as outputs, that is, the legal binding regulations implemented by states, rather than their implementation (for a discussion on this difference, see Helbling et al. 2017, 83–84). This restriction does not allow for Hammar's (1985) central point that despite immigrants' equal access to the economic and social political sphere, they might encounter further barriers such as discrimination, positive or negative, that affect their outcomes and participation in society. However, it is the effect of those legally binding decisions on immigrants' poverty levels that this book is interested in explaining.

Summing up the discussion in this chapter, three broader fields of policies can be distinguished which are relevant for immigrants and thus central to the analytical framework to explain immigrants' poverty: (1) *immigration poli-cies* controlling the admission of immigrants to the territory, (2) those related to *immigrants' social rights* regulating their access to paid employment and welfare benefits and the (3) *labour market and welfare system (labour mar-ket and social policies)*. The following section elaborates on how these three policy areas are connected to each other.

The Relation between Immigration, Immigrants' Social Rights and Welfare States

Different scholars have focused on the interconnections and tensions of these three different fields – immigration, immigrants' social rights and the welfare state. The bulk of this research has dealt with the impact of immigration on the viability of the welfare state in relation to potential fiscal pressure or erosion or social solidarity. One strand of literature argues that immigration could put welfare states under pressure due to higher social expenditure resulting from the disproportional reliance of immigrants on welfare benefits compared to non-immigrants. Following this mainly economic line of argument, generous welfare states act as magnets for low-skilled (and high-skilled) immigrants to migrate to a specific country (for an overview, see Borjas 1989, 1994, 1999; Nannestad 2007). Borjas's (1999) findings for the United States show that foreigners not only immigrate more often to states with higher social transfer but also make more use of social programmes than citizens (see also Borjas and Hilton 1996). Limited evidence also exists for Europe. While immigrants tend to be over-represented among recipients of non-contributory welfare schemes and education-related programmes, they rely less on social programmes related to sickness, unemployment insurance and pensions com-pared to natives (Brückner et al. 2002; Boeri 2009; Razin and Wahba 2015).[21] In general, these studies start from the premise that immigrants have compre-hensive social rights and thus full access to welfare programmes.

A second strand of research suggests that immigration undermines social solidarity and thus the willingness to fund welfare states. Among the first were American researchers who argued that a migratory open border would lead to the 'Americanization of European welfare politics', and thus the dismantling of the welfare state (Freeman 1986; Borjas 1994; Alesina and

Glaeser 2004; but see Taylor-Gooby 2005; Crepaz 2008).[22] They argued that welfare systems historically introduced with the establishment of the nation state were developed with citizens in mind, and were therefore supposed to be closed to non-citizens (Ryner 2000). However, immigrants have been steadily granted access to welfare benefits for different reasons, for example, the post-national forces mentioned earlier. Consequently, 'migrants receiving benefits, therefore, pose a threat to the logic of welfare state' (Freeman 2004, 955) because it erodes the traditional basis of support for the redistributive welfare state as claims for scarce welfare resources are related to 'a visible and subordinated minority' (see also Miller 1995; van Oorschot 2008; but see Banting and Kymlicka 2006).

Welfare attitude research provides mixed empirical evidence for the argument that immigration erodes social support. For instance, Mau and Burkhart (2009) show by combining individual-level and macro-level data that ethnic diversity reduces welfare state solidarity (for similar results on support for welfare state spending in Sweden, see Eger 2010). Experimental persuasion designs also show that welfare support is sensitive to the issue of immigration. Broad initial support for a basic income proposal was reduced when Norwegian respondents were asked to extend the proposal to resident non-citizens (Bay and Pedersen 2006). In contrast, other studies find no impact of immigration on welfare attitudes (Crepaz 2006) or show that other contextual factors, such as a country's prevailing type of welfare regime and unemployment rates, are more important determinants (Mau and Burkhardt 2009). Recent research even points out that ethnic diversity, measured as net migration and change in foreign-born population, increases support for the government reducing differences between the rich and poor (Brady and Finnigan 2014). These studies suggest that the mechanisms behind immigration and public support for redistribution seem to be more complex (e.g. the role of various motivations moderating the relationship between welfare and immigration attitudes; see Emmenegger and Klemmensen 2013). They depend on how nation states and their citizenry define the welfare state boundaries and thus depend on not only who is entitled to welfare benefits but also who is perceived to be a legitimate recipient, which are both related to different interpretations and conceptions of community, belonging and membership (see Geddes 2003).

But welfare attitude research has also dealt more specifically with the social rights of immigrants. This restrictive view, which builds on the idea that 'welfare services should be restricted to "our own"', is known as welfare chauvinism (Andersen and Bjørklund 1990, 212; see also Kitschelt and McGann 1997, 22–23). Empirical evidence indicates that welfare chauvinist attitudes are not only related to individual-level factors such as lower educational attainment, lower income, higher perceived material risks, authoritarianism, higher cultural insecurity and individuals with principles of redistributive justice based on need (e.g. van der Waal et al. 2010; Mewes and Mau 2012; Reeskens and van Oorschot 2012). This literature also shows that welfare chauvinism is prevalent in all European countries, although the majority of respondents agree with the conditional inclusion of immigrants such as those living and working for at least one year in the country. Nonetheless, when Europeans are asked about concerns regarding the living conditions of needy people, immigrants are considered the least deserving of relief, then the unemployed, then the sick and disabled and finally the elderly who are considered the most deserving (van Oorschot 2006; van der Waal, de Koster and van Oorschot 2013). However, the level of welfare chauvinism varies between countries (see also van der Waal, de Koster and van Oorschot 2013). In line with classic welfare attitude research, the authors explain this finding as being due to the institutional structure of welfare regimes (for a state-of-the-art review, see Larsen 2008; Svallfors 2012).[23] In other words, the encompassing and universal character of welfare regimes that gives rise to higher social solidarity between citizens extends to foreign minorities. This influence is attributed to egalitarian norms and non-discriminatory practices, among others, which make it harder to justify the exclusion of particular social groups such as immigrant newcomers (Crepaz and Damron 2009; see also Römer 2017) or establish that more generous social benefits reduce economic competition over scare resources among those in need (Sides and Citrin 2007; van Oorschot and Uunk 2007). As mentioned at the beginning of this chapter, the differentiated version of welfare chauvinism at the macro-level also draws on this argument but proposes two distinct forms: external exclusion of immigrants from the welfare state through restrictive immigration policies at the border and internal exclusion of immigrants from the welfare state through restrictive access to social programmes (see also Banting 2000; Boräng 2015). These scholars argue that the structure and generosity of the welfare state influences which immigrant exclusion form is employed; more encompassing or universal welfare states tend to adopt the external exclusion form, whereas more basic or liberal welfare states tend to select the internal exclusion form (see also Faist 1995).

Generally speaking, this argument that immigration and welfare regimes are complementary seems quite appealing and convincing. But several objections can be raised, in addition to the scant empirical evidence, at least for the external exclusion form. First, as already mentioned earlier, nation states cannot completely control their borders. Nation states have to comply with certain international standards, for example, admitting refugees or the right to family reunification (see Boräng 2015). Comparably, the principle of free movement within the EU, which confers EU citizens with the right to settle and work in any other EU member state, restricts the scope for nation states to limit immigration within the EU.[24] Nevertheless, nation states still have scope when implementing these international rules, as the recent refugee inflow in Europe shows (see also Goodman 2012 on the right to family reunification).[25] Second, it further depends on how the (welfare) community is defined, that is, who is perceived to be a legitimate welfare target group (e.g. Geddes 2003; van Oorschot 2008), and if these perceptions in turn are politically mobilised (e.g. the issue of welfare abusers in election campaigns). Related to this point and based on citizenship literature, national traditions of immigrant incorporation in general might also play a role. Conceptions of citizenship that depend on the cultural and historical-institutional context could explain which logics influence the legal status and citizenship rights granted to immigrants. Sainsbury (2006, 2012) actually follows this line of argument and claims that immigrants' social rights are not just a derivative of welfare regime properties, as Faist (1995) and Banting (2000) postulate, but also depend on how inclusive incorporation regimes are in general (e.g. regarding citizenship acquisition, residence and work permission regulation, family reunification, settlement programmes for newcomers, anti-discrimination legislation and participatory rights; see Sainsbury 2012, 16–19). Her case selection is driven to maximise variation concerning incorporation regimes. Her analysis finds that, with some minor exceptions, social rights of immigrants are comparable within varying types of welfare regimes. The United States and the United Kingdom, which are both liberal welfare regimes, have introduced bans to exclude newcomers from obtaining social benefits. However, British immigration legislation, reflecting the imperial/postcolonial incorporation regime, makes it more difficult to obtain a legal settlement status compared to American regulations. Concerning the corporatist welfare regime, where social entitlement is based on work, Sainsbury shows that immigrants' social rights of the ethnic German and the civic French incorporation models converged, whereby work requirements and civic knowledge tests became important in both countries. Turning to the social-democratic welfare regime, immigrants' social rights are comparable in Sweden and Denmark with the major exception of social assistance. The restrictive stance of Denmark is also evident regarding permanent resident status and citizenship. Although Sainsbury's analysis does not consider immigration policies explicitly, her findings tend to partially support the hypothesis that immigrants' social rights and welfare regimes are linked (see also chapter 3).

FRAMEWORK TO EXPLAIN IMMIGRANTS' POVERTY

In this section, the analytical framework focuses on how immigrants' social citizenship rights that are related, on the one hand, to a country's labour

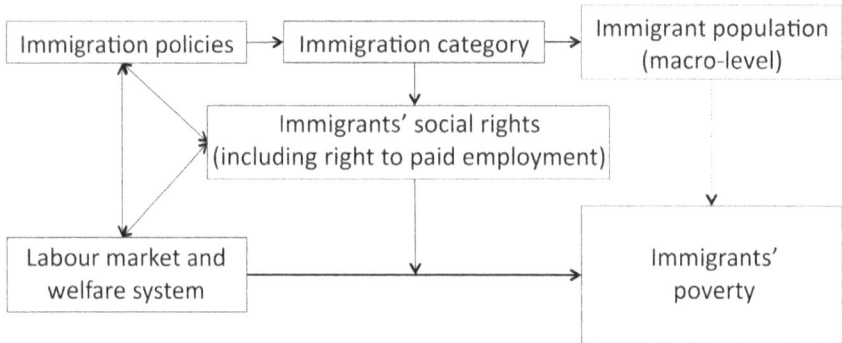

Figure 1.1   **Framework.** *Source*: **Adapted from Eugster, Immigrants and Poverty, and Conditionality of Immigrants' Social Rights,** *Journal of European Social Policy* **(forthcoming) p. 5, Figure 1. Copyright © [2018] (Beatrice Eugster). Reprinted by permission of SAGE Publications.**

market and welfare system and, on the other hand, to immigration policies can explain immigrants' poverty. First, how the labour market and welfare system affects poverty in general is examined. Then, the argument that immigrants' social citizenship rights, including their right to paid employment, condition the impact of the labour market and welfare system on immigrants' poverty is posed. Finally, there is a discussion on how immigration policies influence immigrants' poverty through the immigration category that immigrants are assigned and more indirectly by steering a country's immigrant population. The analytical framework is summarised in figure 1.1.

The Labour Market and Welfare State System

Based on comparative welfare state literature, the institutional setting of the welfare state and labour market serves as a starting point for the analytical framework to explain immigrants' poverty outcomes (bold arrow in figure 1.1). Several scholars have suggested considering the welfare state and labour market arrangements together (e.g. Esping-Andersen 1990; Esping-Andersen and Kolberg 1992; Huber and Stephens 2001; Andress and Lohmann 2008). The main reason is that nation states can intervene not only in the redistribution of income through welfare state arrangements but also in the distribution of economic resources by means of labour market institutions (see also Brady 2009). In brief, the labour market and the welfare system influence a country's prevailing poverty in two ways. On the one hand, states can affect poverty directly by providing social programmes such as unemployment compensation, family provisions and social assistance. On the other hand, states can influence poverty indirectly through labour market policies that influence individuals' earnings and wages. As the literature shows, earnings from labour market participation serve as the main source of households' income (Crettaz and Bonoli 2010). Two of the most important earnings-related labour market arrangements affecting poverty are wage-setting institutions and minimum wage laws. The idea that the (welfare) state's function is confined to redistribute income not only ex post but also ex ante, by shaping the structure of the labour market, is central to this book. However, it should be emphasised that the same logic is expected to be employed in both the labour market and the welfare state.

Moreover, labour market and welfare state arrangements are closely related to each other. First, welfare state arrangements affect an individual's decision to participate in the labour market (see also Esping-Andersen and Kolberg 1992). On the one hand, workers are conferred specific (redistributive) social rights by participating in the labour market and engaging in paid employment. Through the payment of social security contributions in the form of payroll taxes, workers gain access to social insurance funds and pensions. On the other hand, the existence of welfare state programmes – that is, the extent of de-commodification – also affects an individual's decision to exit the labour market. Whether a person considers joining the workforce again depends on the level of social benefits, that is, the social wage a worker receives when he stops working, as well as the tax system and the average effective tax rates, that is, the net earnings of working individuals. In addition, welfare states influence working decisions by providing social services such as childcare, which allows mothers to enter the labour market, or by increasing employment in the public sector (Esping-Andersen 1999).

Second, the argument that social protection can be pursued through not only the welfare state but also the labour market has also been exemplified and discussed in comparative welfare state literature using the example of Australia and New Zealand. Their social protection systems are mainly driven by interventive labour courts conceding workers many wage and non-wage benefits, and are supplemented by residual, income-tested social programmes (Castles and Mitchell 1993; Huber and Stephens 2001).[26] These two forms of state intervention should therefore be considered complementary. States can either implement labour market or social policies, leave the labour market and the welfare state unregulated, or combine both alternatives to different extents.

Addressing Poverty through the Labour Market

As the political economy and comparative welfare state literature suggests, two particular types of labour market regulations can be related to poverty, namely wage-setting institutions and minimum wage laws.

First, regarding *wage-bargaining systems*, the standard argument relates wage-setting institutions to wage equality. Higher centralisation and coordination produce wage compression because they reduce the spread of inter-firm and inter-sector earnings by including a majority of firms and sectors into a sole wage agreement (Pontusson, Rueda and Way 2002, 289).[27] The results so far indicate that more centralised and coordinated wage-setting mechanisms not only reduce a country's wage dispersion, especially at the bottom of the wage distribution, but that these mechanisms also raise the lowest salaries (Wallerstein 1999; Rueda and Pontusson 2000; Alderson and Nielsen 2002; Blau and Kahn 2002; Pontusson, Rueda and Way 2002; see also Quintini and Saint-Martin 2004). Moreover, the few existing cross-national studies on poverty also find empirical support that higher wage coordination reduces poverty (Moller et al. 2003; Lohmann 2009). The implication of these results and the role of wage-setting institutions are relevant in explaining cross-national variations in poverty insofar as it contributes to raising the lowest salaries above the poverty level and therefore affects poverty directly before any government redistribution.

Second, *statutory minimum wages*, as a specific form of wage setting, ensure that workers are paid fair salaries, which in turn allows them to maintain their families' economic well-being. Minimum wages protect low-paid workers by increasing their earnings to an explicit minimum (floor) and therefore raising their living standards. Moreover, the introduction of an explicit floor at the bottom end of the wage distribution tends to diminish wage dispersion and to benefit workers with earnings just above the minimum wage the most (Fortin and Lemieux 1997).

However, opponents point to the adverse effects of minimum wages on poverty. Minimum wages may destroy cheap labour (i.e. low-cost, flexible and temporary employment; see King and Rueda 2008) or prevent the creation of new jobs if these wages are set above the productivity level of workers (OECD 1998). This employment disincentive is even more pronounced in countries with comprehensive social insurance systems since non-wage labour costs such as payroll taxes and social security contributions paid by the employer cannot be shifted to the employee (Eichhorst and Marx 2012). As a result, lower-skilled workers may find themselves priced out of the market (see also Dolado et al. 1996; Esping-Andersen 1999) and thus may display higher poverty. Overall, the empirical literature suggests that a minimum wage has a negative impact on employment but that this effect is relatively weak (Neumark and Washer 2007). The effect of a minimum wage on wage inequality is less controversial. A higher minimum wage leads to lower wage inequality, at least at the bottom end of the distribution, and reduces the probability of low payment (Dolado et al. 1996; Machin, Manning and Rahman 2003; Crettaz and Bonoli 2010; OECD 2012a). Higher minimum wages not only tend to increase wages in the formal sector but often also tend to serve as a benchmark in the informal sector (see Betcherman 2012). Consequently, higher minimum wages may reduce poverty exposure, as long as the disemployment effect resulting from higher unemployment rates among the low-skilled does not prevail (Fortin and Lemieux 1997).

The few studies analysing the effect of minimum wage legislation on family income and poverty provide mixed empirical findings. Neumark and Wascher (2002) show, based on data from 1986 to 1995 for the United States, that the share of previously non-poor families ending up in poverty is greater than the share of poor families escaping poverty, though this net effect is not statistically significant. Moreover, minimum wages tend to increase the income of those living below the poverty line. Addison and Blackburn (1999) find that increases in the minimum wage during the same period reduced poverty among teenagers and older junior high school dropouts. Studies conducted outside the United States suggest that minimum wages do not substantially reduce poverty. In the German case, this limited effect of statutory minimum wages is explained by the interaction of minimum wages and the tax-benefit system (for the simulation of introducing a minimum wage, see Müller and Steiner 2008), while an Australian study points to the lower labour market participation of poor households. Existing evidence, mainly based on the United States, indicates that poor households often do not work at all or only have a single wage earner (see also OECD 1998). Moreover, several studies suggest that the typical minimum-wage worker tends to live in a middle-income household and is more likely to be female, unmarried, with low educational achievements and an immigrant background (Leigh 2007; see also Dolado et al. 1996; Rycx and Kampelmann 2012). Consequently, the impact of a minimum wage on poverty is not straightforward but depends also on the composition of the household and the characteristics of workers affected by the policy.

Although the literature points to ambiguous effects of minimum wages on poverty, in the case of immigrant outcomes, the effect on earnings might outweigh the effect on employment for several reasons. As Adsera and Chiswick (2007) and Schröder (2010) argue, minimum wages are particularly important for immigrants because they are more likely to experience low pay during their first years in the host country. Moreover, research indicates that higher minimum wages especially affect low-skilled immigrants since immigrant workers often have, on average, lower levels of education, language proficiency and social capital compared to citizens, which are all factors associated with lower earnings (see Orrenius and Zavodny 2008). But the impact of minimum wage regulation further depends on where immigrants are situated in the earnings distribution; those at the bottom benefit most from the resulting wage compression (see literature review, in Schröder 2010).

Chiswick, Le and Miller (2008) corroborate this finding when comparing immigrants' earning distribution in Australia and the United States. But they further show that economy-wide institutional wage setting, as prevalent in Australia, has a negative effect on the upward earnings mobility of high-skilled immigrants compared to their American counterparts. With this in mind and focusing on immigrant outcomes at the margins of society, the resulting assumption is that the poverty-reducing effect of (minimum) wage setting prevails for immigrants.

Addressing Poverty through the Welfare State

As mentioned earlier, countries can also address poverty ex post by providing social programmes that target different sections of the population. Three types of social programmes have been found to be especially important for tackling poverty, namely social assistance, family allowance and unemployment compensation (see also Huber and Stephens 2001). Besides targeting different groups within the working-age population, these programmes are also based on different logics of redistribution. While entitlement to unemployment programmes depends, in the majority of countries, on former contributions, family-related benefits are often provided on a universal basis. In contrast, social assistance is provided based on means and income tests.

First, the initial goal of *social assistance* programmes is to tackle poverty. By providing a guaranteed minimum income, they improve the standards of living, primarily of those individuals and families in vulnerable financial positions at the margins of society. Nevertheless, the role of targeted programmes as the sole means of welfare state efforts to reduce poverty has been disputed. Critics call attention to the reluctance of recipients to rely on means-tested benefits and thus the associated stigma that beneficiaries are associated with. They also refer to the political dynamics affecting the generosity of social assistance. Because the majority of the population does not directly benefit from means-tested programmes, for example, the middle and working class, it is hard to achieve a political majority in favour of more generous targeted benefits. Lack of political support leads, in the long run, to a reduction in spending on poverty. In contrast, it has been argued and shown that non-means-tested programmes enjoy higher electoral support (Nelson 2004). This leads to a higher redistributive budget, which goes along with more generous means-tested benefits and thus greater poverty reduction. Korpi and Palme (1998) label this observation that targeting the poor does not yield the expected effect on poverty reduction and redistribution as 'the paradox of redistribution and strategies of equality'. As a result of this influential contribution, welfare state literature scholars have devoted their attention to the effects of welfare state efforts on poverty in general rather than only on social assistance.

Nonetheless, empirical evidence provides mixed support for the paradox of redistribution. The association between targeting, universalism and redistribution has declined since the mid-1990s, as two studies show. Kenworthy (2011, 56) finds that since the mid-2000s, universalism no longer influences the redistributive budget size. His results are supported by the research of Marx, Salanauskaite and Verbist (2013), who show that decreased targeting is accompanied by higher redistribution only in the case of family benefits. On the contrary, the decomposition analysis of specific social programmes indicates that increased targeting of social assistances goes along with higher redistribution. However, most poverty studies found no significant effect of social spending on means-tested benefits on poverty reduction between 1970 and 2000 (e.g. Moller et al. 2003). Sainsbury and Morissens's (2002) study analysing the decomposition of poverty reduction due to means-tested and other social benefits indicates that means-tested benefits often do not suffice to lift households out of poverty and that other social benefits are more important. Using institutional data, Nelson (2004) also confirms that social assistance levels are often set below the poverty line. The difference between the definitions of poverty used in empirical studies, that is, relative and absolute poverty,[28] and official poverty lines used to determine the level of social assistance, which are clearly set below the relative poverty lines, can also partly explain why empirical studies fail to confirm the impact of social assistance on poverty alleviation (see Bahle, Pfeifer and Wendt 2010). Recent research on poverty has moved from poverty conceptions to material deprivation, defined as a set of basic needs (e.g. financial capacity to keep the home adequately warm or to be able to afford to buy meat every second day if desired), and shows that these two conceptions are only partly congruent (Nolan and Whelan 2010).[29] However, empirical studies using material deprivation as a dependent variable indicate that the generosity of social assistance schemes has a significant impact (Nelson 2012). This discussion indicates that the generosity of the welfare state might possibly be associated with generous social assistance and thus with lower poverty.

Second, *family-related programmes* are aimed at other ways, such as reconciliation of work and family and gender equality (see Thévenon 2011), of reducing poverty (see Gornick, Meyers and Ross 1997). Families are exposed to higher poverty risks not only because they have more mouths to feed but also because they have to organise the care of their children, either by reducing the workload of one parent or by paying for external childcare facilities. Welfare states can help families by designing respective policies. Two forms of family programmes can be differentiated: on the one hand, traditional family support such as cash and non-cash benefits as well as tax allowances, and, on the other hand, policies that support the employment of parents (Misra, Moller and Budig 2007). The former's objective is to augment the family income. In contrast, parental support, including not only paid and unpaid parental leave but also the provision of external childcare either subsidised or provided by the state, can be seen as an alternative strategy to reducing a family's poverty by supporting dual-earner households, that is, mothers' employment. However, scholars contend that employment support for parents creates a 'Matthew effect', the sociological phenomenon of accumulated advantage: mothers with higher education are more likely to pursue and be in paid employment and thus to rely more often on these programmes compared to less-educated mothers. Consequently, these social programmes mainly benefit higher-income families and thus do not primarily contribute to reducing poverty (Cantillon 2011).

Empirical studies confirm the impact of both types of family-related policies on poverty, although there is empirical evidence for the Matthew effect concerning parental leave (for a comprehensive discussion and analysis, see van Lancker 2014). Misra, Moller and Budig's (2007) analysis of nine countries between the mid-1990s and 2000 shows that more generous traditional family allowances, the support of childcare and family leave (paid and unpaid) are all related to lower poverty levels.[30] Further studies show not only that the effect of family-related policies is even stronger for single mothers compared to two-parent families but also that the poverty-reducing effect is indirectly related to mothers' employment (Misra et al. 2012). In contrast, paid maternal leave has no significant effect on poverty. Bäckman and Ferrarini's findings (2010) corroborate the poverty alleviating effect of dual-earner policies and traditional family policies. However, the latter only have an effect if the poverty risks of female-headed households are considered. Their results further show that, when controlling for publicly provided childcare services, the dual-earner policy as well as the traditional family policy effects are reduced, but the latter significantly reduces poverty. The findings are robust when looking at twenty-one countries, including those in Eastern and Central Europe or sub-samples.

Finally, the third type of social programme refers to *unemployment benefits*. The basic idea of unemployment insurance is to balance out the financial situation of workers and their families during business fluctuations and to compensate for the respective loss of market income (Sjöberg, Palme and Caroll 2010). However, the benefit of unemployment insurance is contested in the literature as it is directly related to the functioning of the labour market by affecting work incentives. Some scholars maintain that the generosity and longevity of this social programme promote prolonged dependency on unemployment benefits (see Danziger, Haveman and Plotnick 1981; Sjöberg

2000). But unemployment benefits may also have positive effects on the labour supply as well as a country's overall economic success. On the one hand, the existence of unemployment programmes allows jobseekers to find employment that matches their skills. On the other hand, unemployment insurance in combination with other forms of employment protection reduces the wage uncertainty in a worker's career and increases the benefits of investing in human capital, in particular skill-development (Estevez-Abe, Iversen and Soskice 2001).

The majority of empirical studies suggest that unemployment insurance has a poverty-reducing impact. Bäckman's (2005, 2009) research on sixteen Western countries between 1980 and 2000, for instance, shows that unemployment insurance generosity has a substantive effect on poverty, even when sickness insurance and dual-earner policies are considered. Two specific institutional characteristics of unemployment insurance are important, namely net replacement rates and, to a lesser extent, the duration of unemployment insurance schemes, in contrast to the coverage of the workforce which has no significant effect (Bäckman 2005). These results are corroborated by Kenworthy's (1999) cross-sectional study of fifteen advanced industrialised countries around the year 1991. Higher social wages – measured by the replacement rate in percentage of the median worker income – are related not only with lower relative but also with absolute poverty. However, Scruggs and Allan (2006) did not find any significant effect of unemployment insurance generosity on either relative or absolute poverty in sixteen OECD countries between 1980 and 2000. The results instead showed that the generosity of sickness and pension benefits are more accurate predictors for the prevailing levels of poverty of the working population and the elderly population respectively. The authors point to the sensitivity of the results and the high correlation with other indicators of welfare generosity such as spending, pension and sickness benefits. When excluding these three alternative welfare state measures, the coefficients are, as expected, negative and significant.[31]

In sum, based on comparative welfare state literature, this book expects more regulated labour market institutions, that is, wage-setting systems and statutory minimum wages, as well as more generous social programmes, that is, social assistance, traditional family allowances, dual-earner support and unemployment compensation, to have an alleviating effect on a country's poverty, albeit only when the poverty of citizens is concerned. However, the labour market and welfare system are not expected to have a direct impact on immigrants' poverty. As is argued in the next section, the impact of the labour market and the welfare state system on immigrants' poverty is expected to be conditional on the social rights of immigrants.

Accounting for Immigrants' Social Rights and Their Access to Paid Employment and Social Programmes

Certainly, as long as immigrants are granted full access to the labour market and social programmes, there is no reason to expect that the labour market and welfare system affect immigrants' and non-immigrants' poverty differently, once socio-demographic characteristics are controlled for. However, as discussed earlier in the text, immigrants' social rights not only vary across countries but also depend on the immigration category they are assigned upon entry and during the course of settlement (when margizens become denizens).

In this book, social rights are defined as including the right to paid employment and can range from inclusive to exclusive, where the former puts immigrants on par with natives while the latter imposes different treatment. Access to paid employment, for example, can be restricted to a particular employer or sector or allow immigrants to pursue any form of employment. Analogously, access to social programmes can differ with regard to the extent to which immigrants are eligible. Again, it should be noted that the respective social rights vary depending on the immigration category the residence permit is issued for, namely that some types of immigration categories have more extensive social rights than others. The least privileged are undocumented immigrants who have neither legal access to the labour market nor access to social programmes. Nevertheless, a number of countries ensure that undocumented immigrants receive health care support beyond accident and emergency treatment, for example, related to pregnancy and maternity as in Belgium, the Netherlands, Spain and Italy (see Romero-Ortuño 2004). According to other authors, permanent residents and recognised refugees are on the other end of the spectrum and are granted social and economic rights that are almost equal to those of non-immigrants (Brubaker 1989; Hammar 1990; see also Aleinikoff and Klusmeyer 2002). Taking this into account, a country's inclusiveness of immigrants' social rights depends on the extent to which they include particular immigration categories (e.g. granting full, partial or no access) as well as on the scope of immigration categories included (e.g. only specific immigration categories such as family members or labour migrants versus all immigration categories), the two extremes including incorporation of all or no immigration categories.

Therefore, the analytical framework focuses on the interplay between inclusiveness of immigrants' social rights and the labour market and welfare system in order to explain cross-national variations in immigrants' poverty. Concerning the labour market, more regulated labour market arrangements are expected to have a poverty-reducing effect. Whether they also affect immigrants' poverty, however, depends on immigrants' access to paid employment. In other words, immigrants' work rights are expected to moderate the impact of labour market institutions on their poverty (see bold arrow in figure 1.1). The idea is that immigrants benefit to the same extent as non-immigrant workers from the effects of regulated labour market institutions, as soon as they get access to the labour market and pursue paid employment. Labour market participation, in turn, influences their chances of making a living, and thus their exposure to poverty. This means that immigrants' poverty levels should be considerably lower in countries that combine regulated labour market institutions and inclusive work rights for immigrants than in countries with less-regulated labour market institutions and exclusive work rights, with the two remaining combinations resulting in mid-way levels of poverty. Consequently, the hypothesis proposed is that the poverty-alleviating effect of more highly regulated labour market institutions on immigrants' poverty is conditional on the inclusiveness of immigrants' work rights (labour market hypothesis).

The same logic and argument can also be applied to the effect of welfare state arrangements. Since social programmes augment or replace the income of different segments of the population, such as those in need, families and the unemployed, more generous social programmes should be correlated with lower poverty.

However, immigrants living in countries with generous welfare states might not be in a more fortunate situation compared to immigrants settled in countries with less generous social programmes. Whether this is the case hinges on whether immigrants are actually granted access to welfare benefits. Therefore, the second hypothesis proposed is that the poverty-alleviating effect of more generous social programmes on immigrants' poverty is conditional on the inclusiveness of immigrants' social rights (welfare state hypothesis).

The analytical framework focuses on immigrants' social rights which differ depending on the immigration category. However, as discussed earlier in the text, immigration policies cannot be disregarded when explaining immigrants' poverty. On the one hand, immigration policies are linked to immigrants' social rights via the specific immigration category immigrants are assigned upon entry (e.g. labour migrants, family members, refugees and asylum seekers). On the other hand, as different scholars argue, immigration policies and immigrants' social rights can be interlinked (Faist 1995; Brochmann and Hammar 1999; Banting 2000). For example, states may compensate for restrictive immigration policies with inclusive social rights, and vice versa (see also Helbling et al. 2013, 10), or, in welfare chauvinist jargon, opt for external or internal exclusion. Moreover, more liberal immigration policies towards particular types of immigration inflows influence the composition of the immigrant population living in the country, that is, the outcomes of immigration policy, which, in turn, is related to the poverty of immigrants.

This indirect impact of immigration policies via the composition of the *immigrant population living in the country* is accounted for in the analytical framework. Although immigration policies cannot fully control immigration inflows, they determine who may enter the country and thus, to a certain extent, steer the composition of immigrants living within the territory. Immigrants who were selected based on a country's labour demand and their skills, for example, labour migrants, might face fewer (or other) complications regarding labour market (and social) integration compared to those migrating for family-related or humanitarian reasons, for example, family members, refugees and asylum seekers. The reason is that the former might have already spent time, while still being in their country of origin, in getting familiar with their future country of residence and language and/or the transferability of their skills (see Bauer, Lofstrom and Zimmermann 2000). Based on this argument, this book assumes that in countries with more liberal immigration policies, immigrants' poverty is higher than in countries with restrictive immigration policies. In other words, immigrants' poverty is higher in countries that are less selective regarding immigrants. For this reason, the composition of the immigrant population is taken into account.

In sum, the analytical framework builds on the assumption that the labour market and welfare state system are the main determinants of a country's prevailing poverty level. Yet, it can be argued that its effect on immigrants' poverty is contingent on the inclusiveness of immigrants' social rights granting them access to paid employment and social benefits. Last but not least, the analytical framework accounts for the effect of immigration policies via the immigrant population. Well-established determinants in poverty research, namely economic factors at the macro-level and structural, that is, socio-demographic, factors at the micro-level, are included in the analysis as controls (for a review, see Brady 2009 and chapter 4).

WHAT THE FRAMEWORK DOES NOT CONSIDER

There are several limitations related to the analytical framework. The first relates to its focus on the institutional context. This neo-institutional approach excludes the role of certain actors central to the policymaking process – for example, unions, firms, employers' associations, political parties and government, including ethnic and pro-immigrant networks and organisations. Thus, the focus on policies and national laws neglects by whom, for which reasons and in which broader institutional context particular policies are adopted. Moreover, it gives insights neither into which actors and actor coalitions have been more successful than others in pursuing their interests and preferences, nor to which aims these policies have been adopted. To put it simply, the analytical framework cannot explain why particular policies have been introduced in some countries but not in others (see also Sainsbury 2012).

A second limitation is that the analytical framework concentrates on policy output, that is, legal regulations, rather than their implementation. Equality in terms of formal rights as specified in laws and regulations does not assure that they are implemented by respective agencies. Individuals can be denied certain rights that exist in law and regulations, as they are rarely unambiguous and thus dependent on the discretion of national bureaucracies. Public employees interpret a series of regulations and apply them to each individual case (see also Kumlin and Rothstein 2005, 348–49, on the implementation of needs-tested programmes). This discretionary practice does not have to be detrimental for immigrants. Irregular immigrants in some cases benefit from rights not laid down in law such as medical assistance. The analytical framework considers neither the implementation by governmental agencies nor informal regulations existing in a country. An imperfect proxy for implementation practices could be anti-discrimination laws, which guarantee not only equality before the law but also address racial discrimination. Because they abolish legal obstacles immigrants face in the receiving country (see Mahnig and Wimmer 2000) and define a proactive position a nation state takes towards foreigners,[32] they could affect immigrants' poverty. These constitutional legal enactments also play a role in the labour market by formally ensuring that immigrants are treated the same way as citizens when they are hired or once they are employed.

This point is especially relevant where the labour market is concerned. Here, informal practices in addition to formal labour market access are central issues. Even if immigrants have the same rights as citizens, they might encounter labour market discrimination, with discrimination being defined simply as 'unequal treatment of persons or groups on the basis of their race or ethnicity' (Pager and Shepherd 2008, 182), although other types of discrimination including gender, age and religion could also be present. Labour market discrimination can occur due to (racial) prejudices, the more affective part of attitudes, and due to stereotypes that are associated with inadequate information, the more cognitive part of attitudes, also known as statistical discrimination. The impact of labour market discrimination on the poverty of immigrants can be through limited access to employment or lower wages. Examples in the hiring process are lower call-back rates and wage offers (for a literature review, see Dancygier and Laitin 2014). Although it is difficult to measure labour market discrimination, empirical research indicates that immigrants across post-industrialised countries undergo discrimination. Even if employment and wage gaps have declined over time, they nonetheless differ across job type and the migrant group analysed (see Bassanini and Saint-Martin 2008).

Furthermore, the exclusion of non-governmental organisations such as ethnic and pro-immigrant associations also ignores the possibility that these immigrant networks might act as alternative providers of welfare, comparable to the family or the church as discussed in comparative welfare state literature, and therefore directly influence immigrants' poverty. These organisations might create 'network externalities' such as helping newly arrived immigrants (as well as long-term residents) to obtain central information about the host country related to employment, the creation of small enterprises, or accommodation as well as simply providing basic services (Portes 1998; Fennema 2004; Epstein 2009). For example, migrant networks might inform migrant jobseekers about procedures and employment opportunities (on the role of ethnic communities in disseminating information; see, for example, Borjas and Hilton 1996). Additionally, migrant networks might also help in the recruitment process by reducing employers' expectations regarding skills, job qualifications and previous experience. By doing so, they thus contribute to reducing labour market discrimination. But migrant and especially ethnic networks might also have adverse effects. In the long run, these networks might reduce mobility because immigrants are channelled towards jobs that are common among network members, which have been shown to be often low-wage employment (see Kalter and Kogan, 2014). The concentration of particular ethnic groups and their organisational level in a country might also contribute to explaining cross-national differences in immigrants' poverty.

The analytical framework also does not include the impact of direct integration policies within the labour market and the welfare state that are designed to especially target the needs of immigrants. Examples are programmes facilitating the entry of immigrants into the labour market, or the improvement of their educational qualifications in the form of language courses or additional schooling for socially disadvantaged immigrants. Countries such as France and the United Kingdom provide specific schemes to integrate immigrants into the labour market, while the Netherlands and Germany focus on similar programmes for immigrant youths (Mahnig and Wimmer 2000, 195; see also OECD 2007c, 2008). Policies within this domain can also refer to affirmative action, which focuses on the 'equity of outcomes' rather than on 'equal opportunities' and treatment. The Netherlands and the United Kingdom have introduced quotas in the public and private sector, which allocate a specific number of jobs to immigrants (Mahnig and Wimmer 2000, 197; Koopmans et al. 2005, 66–69). Norway has recently committed to interviewing at least one foreigner when hiring workers in the public sector, and to employing immigrants if their qualifications are the same as those of a native (Liebig 2009). Although these policies and quotas have been introduced to reflect the cultural diversity of a society, affirmative action programmes are relatively rare in this field. Direct integration policies in the domain of the welfare state, such as cash transfers or special treatment (e.g. allocation of housing), are even less common. This is if integration programmes or introduction programmes that grant immigrants a certain amount of money, usually an amount below the level of social assistance, are excluded. Until the 1970s, France and the Netherlands, for example, provided special housing programmes for immigrants (Mahnig and Wimmer 2000, 196). Even though it has been argued that, for efficiency reasons, specific social programmes for immigrants would improve their socio-economic outcomes, they are hard to justify due to their non-universal character (Mahnig 2001; see also Brubaker 1989, 180n22). Moreover, because national majorities perceive these programmes as undeserved privileges for immigrants, supporters of those programmes fail to win a majority in political elections (Mahnig 2001). Thus, a tendency to introduce universal programmes can be observed. These are mainly aimed at supporting immigrants, but also provide aid to disadvantaged citizens.

Finally, the claim that inclusive immigration-related policies are beneficial for immigrants' socio-economic outcomes can be questioned. Indeed, exclusive immigration-related policies may also facilitate the incorporation of immigrants. For example, a country may limit access to paid employment and social programmes only to permanent residents, while at the same time making it very difficult to obtain a permanent residence permit due to strict requirements referring to minimum income and integration, such as knowledge of the host country and acquisition of the national language. However, the efforts 'newly' permanent residents have made in order to get the permit itself might enable immigrants to economically sustain themselves. Proficiency in the national language, for example, is favourable for immigrants' socio-economic outcomes because it reduces social distances and is a valuable resource when seeking adequate employment (for an overview, see Esser 2006, 82–87). On the other hand, inclusive social rights do not necessarily lead to lower poverty. Although immigrants may have a legal claim to social benefits, the reliance on social programmes, in particular, social assistance or other means-tested programmes, can have negative consequences on immigrants' legal status and their residence permits. In a number of countries, such as Switzerland, Germany, Denmark, Austria and the United Kingdom, the self-sufficiency of immigrants is a condition for remaining in the country and renewal of their permits during their first years in the country (see Koopmans, Michalowski and Waibel 2012). In Germany, for example, reliance on social assistance by foreigners or their family members is a reason for expulsion (Kingreen 2010, 46–47). Moreover, in Switzerland, welfare dependency can be a reason for expulsion from the country even for permanent residents.[33] This might be a reason for higher (or lower) immigrant poverty rates despite inclusive (or exclusive) social rights.

Chapter 2

Dealing with Immigrants: Poverty

This chapter gives a descriptive overview of cross-national variations in immigrants' poverty. Its main aim is to identify specific poverty patterns in advanced industrialised countries. The first section focuses on immigrants' poverty and distinguishes between *poverty before* and *after taxes and transfers*. The former is based on market income, which includes incomes from wages and salaries, self-employment, property and private pensions, while the latter is based on disposable income that takes taxes and social transfers into account. As well as being a common convention, this differentiation is necessary as poverty rates before and after taxes and transfers are expected to be affected by different determinants and mechanisms, namely labour market institutions in the former case and social programmes in the latter case (see also Moller et al. 2003; Lohmann 2009). Poverty reduction, which accounts for households that are defined as poor based on market income but move out of poverty due to the tax and welfare system, is also assessed. The results are presented for three different types of households: immigrants, non-immigrants and mixed households. The analysis is complemented with alternative poverty measures: income gaps, which give some insights into how well poor households fare, and the intensity measure, which combines income gaps with poverty rates.

The second section of this chapter focuses on poverty after controlling for the effect of households' socio-demographic characteristics. One suggestion raised in migration literature is to compare immigrants' outcomes to the national average in general rather than to comparable non-immigrant groups (see Wimmer and Glick Schiller 2003, 584). In order to address this criticism, the poverty gaps between immigrants and non-immigrants have been calculated. Based on logistic regression analysis, the average marginal effects (AME) of being an immigrant household are calculated using the position of the household relative to the poverty line as the dependent variable. The last section combines both measures and identifies different patterns of poverty related to a country's poverty level and poverty gaps between immigrants and non-immigrants: a universalist type (low level of immigrant poverty and low poverty gap), a residual/liberal type (high level of immigrant poverty and low poverty gap), a segmented/stratified type (low level of immigrant poverty and high poverty gap) and a welfare chauvinism/dualism type (high level of immigrant poverty and high poverty gap).

THE IMPORTANCE OF THE IMMIGRANT BACKGROUND . . .

Poverty rates based on the market and disposable incomes of nineteen advanced industrialised countries are presented in this section for the year 2007.[1] Following comparative research on poverty (e.g. Korpi and Palme 1998; Hicks and Kenworthy 2003; Brady, Fullerton and Cross 2009; Lohmann 2009), poverty rates have been defined in relative terms as the share of households with an income below the poverty line, here defined as 50 per cent of a country's median income, while adjusting for the household size using the modified OECD equivalence scale.[2] The results discussed below are confined to the working-age population, defined as those aged between twenty-one and fifty-nine. Since this definition of poverty is not based on an absolute cross-country measure, it should be rather considered as an indicator for poverty risk, which allows the standard of living in a particular country to be taken into account (Brady 2009; Bäckman and Ferrarini 2010). Three different types of households are distinguished based on the country of birth of its adult members: non-immigrant households, immigrant households and mixed households (which include at least one household member born in the country of residence and one born abroad – see methodological appendix for further information).

Poverty Rates Based on Market Income

On average, pre-tax and transfer poverty are around 19 per cent across all countries, indicating that one out of five households are living below the poverty threshold ($SD = 2.9$). However, when distinguishing between poverty rates of non-immigrant and immigrant households, considerable differences emerge. A non-immigrant poverty rate of around 18 per cent is slightly below the mean (M, $SD = 3.3$), while the poverty rate for immigrant households is twice as high, with a grand-mean across all nineteen countries of 35 per cent ($SD = 11.5$, see appendix table 2A.1). The high standard deviation (SD) of immigrant households points to cross-national variations in poverty rates before taxes and transfers, which are presented in figure 2.1. The first bar refers to non-immigrants' poverty rates, followed by those for mixed and immigrant households.

Three observations can be made. First, the pre-tax and transfer poverty rates of non-immigrant households are more or less comparable across and within welfare regimes, ranging between 16 per cent and 21 per cent. The major exceptions are Switzerland and Sweden, which have markets that generate less poverty (9 per cent and 13 per cent, respectively); while Ireland is an outlier at the top end (26 per cent). Second, poverty rates of mixed households are comparable to those of non-immigrant households. In the majority of the countries analysed, the difference is less than 3 percentage points. In several countries, poverty rates of mixed households are even lower, such as in Norway, Australia and Ireland.[3] By contrast, the share of mixed households that are below the poverty line compared to non-immigrants is substantially higher in Belgium, Germany and France (e.g. 24 per cent versus 17 per cent).

Last but not least, immigrants' poverty rates are higher than those of non-immigrants in all countries. Moreover, they tend to cluster across welfare regimes. The highest rates of poverty can be found in the Nordic countries

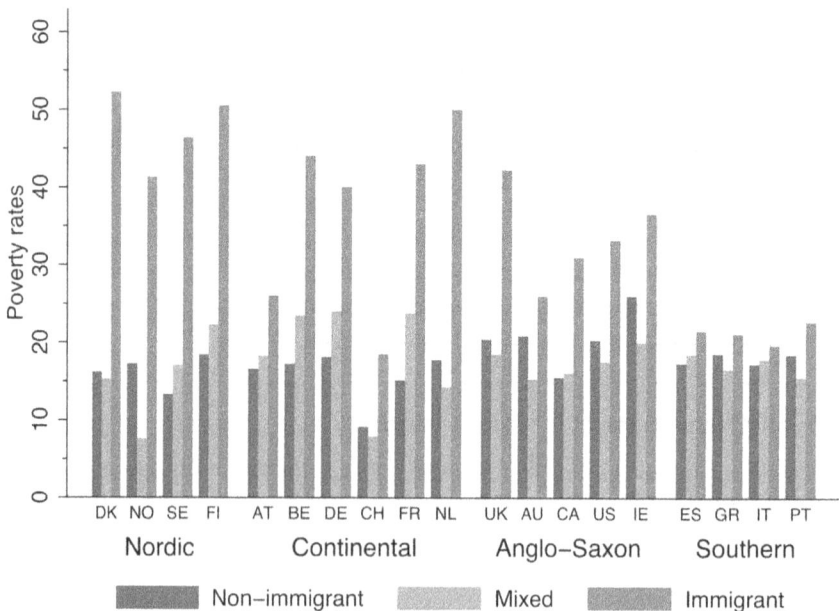

Figure 2.1 **Poverty rates based on market income (50 per cent of median income).** *Source*: **EU-SILC (European countries), HILDA (Australia), SLID (Canada) and CPS (United States).**

(around 48 per cent), followed by Continental European countries (around 41 per cent, excluding Switzerland) and Anglo-Saxon countries (around 34 per cent). In Southern European countries, immigrants' poverty rates are the lowest and most comparable to those of non-immigrant households. In other words, immigrant households in the Nordic countries are almost three times more likely to fall below the poverty threshold, while the ratio is below 1.2 in Southern European countries.[4] For Continental European countries, the ratio is more than twice as high, compared to 1.6 in Anglo-Saxon countries. Within the country groups, however, variations can be observed. For Continental European countries, immigrants' poverty rates are considerably lower in Switzerland (19 per cent) and Austria (26 per cent) compared to Belgium (44 per cent) and the Netherlands (50 per cent). In Anglo-Saxon countries, poverty rates of immigrants living in Canada are lower than those of their British counterparts (31 per cent and 42 per cent, respectively). Although the differences between countries are less pronounced in the Nordic countries, the share of immigrant households considered poor is higher in Denmark (52 per cent) than Norway (41 per cent).

So far, the economic situation of immigrants in Southern Europe looks quite rosy. However, the results presented earlier in the text do not take into account residents working in the informal sector, both natives and immigrants, or irregular immigrants.[5] Concerning the former, both immigrants' and non-immigrants' poverty rates may be overestimated in certain countries if a high share of the population, and in particular of the household members, is employed in the informal sector as these additional earnings that supplement a household's income are not included in the official income surveys used for the analysis. According to Feld and Schneider (2010, 134), the estimated size of the shadow economy in 2007 was highest in Southern European countries (above 19 per cent of official GDP), closely followed by Belgium (19 per cent) and the Nordic countries, as well as in Germany (around 15 per cent).[6] Although there is no reliable data on the number of irregular immigrants in the informal economy, studies so far suggest that they make up a considerable proportion (see King and Rueda 2008, 285–86). However, taking into account that irregular immigrants have to rely on their own means to maintain themselves financially and thus may have a higher probability to participate in the informal sector, crude estimates on the proportion of irregular immigrants can be made.

Although all advanced industrialised countries experience some forms of irregular migration, they are exposed to clandestine migration to different degrees (see Düvell 2008; OECD 2009). Despite the difficulties of getting reliable estimates on the size of clandestine immigration, several studies show that Southern Europe and also the United Kingdom and the United States have higher shares of illegal immigration (e.g. Kovacheva and Vogel

2009; OECD 2009). For example, irregular immigration in Greece has been estimated to be between 172,000 and 209,000 (19–24 per cent of the foreign population), while in the United Kingdom, the estimates fluctuate between 417,000 and 863,000 (11 per cent to 24 per cent of the foreign population; see also chapter 3).

Taking these considerations about irregular migration and the informal sector into account, one could assume that immigrants' poverty rates might be even lower than the ones based on official statistics in specific countries. However, this argument has to be put into perspective. On the one hand, earnings and wages in the informal economy are usually lower compared to in the formal economy and, on the other hand, immigrants staying irregularly in a country usually have no access to social programmes and are only granted a few basic rights related to health care (urgent emergency) and children's education (see FRA 2011).

Poverty Rates Based on Disposable Income

Moving to post-tax and transfer poverty, the cross-country mean lies at 9 per cent (SD = 3.1), which is half of the size of pre-tax and transfer poverty discussed earlier in the chapter. Nevertheless, differences between immigrants and non-immigrants persist. On average, immigrants' poverty rates in the nineteen industrialised countries are at 20 per cent (SD = 5.1), almost 2.5 times the relative value for non-immigrants, whose poverty rates lie at 8 per cent (SD = 3.1).

Turning to cross-national variations of non-immigrants' poverty risk, the evidence in figure 2.2 points to a cluster predicted by comparative welfare state literature. The Nordic and Continental European countries feature the lowest poverty rates (around 6 per cent), followed by Anglo-Saxon countries (around 10 per cent) and Southern European countries (around 12 per cent). Germany is closer to the Anglo-Saxon countries with poverty levels around 9 per cent, while poverty rates in the United States reach almost 15 per cent.[7] The poverty risk of mixed households is closer to those of non-immigrants once taxes and transfers are taken into account. In Norway and Australia, mixed households experience an even lower poverty risk than non-immigrant households. Interestingly, the pre-tax and transfer difference between non-immigrants and mixed households living in Germany disappears.

However, the welfare regime pattern is less consistent when looking at immigrants' poverty rates. Immigrant households' poverty levels are still considerably higher than those of non-immigrant or mixed households. But the stair-like trend in figure 2.1 (i.e. higher poverty rates in Nordic and Continental Europe followed by Anglo-Saxon and Southern European countries) disappears when looking at immigrant-specific poverty. The poverty rates of

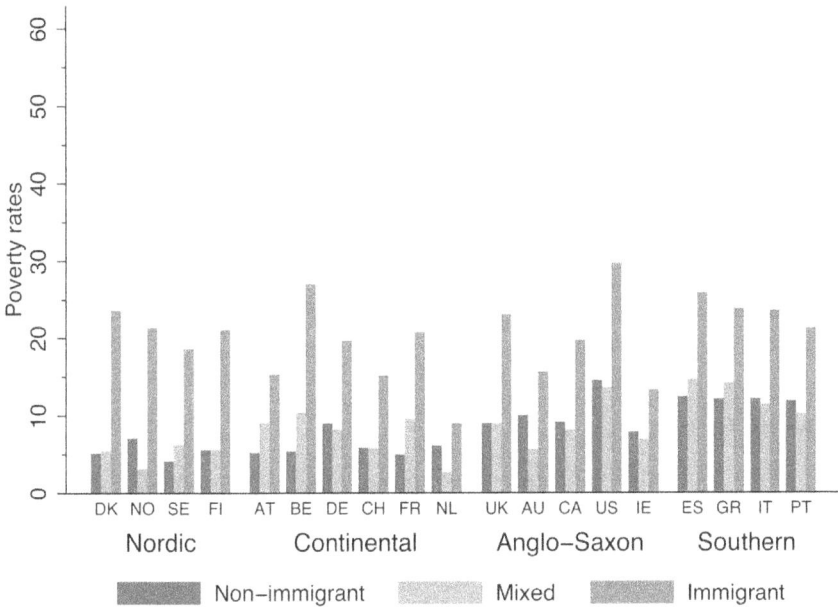

Figure 2.2   **Poverty rates based on disposable income (50 per cent of median income).**
Source: **EU-SILC (European countries), HILDA (Australia), SLID (Canada) and CPS (United States).**

Southern European immigrant households are now around the cross-country mean. The Nordic and Southern European countries are still relatively homogeneous, with country group averages of 21 per cent and 24 per cent, respectively; but higher variation exists in Continental European and Anglo-Saxon countries. Immigrant households living in the Netherlands (9 per cent) and Ireland (13 per cent) experience the lowest poverty risk, followed by those in Switzerland, Austria and Australia (around 15 per cent). In contrast, one out of four immigrant households in Belgium and the United States are living with an income below the poverty threshold. But the classification of countries according to their immigration history does not considerably contribute to explaining cross-national variations (Hollifield, Martin and Orrenius 2014; see also Castles and Miller 2009). The three major groups proposed by these authors and presented in more detail in the next chapter distinguish between *traditional immigration countries*, including Australia, Canada and the United States, *latecomers to immigration,* including Southern Europe, as well as Finland and Ireland and finally, *countries of immigration*, including those countries with a 'guest worker' tradition (e.g. Germany, Belgium, Sweden and Denmark) and a colonial past (e.g. France, the Netherlands and the United Kingdom).

A final observation is that the relative difference between poverty rates of immigrants and non-immigrants varies. In Nordic countries, they are more than four times more likely to live in poverty, compared to three times more likely in Continental Europe and two times more likely in Anglo-Saxon and Southern European countries. The highest differences between non-immigrant and immigrant households can be observed in Belgium, Sweden and Denmark, and to some extent in France, where immigrant households are 4.5 times more likely to live below the poverty line. In contrast, poverty rates for both groups are more comparable in the Netherlands and Australia, with the probability for immigrants living in poverty being around 1.5 times higher than for non-immigrants.[8]

Poverty Reduction

In order to facilitate the comparison of poverty rates before and after taxes and transfers, *poverty reduction effectiveness (PRE) scores* are calculated (Mitchell 1991). The resulting scores are simply the difference between poverty rates based on market and disposable income, standardised by the poverty rates based on market income. A value of 70 indicates that 70 per cent of the poor households move out of poverty, while a value of −20 means that the share of poor households increases by 20 per cent when taking taxes and transfers into account. Higher PRE scores can thus be associated with higher effectiveness of countries, or welfare states, in reducing poverty, and vice versa (see Mitchell 1991, 65; Moller et al. 2003, 33; Morissens and Sainsbury 2005).[9]

The PRE scores are on average around 50 ($SD = 17$), indicating that 50 out of 100 poor working-age households can be lifted out of poverty. The respective PRE scores by country and immigrant group are presented in figure 2.3. In almost all countries, the PRE scores of immigrant households are lower compared to non-immigrant households. While across all countries over 50 per cent of poor non-immigrant households attain a socially acceptable standard of living ($M = 52$, $SD = 15$), this is the case for only 34 per cent of immigrant households ($M = 34$, $SD = 29$). For non-immigrant households, the values range from 28 to 70, and for immigrant households, from −20 to 81.

Non-immigrants' PRE scores cluster relatively coherently within types of welfare regimes, with the highest scores found in the Nordic countries (66), closely followed by Continental European countries (60) and Southern European countries (32). However, in Anglo-Saxon countries, the PRE scores vary considerably. Almost 70 per cent of Irish native households can be lifted out of poverty, while this is the case only for 29 per cent of US-American households. The PRE scores for mixed households are in general somewhat lower, though five countries differ from this pattern, namely Finland, Canada,

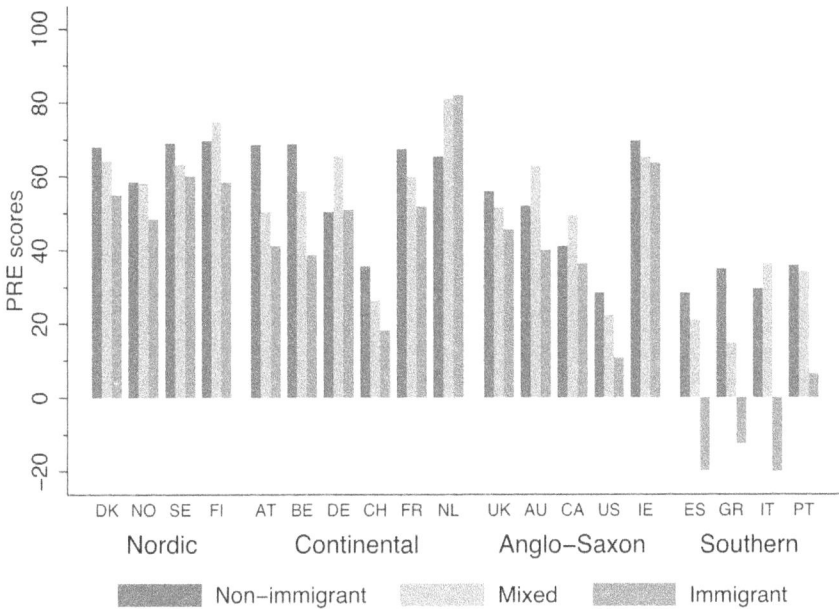

Figure 2.3   Poverty reduction (50 per cent of median income). *Source*: **EU-SILC (European countries), HILDA (Australia), SLID (Canada) and CPS (United States).**

Australia, Germany and the Netherlands (PRE scores are between 5 and 15 points higher than for non-immigrants).

The Netherlands is also a major exception when looking at PRE scores of immigrant households, where more than eight out of ten immigrant (and mixed) households can be taken out of poverty. In the remaining countries, immigrants' PRE scores are lower following the same pattern described earlier in the text: northern countries (55), Continental European countries (47) and Anglo-Saxon countries (39). Southern European countries are at the bottom of the league, where the share of poor immigrant households increases on average by 11 per cent after taking the tax and welfare system into account. However, this does not mean that immigrants living in Greece, Spain or Italy are excluded from receiving social benefits nor that they pay more taxes than the amount they receive in social benefits.[10] Moreover, the PRE scores represent the net share of poor households that move out of poverty and thus conceals that some households move into poverty while other households move out of poverty. In fact, every fifth poor immigrant household is lifted out of poverty in these three countries. But the share of poor households that were non-poor based on market income increases by 34 per cent after taking taxes and transfers into account, thus resulting in an average net PRE score of −11 for Southern European countries (see appendix table 2A.1).

In Southern European countries, the differences between immigrant and non-immigrant PRE scores are the highest compared to Nordic and Anglo-Saxon countries (except the United States), where they are much lower. In Continental European countries, the traditional guest worker countries, differences are also quite high, except in Germany. This could be an indication of the stronger focus on work-related social programmes, which depend on previous employment, in Continental European countries. In Austria and Belgium, for example, around 70 per cent of poor non-immigrant households can be lifted out of poverty, compared to 40 per cent of immigrant households. In contrast, the scores for immigrants and non-immigrants are almost identical in Germany (PRE score = 50). This is an interesting finding, as some studies suggest that immigrants were disproportionately affected by the Hartz IV reforms (see Butterwegge and Reißlandt 2005). Moreover, the difference between immigrants and non-immigrants' PRE scores is also relatively low in Canada, Ireland and Sweden.

Finally, two outliers with considerably lower immigrant PRE scores are worth mentioning. Switzerland and the United States do relatively poorly when it comes to reducing the poverty rates of immigrant households. In Switzerland, only one out of five poor households reaches a socially acceptable standard of living, and this is the case for only 11 per cent of immigrant households in the United States. However, while in the former, the poverty rates based on market income are among the lowest across the countries (19 per cent), the respective value for the United States is almost twice as high (33 per cent).

In sum, the comparison of these three poverty indicators yields four main findings. First, immigrant households are more likely to live below the poverty line than non-immigrant and mixed households, regardless of whether these are measured by poverty rates before or after taxes and transfers. Second, across all countries, immigrants are less likely to move out of poverty than non-immigrants. Third, the results also show that poverty rates of non-immigrant households, at least when measured in terms of disposable income, are ranked according to welfare state literature proposals. Non-immigrant households living in Nordic and Continental European countries experience lower poverty risk than their counterparts in Anglo-Saxon and Southern European countries. Finally, these findings partly apply to immigrant households when considering the similarity within country groups but not regarding the level of poverty rates. On the one hand, variations in immigrants' poverty rates within the Nordic and Southern European countries are relatively small. By contrast, in Continental European and Anglo-Saxon countries, immigrants' country of residence makes a significant difference.

The poverty rates after taxes and transfers are considerably higher in the United States, Belgium and the United Kingdom with almost or over 25 per cent of poor immigrant households, compared to the Netherlands and Ireland (below 14 per cent). On the other hand, no clear pattern emerges with regard to the levels of immigrant poverty. The respective values are not considerably lower in Nordic countries, but comparable to Southern European countries (around 20 per cent). Moreover, when disregarding the outliers Belgium and the United States, poverty rates of immigrant households are actually lower in Continental European and Anglo-Saxon countries.

However, poverty rates do not provide information on how poor households fare. For instance, two countries with the same poverty rates may hide the fact that poor households on average have considerably different financial budgets. In one country, poor households in general may live with an income just below the poverty threshold, while in another country, the average income of poor households may be less than half of the poverty threshold. For this reason, two alternative poverty measures are presented in the next section.

Alternative Measures of Poverty – Income Gaps and Intensity

The first measure, income gaps, captures the difference between the average income of poor households and the poverty threshold, standardised by the poverty threshold. The indicator ranges between 0 and 1, with higher values indicating that the income of poor households is substantially below the poverty threshold. The second measure, intensity, is simply the product of the poverty rate and the income gap (see Brady 2003, 2009).

The *income gap based on market income* across countries is, on average, .62 (SD = .07). In other words, in the majority of the countries studied, poor households live with a market income that is less than 50 per cent of the poverty threshold. One possible reason for this is that poor household members have low labour market attachment levels and consequently no earnings from employment. The relative values for immigrant and non-immigrant households are comparable, with an average around .63, but with a higher standard deviation for immigrant households (SDs = .13 and .07). Mixed households fare comparatively better with a mean of .56 (SD = .09).

The income gaps based on market income by country are summarised in figure 2.4. Generally speaking, immigrants fare worse compared to non-immigrant households in the Nordic and Continental European countries as well as in Ireland. The opposite is the case for poor immigrant households in Southern European countries and the United States who have market incomes that are closer to the poverty line than the non-immigrant poor. Taking Greece as an example, immigrant households live, on average, with a yearly

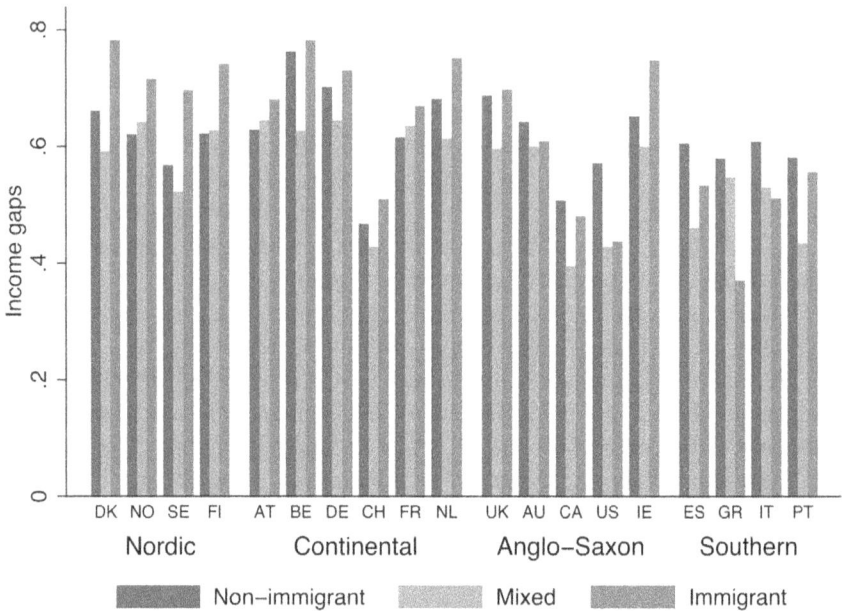

Figure 2.4   Income gaps based on market income (50 per cent of median income). *Source*: **EU-SILC (European countries), HILDA (Australia), SLID (Canada) and CPS (United States).**

income of 63 per cent of the poverty threshold, here €4,900, compared to 42 per cent for non-immigrant households. This finding can also be observed in Australia and Canada, though to a lower degree.[11]

When taking taxes and transfers into account, the *income gaps based on disposable income* are, on average, considerably lower ($M = .32$, $SD = .05$). The grand-mean is comparable for non-immigrant and immigrant households ($M = .33$, $SD = .05$ and $M = .34$, $SD = .08$). These results indicate that the disposable income of poor households, though not enough to lift them out of poverty, is closer to the poverty threshold. This finding is also supported when comparing the values across countries (see figure 2.5).

However, in contrast to income gaps based on market income, no clear patterns can be observed across country groups. First, in a number of countries, immigrant households are less poor in terms of income than non-immigrant households. Examples are Finland, Norway and Germany and also Canada, the United States and Greece. Second, the depth of poverty varies within country groups. Within the Nordic countries, the respective values for immigrant households are much lower in Finland (below .2) than in Denmark (almost .5), one of the countries with the highest values along with Ireland

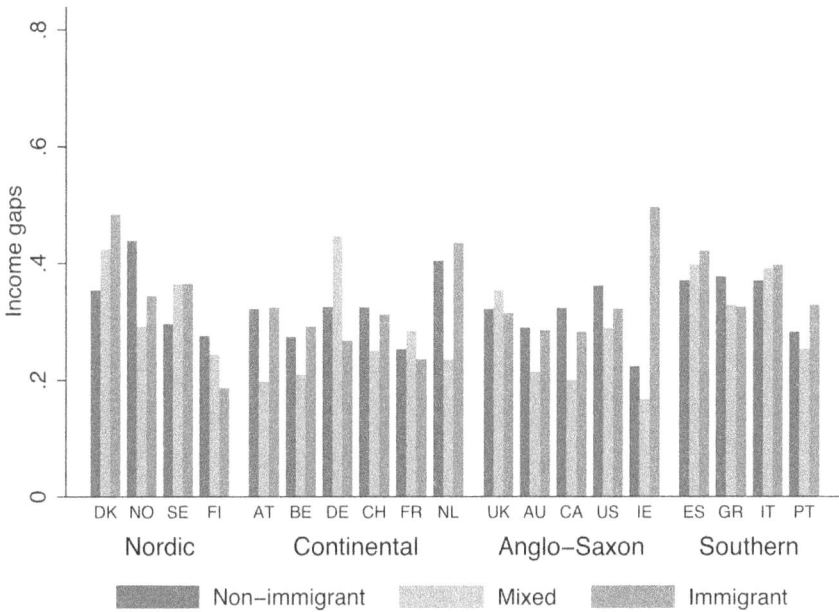

Figure 2.5   Income gaps based on disposable income (50 per cent of median income). *Source*: EU-SILC (European countries), HILDA (Australia), SLID (Canada) and CPS (United States).

and the Netherlands. Differences also exist in the other country groups, for example, between France and the Netherlands or Canada and Ireland. Finally, what is of particular interest is that countries with relatively low immigrant poverty rates, such as the Netherlands and Ireland, exhibit relatively large income gaps. In other words, although the number of Dutch and Irish immigrant households living in poverty is relatively low, their disposable income is considerably below the poverty threshold.[12]

The second indicator, *intensity*, simply combines the information of a country's poverty rate and its income gaps. It therefore provides a measure that considers quantity as well as depth of poverty.

Using the measure *intensity based on market income*, the grand-mean lies at 12 (*SD* = 2.6). According to the findings discussed earlier, the average for immigrant households (*M* = 23, *SD* = 11.0) is higher than for non-immigrant households (*M* = 11, *SD* = 2.7). Figure 2.6 presents intensity broken down by country. First, the poverty risk for immigrant households is still higher than for non-immigrant households in all countries, with the exception of Greece and Italy, while the statistics for mixed households are closer to those of non-immigrant households. Second, the pattern hardly differs compared to the

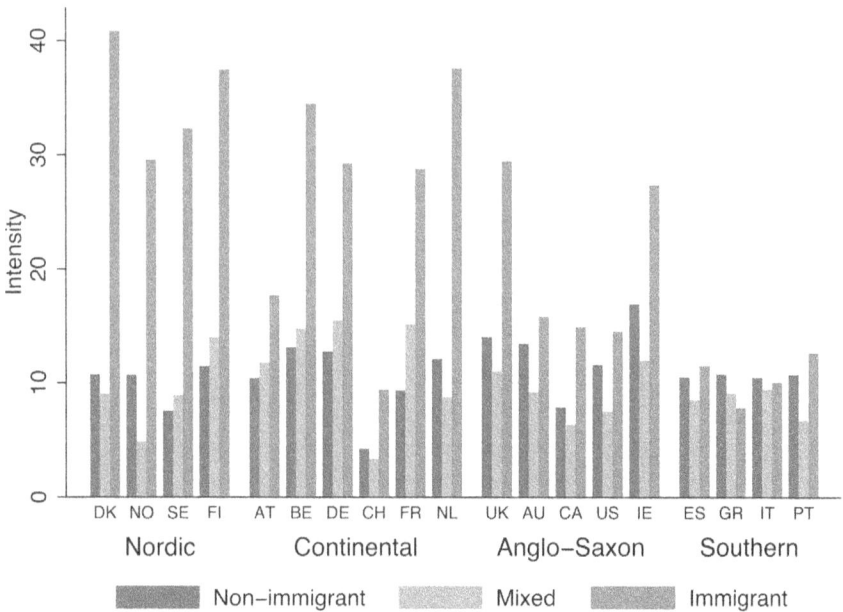

Figure 2.6   Intensity measure based on market income (50 per cent of median income). *Source*: EU-SILC (European countries), HILDA (Australia), SLID (Canada) and CPS (United States).

respective figures on poverty rates based on market income (see figure 2.1). The correlation between these two indicators is also very high for all three groups (above .9, see appendix table 2A.2).

Figure 2.7 presents the *intensity measure based on disposable income*.[13] Here, the difference between non-immigrants and immigrants decreases compared to poverty rates based on disposable income.[14] In addition, the intra-country group variation increases, in particular, in the Nordic and Southern European countries. For example, the poverty risk of Danish immigrants is almost three times higher than those of Finish immigrants. In contrast, differences within the Continental European and Anglo-Saxon country groups diminish. Belgium, still the laggard in terms of poverty based on intensity, is closer to Germany and France. Comparably, the Netherlands moves to the group mean, though remains the country where immigrants are exposed to the lowest poverty risk. Analogous to Belgium, the intensity measure for immigrant households decreases in Canada and Australia; both are even lower compared to Ireland.

The descriptive analysis of alternative measures of poverty, such as income gaps and intensity, emphasises the fact that the financial situations of poor households differ across countries. For example, the income gaps of poor

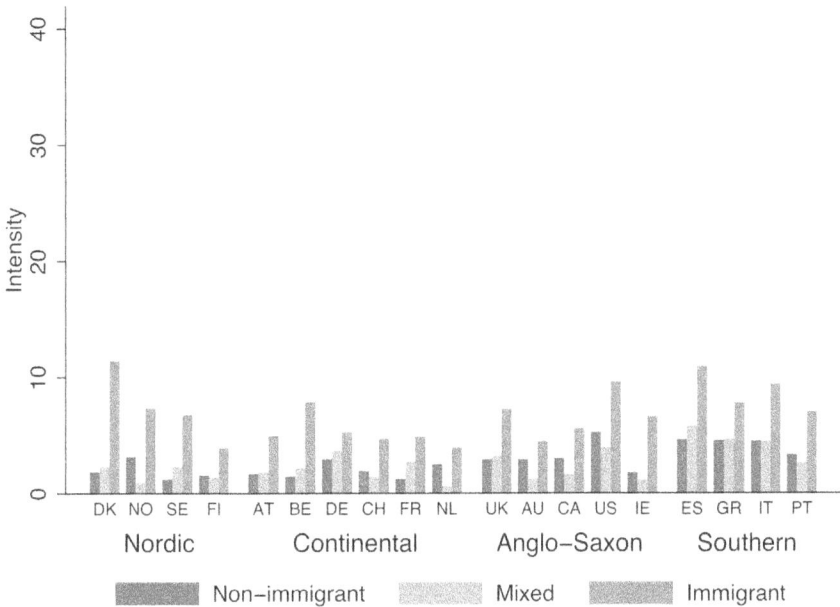

Figure 2.7 **Intensity measure based on disposable income (50 per cent of median income).** *Source*: **EU-SILC (European countries), HILDA (Australia), SLID (Canada) and CPS (United States).**

Irish and Dutch immigrant households show that their financial situations are worse than those of their counterparts living in Finland. This is also reflected in findings based on the intensity measure. However, a comparison of the country ranking using intensity measures and the more basic poverty rates shows that the order of the countries remains more or less stable, with the exceptions mentioned earlier, and that the correlation of these different measures is quite high. Considering that the interpretation of the intensity measure is not straightforward, this book chooses to rely on poverty rates based on market income and disposable income as dependent variables for further analysis.

The poverty indicators used so far are aggregated measures comparing the immigrant and the non-immigrant population in general. However, this method of comparing immigrants' outcomes with those of non-immigrants', the national mean, might hide the fact that socio-demographic factors vary systematically between these two groups. Therefore, it is important to account for potential variations between the immigrant and non-immigrant population. Just imagine the fictive case where all immigrants in country A are employed in low-paid service jobs, while all immigrants in country B are working in high-paid professional and managerial jobs. Higher poverty levels of immigrants in country A would be mainly the result of the type of employment pursued by immigrants rather than their immigrant background. Although this example is far-fetched, immigrants' higher poverty risk may not be due to their immigration history but rather due to other factors that have been identified in previous studies such as important individual determinants of poverty (e.g. education and labour market participation), or a combination thereof.[15] The next section presents how immigrants fare compared to non-immigrants when controlling for a range of socio-democratic characteristics such as skill and education, family composition and labour market participation.

. . . IN COMBINATION WITH SOCIO-DEMOGRAPHIC FACTORS

To identify the immigrant-specific effect on immigrants' poverty risk, this section analyses poverty gaps, that is, the difference between immigrants' and non-immigrants' poverty risk after controlling for socio-economic factors. They are assessed using logistic regressions and calculating the average marginal effects (AME) of having an immigrant background on poverty risk. The advantage of this approach is that it allows the impact of socio-demographic factors and the immigrant background to be contrasted. However, the immigration-related AME coefficients can be interpreted only when using a country's non-immigrant population as a reference. Thus, rather than comparing the 'net' poverty rates of immigrants across countries, differences in poverty risk between immigrants and non-immigrants between countries can be compared. First, this section presents AME coefficients, including only the immigrant household characteristics as an explanatory factor. This serves as a benchmark for capturing the distinct effect of socio-demographic characteristics. Then, socio-demographic household characteristics are added as control variables. This is done separately for poverty based on market income and disposable income.

When comparing the *poverty gaps between immigrants and non-immigrants based on market income without controlling for socio-demographic factors*, the likelihood for immigrants to live in poverty is around 14 percentage points higher than for non-immigrants.[16] The results calculated for each country separately are reported in figure 2.8. In line with the findings discussed earlier, immigrants across the countries tend to be exposed to a higher poverty risk when compared to non-immigrants. In principle, these AME are just an alternative way to compare poverty rates of immigrants and non-immigrants as in figure 2.1.

In the Nordic countries, the difference between non-immigrants and immigrants is most pronounced. Here, the likelihood for immigrants to live in

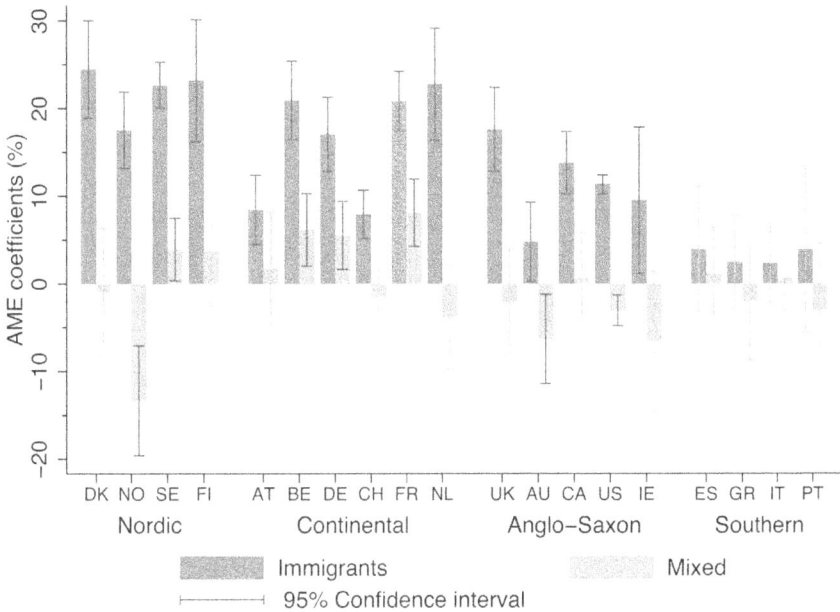

Figure 2.8 **Poverty gaps based on market income (50 per cent of median income, excluding control variables).** *Source*: **EU-SILC (European countries), HILDA (Australia), SLID (Canada) and CPS (United States).**

poverty is more than 22 percentage points higher, followed by Continental European countries ($M = 16$) and the Anglo-Saxon countries ($M = 11$). The poverty gaps are considerably lower in Australia (below 5, $p < .5$) and Southern European countries (coefficients not significant at the 5 per cent level, see grey-coloured confidence interval in figure 2.8). Across the countries, immigrants' risk of living in poverty ranges from +24 percentage points in Denmark to +2 percentage points in Italy (see appendix table 2A.3).

Turning to mixed households, in the majority of countries they are exposed to comparable poverty risk as non-immigrants; that is, the coefficients are not significant. Only mixed households in France, Belgium and Germany have a significantly higher risk of living in poverty (above five, see appendix table 2A.3). In contrast, Norwegian members of mixed households have a 15 percentage points lower probability of ending up in poverty compared to non-immigrants. This is also the case in Australia and the United States.

Poverty gaps based on market income change once socio-demographic factors such as skills and education, and labour market participation are controlled for.[17] The AME of the immigrant background across countries decreases from +14 percentage points to around +6 percentage points

higher poverty risk for immigrants ($p < .001$). Figure 2.9 supports this finding when comparing the *poverty gaps accounting for the control variables*
by countries. Three major differences should be highlighted. First, the net
AME coefficients are much lower for both immigrants and mixed households, indicating that socio-demographic factors play an important role in
explaining poverty differences between immigrants and non-immigrants.
The values range between 0 and 9 for immigrants, and between −4 and 6 for
mixed households. It should be noted that the majority of the coefficients for
mixed households are now positive, with the exception of Norway and the
Netherlands, though these numbers are significant only for Sweden, Belgium,
Switzerland, France, the United States and Italy.

Second, the poverty risk of immigrant and non-immigrant households
becomes more similar when controlling for socio-demographic factors and
even disappears as the confidence intervals suggest. For example, for Austria and the United Kingdom, the differences between immigrants and non-
immigrants are no longer significant, while in the Danish and Finnish sample,
the AME coefficients are significant at only the 10 per cent level (see
appendix table 2A.3). Therefore, socio-demographic factors rather than the

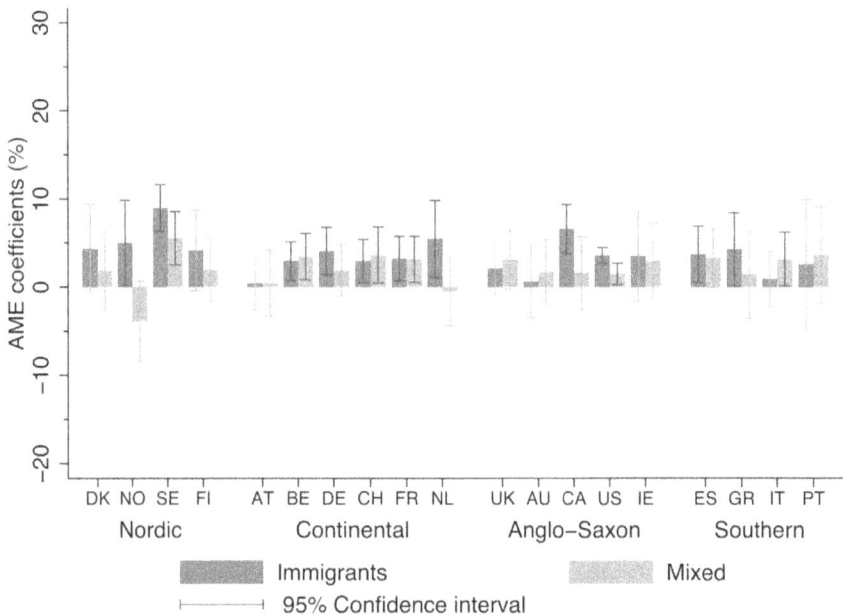

Figure 2.9 **Poverty gaps based on market income (50 per cent of median income,
including control variables).** *Source*: **EU-SILC (European countries), HILDA (Australia),
SLID (Canada) and CPS (United States).**

immigrant background account for a considerable part of the variations in poverty risk beyond immigrant background in those countries.[18] One of the most important determinants is labour market participation. Households with at least one employed person or multiple earners have a considerably lower probability of ending up in poverty. On the other hand, households where all members are employed atypically or self-employed have a higher poverty risk. Although the poverty gaps have decreased after controlling for socio-demographic characteristics, they still remain significant in a number of countries. Moreover, the poverty risks of immigrant households living in Spain and Greece become significant ($p < .05$).

Finally, intra-country group variation persists when comparing the AME coefficients with and without control variables in figures 2.8 and 2.9. Immigrants living in Austria experience comparable poverty risks based on market income as non-immigrants, in contrast to Dutch immigrants who experience considerably higher poverty than Dutch non-immigrants. Turning to Anglo-Saxon countries, the poverty risk differs less between immigrants and non-immigrants in the United Kingdom (around 2 percentage points, not significant) than in Canada, where the poverty risks of immigrants are almost 7 percentage points higher than those of non-immigrants ($p < .001$). Within country groups, variations can also be observed in Southern European countries, with immigrants living in Italy experiencing comparable poverty risk to non-immigrants in contrast to Greece, where immigrants' poverty risk is 4 percentage points higher ($p < .05$).

When turning to *poverty gaps based on disposable income excluding control variables*, immigrants in general experience a much higher poverty risk than non-immigrants, 14 percentage points higher (grand-mean). The respective results when taking taxes and transfers into account are presented in figure 2.10. In accordance with the findings discussed earlier, AME coefficients are positive and significant in all countries (except Ireland and the Netherlands), indicating that immigrants across the board have a higher poverty risk than non-immigrants. However, when compared to raw AME coefficients based on market income, the values are lower and range between two and thirteen times ($M = 8$, $SD = 2$), compared to between two and twenty-four ($M = 14$, $SD = 8$). For mixed households, raw coefficients based on market income and those based on disposable income are highly correlated ($r = .78$) in contrast to the respective values for immigrants ($r = .10$). This low correlation can be explained by the Nordic countries moving down to the cross-country average and Southern European countries moving up. Immigrants living in Southern Europe now have not only a significantly higher poverty risk compared to non-immigrants (around nine) but also a poverty risk that is comparable to those of immigrants living in Nordic countries.

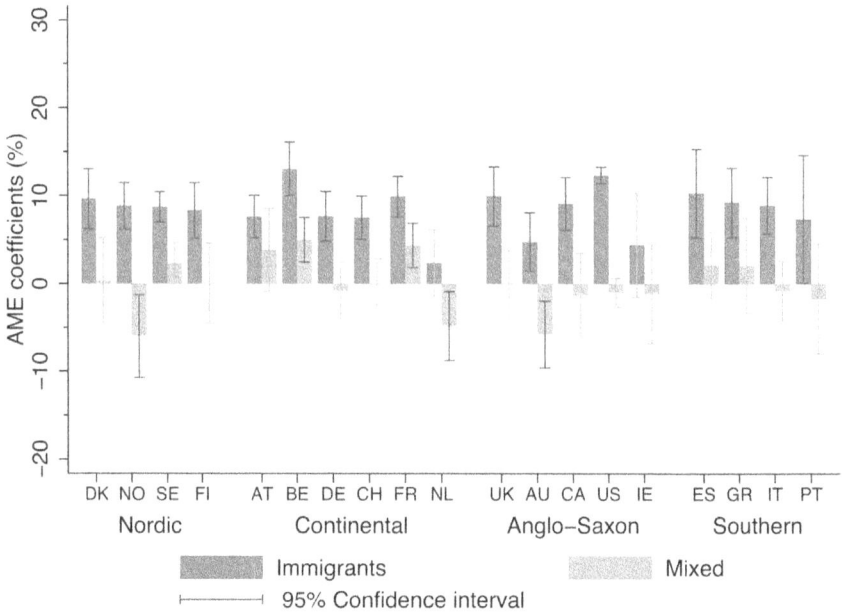

Figure 2.10 **Poverty gaps based on disposable income (50 per cent of median income, excluding control variables).** *Source*: **EU-SILC (European countries), HILDA (Australia), SLID (Canada) and CPS (United States).**

Overall, cross-national differences in poverty gaps based on disposable income are less pronounced than those based on market income, at least when only relying on immigrant background. Major exceptions are Belgium and the United States at the upper end, and the Netherlands and Ireland at the lower end.

When looking at *poverty gaps based on disposable income after controlling for socio-demographic characteristics*, the cross-country mean when including all observations reflects a 7 percentage points higher probability of immigrant households ending up in poverty compared to non-immigrant households. The AME coefficients by countries, as shown in figure 2.11, are lower than those excluding control variables. According to the country-specific coefficient, the likelihood of immigrants compared to non-immigrants ending up in poverty is higher and ranges between 0 and 10.[19]

Moreover, poverty gaps between immigrants and non-immigrants have ceased to be significant, that is, the same trend as in the case of poverty gaps based on market income. Examples are Denmark and Finland, but the effect also fades for Germany ($p < .1$). For those countries, factors such as education, labour market participation and type of employment (atypical or self-employment) are better predictors than place of birth.

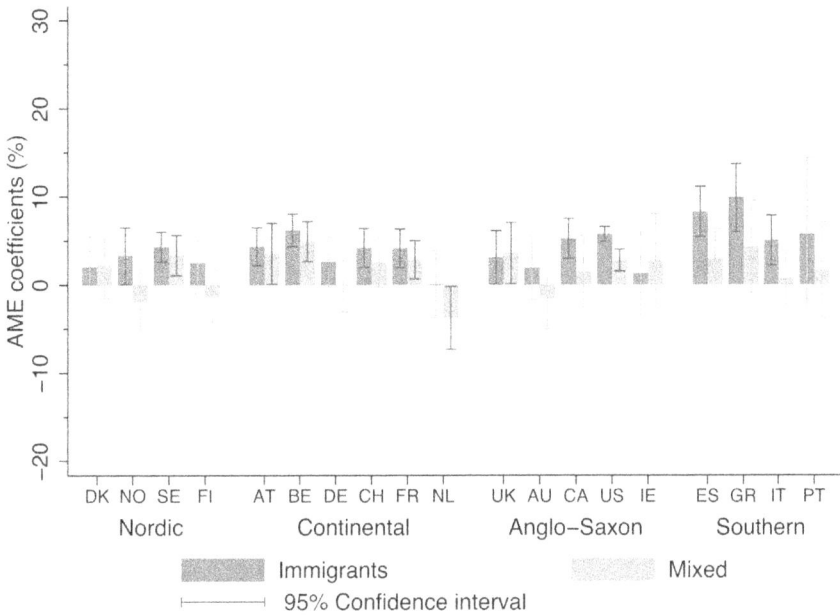

Figure 2.11   **Poverty gaps based on disposable income (50 per cent of median income, including control variables).** *Source*: **EU-SILC (European countries), HILDA (Australia), SLID (Canada) and CPS (United States).**

Finally, intra-group variations can be observed not only in the Nordic countries, with a significantly higher poverty risk for immigrants compared to non-immigrants in Sweden and Norway, while socio-economic factors account for most of the poverty differences in Denmark. This can also be observed in Continental European countries, where the poverty gap is high in Belgium compared to negligible poverty differences in the Netherlands. Considering Southern European countries, the poverty risk of immigrants in Greece or Spain is almost 10 percentage points higher compared to native-born residents, in contrast to Portugal and Italy, where the respective poverty gaps are less pronounced. Looking at the Anglo-Saxon countries, poverty gaps in Ireland and Australia are insignificant in contrast to Canada and the United States. The latter can be explained by the fact that immigrants, including those with permanent residence permits, are, in accordance with the Welfare Reform Act of 1996, excluded from federal means-tested cash and non-financial social service for the first five years (see van Hook, Brown and Bean 2006, 644).

Overall, the results so far suggest, first, that poverty gaps before and after taxes and transfers are considerably lower once socio-demographic charac-teristics are controlled for. Second, despite this reduction in poverty gaps, immigrants in a number of countries are still exposed to a significantly higher poverty risk than non-immigrants. And finally, the poverty gaps between immigrants and non-immigrants vary across countries without clustering according to the welfare regime typology or immigration history (Castles and Miller 2009; Hollifield, Martin and Orrenius 2014).

CROSS-NATIONAL PATTERNS OF IMMIGRANTS' POVERTY

So far, this chapter has focused separately on poverty rates and the remaining difference in poverty risk between immigrants and non-immigrants within a country after controlling for socio-demographic factors. The former poverty measure allows comparing immigrants' poverty levels in general between countries, while the latter assesses how immigrants fare in terms of poverty compared to non-immigrants within a country. Consequently, can certain poverty patterns be identified across countries?

Combining both poverty measures – high/low immigrant poverty levels and poverty differences/no poverty differences between immigrants and non-immigrants – four different combinations are theoretically possible: a *universalist type* where immigrants' poverty rates compared to other countries and compared to non-immigrants living in the same country are low; a *residual type* where poverty rates of immigrants are high but comparable to those of non-immigrants (no native/immigrant poverty gap); a *segmented/stratified type* where immigrants in terms of poverty fare relatively well compared to immigrants in other countries, though poverty differentials regarding the country's non-immigrant population exist; and finally, the *dualist/welfare chauvinist type* where immigrants are exposed to both higher poverty risk vis-à-vis immigrants in other countries and poverty gaps vis-à-vis non-immigrants within the same country.

Figure 2.12 presents *poverty measures based on market income*. It displays how immigrants' poverty rates (horizontal axis) and poverty gaps between immigrants and non-immigrants (vertical axis) are related. The bold line shows the respective average and the dotted lines refer to the average ±1 standard deviation. In addition, the markers indicate whether AME coefficients are significant (filled) or not (unfilled).

Starting with the *universalist type*, Italy is a representative thereof. Here, immigrants' poverty rates are relatively low compared to the rest of the countries and poverty gaps are non-existent (both measures are below 1 standard deviation; see bottom left in figure 2.12). Additionally, Austria and Australia with somewhat higher poverty rates can be said to represent 'soft' versions of this type. The *dualist/welfare chauvinist type* prevails in Sweden and the

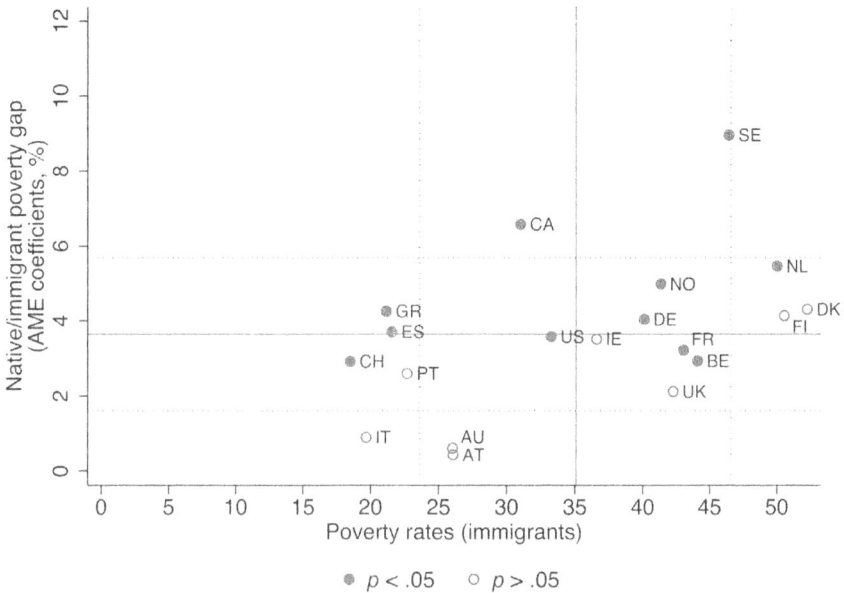

Figure 2.12   **Poverty measures based on market income (50 per cent of median income), immigrants.** *Source*: **EU-SILC (European countries), HILDA (Australia), SLID (Canada) and CPS (United States).**

Netherlands, with both measures considerably higher than the grand-mean of immigrants' poverty rates and poverty gaps. The United Kingdom comes closest to the *residual/liberal type*, combining low poverty gaps with higher immigrant poverty levels. No country belongs clearly to the *segmented/ stratified type*. However, Switzerland, despite its lower than mean AME coefficient, as well as Canada, with immigrants' poverty levels closer to the grand-mean, represents a 'soft' version of the segmented/stratified type.[20]

For two groups of countries, the assignment is less clear-cut, in particular when using alternative poverty thresholds (40 per cent and 60 per cent) and equivalence scales (squared root). Focusing on the Southern European countries (Spain, Greece and Portugal), they all score low on the immigrant poverty dimension but are around the mean regarding poverty gaps. Thus, they can be considered cases that fall in between the *segmented/stratified* and *universalist type*. The opposite is the case for the two Nordic countries, Finland and Denmark, that is, as cases between the *dualist/welfare chauvinist* and the *residual/liberal type* where immigrants are exposed to higher poverty risks, while poverty gaps are close to the grand-mean. The remaining countries cannot be clearly assigned to a particular type. Some countries display significant poverty gaps combined with slightly higher than grand-mean of immigrant poverty, namely in Norway, Germany, France and Belgium, while in the United States, immigrants' poverty rates are slightly below the average.

When turning to the comparison of *poverty measures based on disposable income*, one can observe that countries do not line up as one would expect according to welfare regime typology, although immigrants' poverty and poverty gaps are related to each other (see figure 2.13).[21] As discussed earlier in the chapter, immigrants' poverty and poverty gaps are relatively low in Ireland and the Netherlands, which can therefore be classified as *universalist types*.[22] This is also partly true for Australia, which represents a borderline case. At the other end of the spectrum, Spain characterises the *dualist/welfare chauvinist type*, with Greece, Belgium and the United States coming close to this type, combining high poverty gaps and immigrant poverty levels. Again, no country can be clearly identified as a *segment/stratified type*, though Switzerland and Austria can be seen as 'soft' versions; immigrant poverty levels are relatively low compared to the other countries and the poverty gaps between immigrants and non-immigrants prevail.

It is evident in figure 2.13 that a number of countries cannot be clearly identified as belonging to a certain type. The poverty risks of immigrants living in those countries are close to the grand-mean. Nevertheless, high poverty

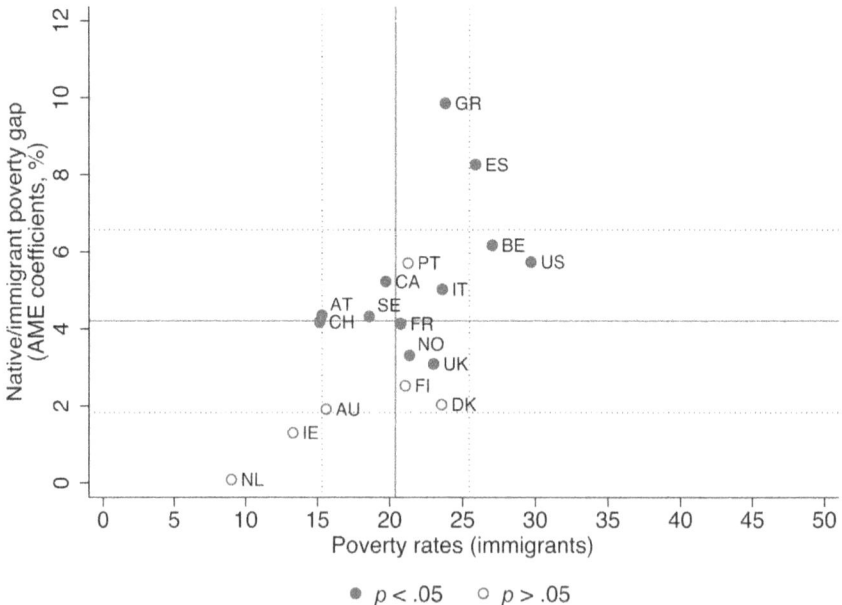

Figure 2.13   **Poverty measures based on disposable income (50 per cent of median income), immigrants. *Source*: EU-SILC (European countries), HILDA (Australia), SLID (Canada) and CPS (United States).**

gaps prevail in Sweden, Canada, France, Norway and Italy, while the opposite is true in Australia, Germany, Finland, Portugal, the United Kingdom and Denmark.

This is also the case when comparing the poverty measures of mixed households, where the majority of countries cannot be clearly assigned to a particular type (see appendix figure 2A.1). Using the poverty measures based on market income, only Norway, and to a certain extent the Netherlands, can be clearly classified as *universalist types*, while mixed households living in Switzerland belong to the *segmented/stratified type*. Turning to poverty measures based on disposable income, Norway and the Netherlands are joined by Finland and Australia, which all have relatively low poverty rates and poverty gaps between non-immigrants and mixed households.

SUMMARY OF FINDINGS

This chapter provided a description of immigrants' poverty levels and differences in poverty risks between immigrants and non-immigrants. In general, immigrants are more often exposed to poverty than non-immigrants, regardless of the poverty measurements used. Moreover, the results suggest that there is variation between countries, which can be explained by neither the welfare regime typology nor a country's immigration tradition. The main three relevant findings can be summarised as follows.

First, immigrants' poverty levels across countries are higher than that of non-immigrants and mixed households, regardless of whether poverty is measured according to market income or disposable income. However, the income gaps show that although immigrants have a higher probability of ending up in poverty, their financial situation does not have to be worse when compared to poor native-born households, for example, in traditional immigration countries (Australia, Canada and the United States) and Southern European countries (based on disposable income, this is also true in Finland, Norway, Germany and France).

Second, the analysis of the poverty gaps also indicates that immigrants fare worse in terms of socio-economic outcomes when compared to non-immigrants, but that the effect of socio-demographic factors should not be underestimated. In a number of countries, the differences between immigrants and non-immigrants disappear after controlling for household-level characteristics such as labour market participation and type of employment. This finding thus suggests that these factors are central to assessing poverty risks, in general, and immigrants' poverty, in particular.

Finally, no clear patterns can be identified regarding country clusters when relating both poverty measures to each other, namely poverty levels comparing immigrants' situations among countries and poverty gaps comparing the situation of immigrants and non-immigrants. Distinct cases can only be identified concerning the *universalist type* (low poverty/no gap, with Italy based on market income and the Netherlands and Ireland based on disposable income) and the *dualist/welfare chauvinist type* (high poverty/high gap, with Sweden and the Netherlands based on market income and Spain based on disposable income). In other words, there is a tendency for poverty levels and poverty gaps to co-exist.

Overall, findings of this chapter show not only that variation within welfare regimes exists but also that socio-demographic characteristics do not suffice to explain differences between immigrants' and non-immigrants' poverty risk. Alternative explanations, such as the political-institutional setting and, in particular, immigrants' social rights in terms of their access to the labour market and the welfare state, have to be taken into account. Immigrants' social rights and thus the inclusiveness of a country's prevailing labour market and welfare system towards immigrants are considered in more detail in the next chapter.

Chapter 3

Dealing with Immigrants: Immigrants' Social Rights

This chapter provides a descriptive overview of immigrants' social and work rights in advanced industrialised countries. It focuses on *immigrants' access to paid employment* and *social programmes*. The analysis distinguishes between different types of immigration categories, including labour migrants and permanent residents as well as the family members of both categories. As discussed in the previous chapter, these social and work rights are expected to moderate the impact of the labour market and welfare system on immigrants' poverty. The last section contributes empirically to the welfare chauvinism thesis – that 'welfare services should be restricted to "our own"' (Andersen and Bjørklund 1990, 212) – and thus the claim that welfare states and immigration can be reconciled only if nation states choose to *limit immigrants' access to social programmes*. The more nuanced version of Banting's (2000) welfare chauvinism is tested, namely if the internal exclusion of immigrants is less pronounced in more generous welfare states (e.g. the Nordic and Continental European countries) than in more basic welfare states (e.g. Anglo-Saxon countries). Before turning to immigrants' social and work rights, this chapter will begin with a brief overview of the composition of the immigrant population and immigration history for the advanced industrialised countries included in this study.

ADVANCED INDUSTRIALISED COUNTRIES AND THEIR IMMIGRANT POPULATION

Since mankind's earliest days, humans have migrated for a variety of reasons (Manning 2005). Although migration in world history has varied geographically and over time, the advanced industrialised countries covered in this book have experienced a growth in immigration over the past decades (e.g. OECD 2007c). By 2007, more than 10 per cent of residents were born outside their country of residence in most advanced industrialised countries.[1] The countries in table 3.1 are ordered according to their historical immigration tradition, which is a simplified classification. The clustering of countries largely coincides with classic welfare regime typology, with the United Kingdom, Finland and Ireland being the major exceptions.

Generally speaking, three different traditions of immigration can be distinguished in advanced industrialised democracies (Hollifield, Martin and Orrenius 2014; see also Castles and Miller 2009). First, *traditional immigration countries*, which include Australia, Canada and the United States, which were founded as nations of immigrants. These countries had already experienced continuously permanent immigration inflows before 1945, mainly from Europe, and afterwards from Asia and Latin America. Australia and Canada remained favoured destinations, with a foreign-born population of about 20 per cent, as table 3.1 shows, despite adopting more restrictive measures over the past twenty years to control immigration and mainly attract skilled workers. The percentage of foreign-born residents is somewhat lower in the United States at around 13 per cent. Almost 90 per cent of those foreign-born residents originated from non-industrialised countries, a third of which, and by far the largest group, originated from Mexico (OECD 2010, 311). However, these figures do not account for irregular migration, especially from Latin America, which has been estimated to be around 11.5–12 million (OECD 2009, 122). The permit-based statistics between 2003 and 2007 in these countries give some insights into (the success of) their immigration policies (see the columns on the right-hand side in table 3.1). Australia and Canada both pursue a skill-based immigration system (Hollifield, Martin and Orrenius 2014), which is reflected in the fact that around 25 per cent of permits are issued for work reasons. In the United States, which has no official immigration policy (ibid.), permits based on family reasons make up the largest share with 71 per cent. However, the proportion of family-based immigration is also quite high in Australia and Canada (above 50 per cent of issued permits).

The second group refers to *countries of immigration* that do not view immigration as 'a fundamental part of their national identity or their nation-building process' (Hollifield, Martin and Orrenius 2014, 13). After the Second World War, several European countries actively recruited immigrants as temporary 'guest workers' to suit the fluctuating labour demand of their growing economies, a practice that prevailed until the oil crisis in 1973–1974. As the term 'guest' suggests, they were not admitted to stay and become permanent residents. However, this 'guest worker' tradition goes back to even before the outbreak of the First World War, when countries such as the United Kingdom, Germany, France and Switzerland already experienced

Table 3.1. Stocks of foreign-born population and permit-based statistics

	Stocks of foreign-born population in 2007 (%)				Permit-based statistics, 2003–2007 (%)						
	Total in Ths.	Industr. Countries	Only EU15	Only EU12	Work	Family	Humanitarian	Free movement	Others	Total (2007, Ths.)	Net mig. rate (per Ths.)
AU	521 (15%)	52.6	36.1	4.2	25.2	51.3	8.2	14.2	1.0	200	10.7
CA	6,187 (19%)	37.4	25.4	6.4	23.0	60.5	16.5	–	0.1	237	7.4
US	38,048 (13%)	13.1	7.1	2.5	8.4	71.7	11.3	–	8.6	1,052	3.3
AT	1,236 (15%)	42.4	19.7	20.0	2.5	46.0	11.1	39.1	1.3	50	3.7
BE	1,380 (13%)	49.6	43.6	5.0	7.0	35.0	6.2	51.7	–	40	5.0
DK	379 (7%)	34.8	19.6	8.6	16.1	27.3	6.5	43.8	6.3	26	3.2
FR	7,129 (12%)	32.3	26.6	2.9	5.2	57.4	6.0	20.9	10.6	162	1.5
DE	10,529 (13%)	24.6	14.0	10.2	6.1	26.9	8.7	43.1	15.2	233	0.1
NL	1,751 (11%)	25.6	17.7	4.2	11.2	42.9	21.9	24.0	–	70	0.7
NO	445 (10%)	43.1	26.7	10.5	5.7	41.6	17.0	35.7	–	44	7.3
SE	1,228 (13%)	43.5	27.5	9.7	0.6	43.8	18.7	37.0	–	74	5.7
CH	1,571 (22%)	57.8	51.5	3.4	1.7	21.9	4.7	69.4	2.3	122	9.1
UK	6,192 (10%)	39.5	19.7	11.9	26.6	29.6	11.4	24.9	7.5	364	5.0
FI	203 (4%)	40.4	23.7	11.7	11.2	34.4	12.1	38.8	3.4	18	2.7
IE	602 (14%)	79.3	51.6	21.5	8.9	17.3	0.9	72.9	–	68	9.0
GR	1,123 (10%)	28.3	13.0	9.7	–	–	–	–	–	–	1.4
IT	3,433 (6%)	28.4	4.6	22.6	23.8	45.7	2.5	26.0	2.0	571	3.4
PT	651 (6%)	28.1	23.8	0.1	36.4	41.1	0.3	21.0	1.3	43	2.4
ES	6,045 (13%)	38.5	19.9	16.2	26.5	15.9	0.1	57.0	0.5	682	10.0

Note: Data on foreign-born population refer to the following years: Canada and Ireland (2006), Greece and Portugal (2001), Switzerland (2000). Data for permit-based statistics: Denmark and Switzerland (2004–2007), Belgium (2005–2007), Finland (2006–2007) and Spain (2007). Data for Italy refer to stocks of foreign population, based on nationality, are presented.

Source: OECD International Migration Database (2016), OECD (2008, 2009, 2010), UN Population Division World Population Prospects: The 2015 Revision.

high inflows of immigrant workers. For example, the industrialisation of the Ruhr area in Germany from the 1850s attracted many immigrants not only from surrounding countries such as the Netherlands and Italy and other parts of Germany but also from Poland. By 1910, Poles accounted for up to 30 per cent of the residents in certain towns in the Ruhr area (Lucassen 2006, 30–31).[2] Along with Germany, the prime example of the 'guest worker system', Austria, Belgium, the Netherlands and Sweden, as well as Denmark and Norway more recently, actively recruited workers who mainly originated from the less-developed European periphery, such as Southern European countries as well as Ireland and Finland.[3] To facilitate the recruitment, bilateral agreements were signed which not only regulated recruitment procedures but also working conditions and social security arrangements between the receiving countries and the countries of origin (e.g. 'Italiener-Abkommen 1963' between Switzerland and Italy, see Wimmer 1998).[4]

Within these countries of immigration, Castles and Miller (2009) point to the role of immigration from former colonies in the case of France, the Netherlands and the United Kingdom. Although the privileged access of citizens and residents from former ex-colonies to enter the country and get access to special housing or work programmes has been abolished (e.g. exclusion of British overseas citizens from unrestricted settlement in the United Kingdom in the early 1980s; see Mahnig and Wimmer 2000), they still rank among the three largest groups of foreign-born immigrants in 2007 (e.g. in France Algerians and Moroccans constitute 19 per cent and 12 per cent of the foreign-born population, while the largest foreign-born groups in the Netherlands are the Surinamese and the Turks with both at around 11 per cent, and in the United Kingdom, Indians at 9 per cent; OECD 2010). In addition, the percentage of the foreign-born population from non-industrialised countries is larger compared to the traditional 'guest worker' countries.[5]

However, labour migration in these countries of immigration only accounts for a small share of the permits issued between 2003 and 2007 as the permit-based statistics in table 3.1 reveal. They range between 0.6 per cent in Sweden and 26.6 per cent in the United Kingdom. Unfortunately, these figures do not include EU workers who move to other member states and are subsumed in the category 'free movement', which also contains those EU citizens moving within the EU for other non-work-related reasons such as study purposes, retirement or accompanying family members. Migration within the EU facilitated by the introduction of the regulation concerning the freedom of movement for workers within the European Community in 1968 actually makes up one-fifth of all issued permits. Belgium and Switzerland, in particular, and also Denmark stand out as countries with a high number of permits issued to EU citizens (between 44 per cent and 69 per cent of all permits). These figures, however, have to be put into perspective; only a small share, about

13.2 million of 491 million EU27 foreign-born persons (less than 3 per cent), actually lived in another EU member state in 2006 (Castles and Miller 2009, 119).[6] Moreover, internal migration decreased due to the equalisation of earnings and living standards within the EU, while immigration from outside the EU grew (Castles and Miller 2009, 101). Permits issued for family reasons play a major role in France but also in Austria where the federal government restricts immigration through an annual quota (IOM 2009, 140–41). Finally, besides family reunification, permits issued for humanitarian reasons are considerably more common in the Netherlands, Norway and Sweden: countries not only with national identities rooted in liberal values of tolerance and humanism but that are also welfare states inclusive towards immigrants (see the section covering internal exclusion further in the chapter).

Finally, Southern European countries make up the group *latecomers to immigration* and include Italy, Spain, Portugal and Greece, which until 1973 were viewed as emigration countries. These countries experienced immigration inflows from former colonies (e.g. Latin America in Spain and Brazil in Portugal), Northern Africa and neighbouring countries (e.g. 60 per cent of Greek residence permits were issued to Albanians in 2004). This recent immigration trend is also evident when looking at the share of permits issued for work reasons, which is considerably higher when compared to European countries of immigration. Nevertheless, these figures do not reflect that Southern European countries were and are affected the most by irregular immigration, with immigrants either entering without documents or overstaying their visas (OECD 2009, 120–22). Additionally, Finland and Ireland, both situated in the European periphery, represent cases of more recent immigration. For example, in Finland, it was not until the 1980s that immigration exceeded emigration for a prolonged period. Belonging to the Swedish empire until 1809, Finland became independent in 1917 after a period as an autonomous Grand Duchy under the Russian Empire. Until today, Russians represent the largest group of foreigners in Finland. Traditionally a country of emigration, it remained a rather closed society after the Second World War due to geographic and historical reasons, such as the iron curtain, and due to relatively restrictive immigration policies compared to other Nordic and European countries (see Kyntäjä 2003).

In sum, this brief overview shows that all advanced industrialised countries have dealt with immigration over the past decades. Although this rough classification neglects variations within country groups regarding more specific immigration flows, that is, immigration categories, and country-specific peculiarities, it provides a starting point to compare immigrants' work and social rights. As mentioned in the previous chapter, comparative migration literature has only started to systematically assess cross-national differences in immigration policies (e.g. Peters 2015; Helbling et al. 2017). Having said that, the key point for this book is that the foreign-born population does not form a negligible part of the population in advanced industrialised countries. Moreover, as table 3.1 shows, a country's foreign-born population does not only consist of immigrants from industrialised countries or countries benefiting from special treatment, such as the European Union or Nordic countries. Although the percentage of immigrants born in EU15 countries should not be underestimated, the diversity of the immigrant population in terms of country of origin has increased in recent decades (see OECD 2008, 2009, 2010).[7] Keeping this in mind, the following section discusses the rights of immigrants in more detail regarding their access to paid employment and social programmes.

IMMIGRANTS' WORK AND SOCIAL RIGHTS

This section addresses the question of how inclusive immigrants' rights are once they have settled in a country. In order to do so, it focuses on policies that target immigrants directly. The selection of relevant immigration categories for the analysis draws on a study on immigrants' social rights by Aleinikoff and Klusmeyer (2002). Four broad immigration categories are differentiated, which are operationalised based on residence permits, namely (1) holders of temporary residence permits (mainly issued for work, hereafter: labour migrants) and (2) their family members, (3) holders of permanent residence permits (hereafter: permanent residents) and (4) their family members as well. The access of nationals and their family members to paid employment and social programmes serves as a reference point for the comparison (for a detailed coding procedure, see methodological appendix).

Access to Paid Employment

The measure of access to paid employment for these different immigration categories was inspired by Cerna's (2008) and Ruhs' (2011) measures of openness to labour migration. Thus, the access indicator for migrant workers distinguishes four categories: whether employment is tied to a specific employer, whether change of employment is possible but requires a new work permit, whether change is allowed within a specific sector, occupation or region, and whether migrant workers are granted the same full access as nationals.[8] The indicator for the remaining categories is slightly different and takes into account whether individuals from an immigration category are permitted to work at all and, if they are, whether they have to apply for a work permit, are granted unlimited rights or special treatment after a certain period (e.g. no labour market test), or are granted the same full access as nationals.

Using secondary sources to identify the relevant legislation (e.g. IOM 2009), the data were collected relying on immigration laws and regulations related to the entry and settlement of immigrants as well as their employment (for legislative sources, see appendix table MA.3). The data presented in this chapter consider national legislation as of 1 January 2007. One major reason to focus on the year 2007 is the outbreak of the financial crisis in 2007–2008, which has affected advanced industrialised countries and their populations to different degrees (e.g. the Southern European countries). Moreover, the crisis has hit immigrants particularly hard, as recent studies indicate (OECD 2009, 2010).[9]

Table 3.2 summarises the access immigrants from different categories have to paid employment. As is evident, nationals and their family members have the most privileged access to the labour market. In all countries, TCNs married to a citizen are granted full access to the labour market from the beginning of their stay.[10] This is also true for Convention refugees as well as EU citizens moving to another member state and their family members (neither shown nor included in the analysis). The work rights of EU citizens are codified in Article 23 of the Directive 2004/38/EC, which also entitles family members of EU citizens originating from third countries to the right to take up any employment or self-employment. Family members, as defined in the Directive, include not only spouses and children under the age of twenty-one but also the partners of EU citizens as well as the direct relatives in the ascending line of both the EU citizen and their spouse/partner.

Before turning our attention to permanent residents, it should be noted that the understanding of permanent migration varies between countries. As previously mentioned, traditional countries of immigration, such as Australia, Canada and the United States, grant permanent residence permits from the beginning of the stay or allow certain subgroups of immigrants with temporary residence permits to apply for a permanent residence permit (e.g. dual intent). In contrast, becoming a permanent resident in Europe usually requires a five-year habitual residence period in the country of settlement (see last row in table 3.2) among other prerequisites (e.g. language proficiency; see Huddleston et al. 2011).[11]

As is evident in table 3.2, immigrants with permanent residence permits enjoy the same access to employment as nationals in all states. Most countries also allow their family members immediate access to employment. The few exceptions are Greece and Austria, where family members of permanent TCNs have to wait one year before they obtain unrestricted access to employment. Restrictions also exist in Ireland and Spain, where lawfully residing spouses and dependents are required to obtain a labour permit but are exempt from a labour market test (IOM 2009, 330). It should be noted that although family members of permanent residents are often granted unrestricted access

Table 3.2. Immigrants' access to paid employment by immigration category

	Nationals/ family members	Permanent residents/ family members	Labour migrants/ family members	Required time of residence for permanent residents
AU	3	3	2	Depending on type of permit
AT	3	3/2[1y]	1[18m,5y]/0.5[1y]	Depending on type of permit
BE	3	3	1.5 (A=3[4y], B=0)/2	5 years
CA	3	3	1 (permit: 0,2)/1	Depending on type of permit
DK	3	3	1/3	7 years (under certain conditions 5 years)
FI	3	3	2/3	4 years
FR	3	3	2/3	5 years
DE	3	3	2/1[2y]	5 years
GR	3	3/2[1y]	2/2[1y]	5 years
IE	3	3/2	0.5 (<12m:0, ≥12m: 1[5y]) /2	5 years (indefinite leave to remain: 8 years)
IT	3	3	1/3	6 years
NL	3	3	1.5 (general=1, skilled=2;[3y])/2 (general=1, skilled=3)	5 years
NO	3	3	0.5 (general=0, skilled=1)/2 (general=1, skilled=3)	3 years
PT	3	3	1.5 (job list[3y])/3	8 years (under certain conditions 5 years)
ES	3	3/2	2[1y]/2 (no LM test if partner 1y in ESP)	5 years
SE	3	3	1.5 (perm.)/3 (gov. prop.)	not mentioned
CH	3	3	1[5y]/1(no LM test, but no right)	10 years (under certain conditions 5 years)
UK	3	3	2/3	10 years (under certain conditions 5 years)
US	3	3	1/0	depending on type of permit

Note: Labour migrants/*family members* 0 = employment tied to specific employer/*not permitted to work*, 1 = (change of) employment possible but requires new work permit, 2 = change allowed within specific sector, occupation or region/*unlimited working rights after certain period*, 3 = full access as nationals. The period of years to be granted full access to the labour market without having to apply for permanent residence permit is indicated in square brackets.

Source: See appendix table MA.3, information on required time of residence to obtain permanent residence permits; see further IOM (2009).

to employment, this is combined with a temporary residence permit for a probationary period, after which they are granted an unlimited residence permit. For example, in the United Kingdom, spouses and partners are entitled to a leave to enter and stay for a period of two years if their relationship has lasted less than four years; otherwise, they are granted 'indefinite leave to remain', equivalent to a permanent residence permit (IOM 2009, 521). Apart from the exceptions mentioned earlier, permanent residents and their family members, along with recognised refugees and EU citizens (including their direct relatives), are granted almost unrestricted access to employment on the same terms as nationals.

In contrast, countries differ with regard to the restrictions they impose on immigrants with temporary residence permits. For the subsequent analysis, immigrants with temporary residence permits are confined to migrant workers. This analysis thus excludes foreigners residing in the country for other reasons such as retirement or leisure. As table 3.2 indicates, no nation states grant full access to paid employment on the same terms as nationals from the beginning of their stay. Nevertheless, two major practices can be distinguished.

The first common practice is to link the work permit to employment with a specific employer. Having a job offer is a central condition in over 90 per cent of temporary migration programmes (Ruhs 2013, 74), while only 50 per cent of programmes further required a labour market test. In addition, a second practice is widespread, namely to allow labour migrants to accept any job, though restricted to a specific sector, occupation or region. In other words, this practice allows immigrants to change their employers without having to request a new permit. Among the countries that pursue this practice are France, Germany, Greece, Spain and the United Kingdom.[12] Furthermore, in Portugal, migrant workers are allowed to accept employment from a job list published by the government. This practice is usually aimed at high-skilled immigrants. The Canadian Federals Skilled Worker programme and the skilled-independent regional visa in Australia are two examples. But this practice can also be found in Europe. For instance, the Netherlands has implemented a programme, 'kennismigranten' (knowledge migrant workers' scheme), where being able to change employers depends on earning a certain wage (IOM 2009, 410–11).[13]

However, acquiring a permanent residence permit is not a necessary condition to obtain unrestricted access to employment without having to apply for a new permit when changing employer and occupation. A number of countries grant immigrant workers unrestricted access to the labour market after a specific period. This is often accompanied by an unlimited residence permit that foreign workers receive after having been employed in the host country for some years. This unlimited residence permit does not grant further rights – such as protection from expulsion, for example, due to insufficient financial means and conviction, or access to particular social programmes – in contrast to a permanent residence permit (see discussion below). Examples of countries maintaining this practice are Belgium, the Netherlands and Spain, which require up to four years of previous continuous employment. Austria also has a specific preferential procedure for *Schlüsselkräfte* (key persons, that is, a skilled worker permit) who after eighteen months are granted unrestricted access to the labour market ('Niederlassungsbewilligung – unbeschränkt', a specific type of permanent residence permit). Switzerland could also be mentioned, a country where immigrant workers are entitled to unconditional access to paid employment after five years, while TCNs can obtain a permanent residence permit only after ten years of lawful residence.[14]

Broadly speaking, however, unrestricted access to the labour market is usually confined to permanent residents. This does not only apply to traditional immigration countries such as Australia, Canada and the United States. Ireland and Austria can also be mentioned here, as migrant workers, at least those who are not 'key workers', have to wait up to five years to get unrestricted access to employment, the same time required to obtain a permanent residence permit.[15]

Turning to migrant workers' family members' right to work, national policies in general encourage their employment by granting them full access to the labour market from the beginning of their stay. Here, one has to distinguish between two cases: migrating with the family from the beginning of the stay in the host country and family reunification. Concerning the former situation, most countries allow spouses and partners, including children, to join the primary applicant. However, when considering family reunification, the conditions the sponsor and his/her family members have to fulfil to reunify the family vary greatly across countries. The requirements include, among others, the length of habitual residence, language proficiency and integration tests as well as sufficient economic resources (Huddleston et al. 2011). For example, a TCN living in Denmark must have held a permanent residence permit for at least three years, which de facto requires between eight and ten years of residence (IOM 2009, 218; see also Groenendijk 2006, 14). In addition, qualifying sponsors in Greece, Spain and Ireland have to prove a certain length of residence, which is usually up to two years (IOM 2009).[16] Other countries such as Austria, Germany, Norway, the Netherlands and Spain are less strict with regard to the length of residence but demand proof of language proficiency and integration tests from the joining family members. The Netherlands goes so far as to require family members to attend a language and integration test before arriving in the country (for an overview, see Goodman 2010; Huddleston et al. 2011).

Keeping this caveat in mind, the Nordic countries as well as Australia, France, Italy, Portugal and the United Kingdom grant family members of immigrant workers immediate access to paid employment. The second group of countries makes unrestricted access to employment of family members dependent on either the residence permit of the sponsor (e.g. Belgium) or the length of residence in the country of the joining family member (e.g. Austria, Greece, Germany and the Netherlands) or requires family members to request a work permit, albeit without being constrained by a labour market test (e.g. Ireland, Spain and Switzerland). Finally, in Canada,[17] family members receive no preferential treatment and have to individually apply for separate work permits; while in the United States, family members are not allowed to work at all until the sponsor obtains a permanent residence permit.

The least privileged immigration category in terms of access to employment is asylum seekers (results not shown). Countries differ with regard to whether immigrants are allowed to take up paid employment during the asylum procedure and waiting period. In Ireland and Denmark, asylum seekers have no right to employment at all. These two countries also opted out of the Council Directive 2003/9/EC, which laid down minimum standards for the treatment of asylum seekers. The remaining EU/EFTA member countries and Anglo-Saxon countries permit asylum seekers to work during the determination of their immigration status (see EQUAL 2007, 6–7). In Sweden and Norway, asylum seekers can apply for a work permit without having to endure a waiting period, which can be up to twelve months elsewhere (e.g. France, Germany and the United Kingdom). In Australia, the access asylum seekers have to employment depends on whether they have a bridging visa or not (Aleinikoff and Klusmeyer 2002, 96–97).

So far, the analysis of immigrants' access to paid employment has corroborated findings from citizenship literature, confirming that the main divide is not between nationals and immigrants but within different types of immigration categories, in particular between permanent and temporary residents (Brubaker 1989; Hammar 1990; Sainsbury 2006). But it remains unclear if the overall integration of immigrants into labour markets is comparable across countries and how a country's immigrant integration is related to its labour market system. Figure 3.1 provides descriptive evidence to address these questions. On the horizontal axis, the index on immigrants' access to paid employment is plotted. This index is simply calculated as the average of the four immigration categories (permanent residents/labour migrants and their respective family members) and then re-scaled to range from 0 to 1. The vertical axis shows different indicators associated with institutional wage setting and minimum wages (for the operationalisation of relevant labour market institutions and social programmes and descriptive statistics, see methodological appendix and appendix table MA.4 for details).

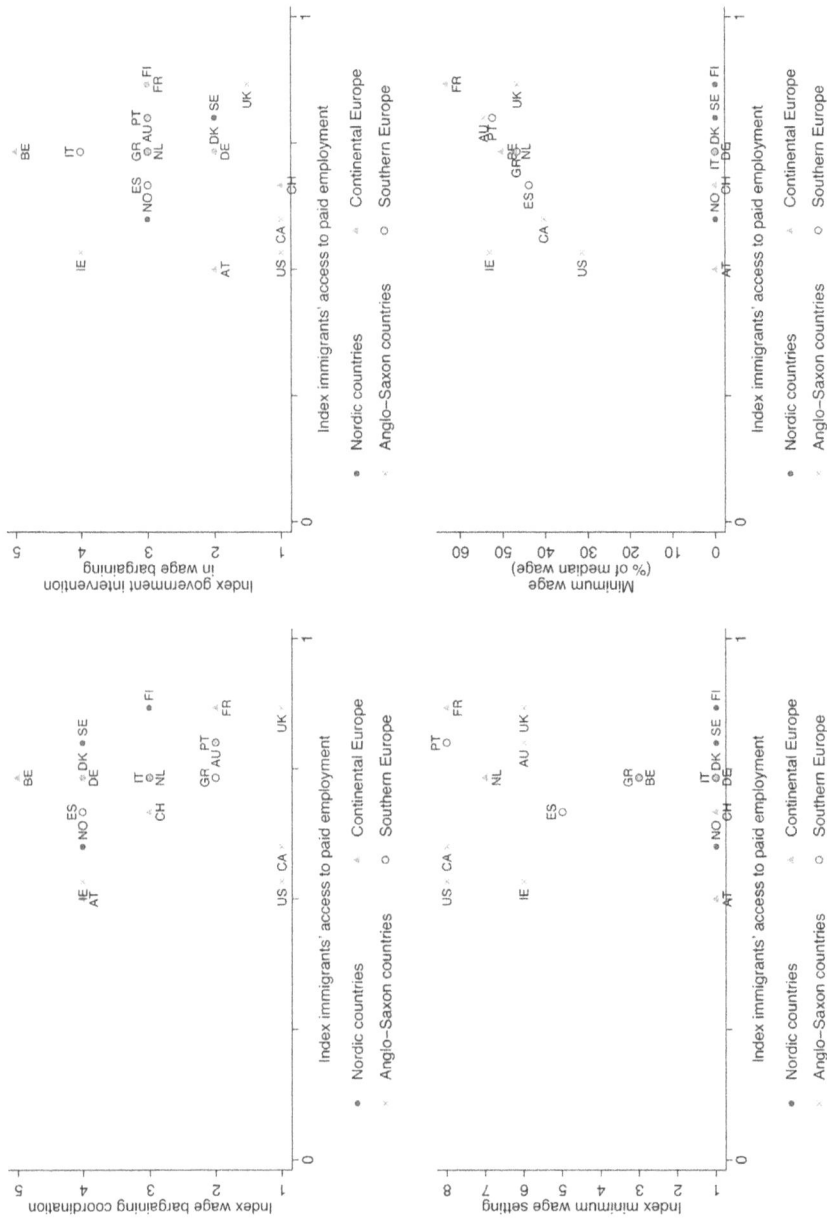

Figure 3.1 Correlation between immigrants' work rights and labour market regulations. *Top left,* coordination of wage bargaining; *top right,* government intervention in wage bargaining; *bottom left,* minimum wage setting; *bottom right,* minimum wage. *Source:* Visser (2013) and OECD (2015c); for work rights, see appendix table MA.3.

Starting with immigrants' work rights, no clear pattern regarding welfare or immigration regimes is evident in figure 3.1 (see horizontal axis). Instead variations within country groups in immigrants' labour market incorporation can be observed. In brief, Finland, France and the United Kingdom are among the most inclusive countries. They only restrict labour migrants' access to paid employment. In contrast, Austria, Ireland and the United States score relatively low, primarily due to the further restrictions they put on both family member categories, as described earlier in the text. Yet, overall labour market access is relatively unrestricted; the countries mainly occupy the right-hand side of the work rights axis.

Before focusing on the relation between immigrant work rights and the labour market system, how do countries coordinate wage setting and regulate minimum wages? Variations among countries can be observed (see vertical axes), though none neatly correspond with different types of welfare regimes. Nonetheless, wage bargaining, measured based on Kenworthy's index (2001), is more strongly coordinated in the Nordic and Continental European countries, along with Ireland and Spain, compared to the Anglo-Saxon and Southern European countries (see the graph in the upper-left corner in figure 3.1). The government only indirectly influences wage bargaining in most Continental and Southern European countries as well as in Australia, Norway and Finland (see the graph in the upper-right corner in figure 3.1). In contrast to Belgium, where the government imposes private sector wage settlements, government intervention is non-existent in the United States, Canada and Switzerland. Eight countries have no statutory minimum wage or any comparable agreement (see the graph in the lower-left corner in figure 3.1). Yet all these cases score relatively high on the wage coordination index. In contrast, all Anglo-Saxon countries as well as France and the Netherlands have a national minimum wage that is set by government, the judiciary or expert committee; tripartite non-binding consultations take place in Spain, while the minimum wage in Greece is set through national agreement between the unions and employers. In terms of generosity, minimum wages range between 30 per cent of the median wage in the United States and more than 60 per cent in France (see the graph in the lower-right corner in figure 3.1).

No systematic pattern emerges between immigrant work rights and the degree of coordination and government intervention in wage setting and minimum wages. The first graph (upper left) only provides scant evidence that immigrants' access to paid employment is more exclusive in countries with economy-wide bargaining than in countries with none, fragmented bargaining or company bargaining. The results are even less clear-cut regarding government intervention in wage bargaining (upper-right graph).

This is also true when turning to minimum wage setting in the lower-left corner of figure 3.1. Immigrants' work rights are unrelated to government involvement regarding wage bargaining and the minimum wage. Yet, when the generosity of the minimum wage as a percentage of a country's median wage is considered, a positive relation with inclusive work rights can be identified.[18]

In sum, there is evidence for cross-national variation in immigrants' work rights but it is not related to a country's wage-setting institutions and minimum wage regulations. Having said that, the main argument of this book does not expect a linear relation between labour market regulations and immigrants' work rights. Moreover, systematic co-occurrences are expected to affect immigrants' poverty. More precisely, the effect of more highly regulated wage bargaining and/or minimum wage setting on immigrants' poverty should be larger in countries with inclusive work rights than in countries with more exclusive work rights. For instance, the poverty-reducing effect of highly coordinated wage bargaining, as evident in figure 3.1, should be larger in Sweden compared to Ireland and Austria. Similarly, government involvement in minimum wage setting should have a stronger impact on immigrant poverty in France compared to the United States. Whether this is indeed the case is tested in the next chapter.

Access to Social Programmes

The right to paid employment, however, is important not only because it allows immigrants to maintain themselves economically and thus escape poverty but also because employment, especially that which builds up contributions, gives access to social security benefits. This section provides an overview of immigrants' social rights in terms of access to unemployment programmes, family-related programmes (traditional and dual-earner support) and social assistance. The data presented here have been collected as outlined further. Based on findings from earlier research (North, de Wenden and Taylor 1997 quoted in Soysal 1994, 123), the measures used in this book focus on the access of immigrants in specific immigration categories as well as their length of residence. The latter accounts for whether countries have implemented a waiting period or ban of several years during which immigrants are prohibited to access specific social programmes that do not require a previous period of contribution, such as universal or means-tested programmes. This approach is often chosen in traditional immigration countries where permanent residence permits are granted from the beginning of the stay. But the length of residence also matters for contributory social programmes, where a certain period of previous employment is required. Combining both factors, whether a specific immigration category is granted access to social programmes and whether a certain length of residence or work period is required, the following categories are distinguished:

0: no access
1: contribution period ≥ fifty-two weeks of employment or waiting period ≥ five years
2: contribution period < fifty-two weeks of employment or waiting period < five years
3: employment
4: full access

The threshold for the length of residence is set at five years because in most countries, this is the time required to be eligible for a permanent residence permit. For contributory social programmes, a lower threshold of fifty-two weeks is required. The main reason here is that for immigrants with temporary residence permits (or labour migrants), job loss affects the renewal of their permits. Finally, a category has been added which considers that merely being in employment grants access to social programmes. Comparable to the measure of immigrants' access to paid employment, national social security laws and regulations were used as primary data sources which were identified using secondary sources such as the information available at the Mutual Information System on Social Protection (MISSOC) website for European countries and country chapters of the OECD Benefits and Wages report (OECD 2007b, see appendix table MA.3). The data sources have been collected and coded separately for each social programme and immigration category.

Before presenting the results in detail, some general remarks on immigrant-specific requirements for claiming social benefits should be made. In line with former contributions, the analysis shows that citizenship/nationality is not a condition for obtaining access to social programmes (Brubaker 1989; Soysal 1994; Aleinikoff and Klusmeyer 2002). These authors also point to the role of other factors in addition to duration of residence, such as physical presence in the country, the legality of residence and work and country of origin. Due to low variation between countries, for example, country of origin has a low significance when compared to legal residence and physical presence,[19] this information has not been considered.[20] Finally, in line with previous research, permanent residence in most countries entitles the permit-holder to full social rights, with the major exception being traditional countries of immigration, which is discussed in more detail further.

Regulating Immigrants' Access to Social Programmes

In general, three major practices granting immigrants access to social programmes can be identified, which are related to types of welfare regimes and more specifically the basis of entitlement, that is, means-tested and universal social programmes.

First, the practice of a waiting period that targets primarily permanent residents was introduced, mainly in Anglo-Saxon countries. These provisions are either laid down in immigration law – in the United Kingdom and the United States – or in social security law – in Australia, Ireland and the United States. The United States, for example, adopted a five-year limited eligibility for federal means-tested public benefits in the case of qualified aliens such as lawful permanent residents with the Welfare Reform Act of 1996 (8 U.S.C. §1613). In other words, permanent residents are barred from these services for the first five years of residence. Furthermore, lawful permanent residents must demonstrate forty quarters of work to be entitled to means-tested programmes such as Supplementary Security Income or Food Stamps.[21] Refugees are exempt from the condition of employment, but their access is restricted to a maximum of seven years (see also Aleinikoff and Klusmeyer 2002).

Australia has also imposed a waiting period before claiming social benefits. Only persons that are Australian residents, defined by law as citizens and holders of a permanent visa (Social Security Act 1991, 7(2)), and who have complied with the newly arrived resident's waiting period, that is, have been an Australian resident for a period of 104 weeks, are granted access to social benefits such as unemployment assistance ('Newstart Allowance') and social assistance ('Special Benefit').

Although Canada has not implemented a specific waiting period, permanent residents and their family members have no access to public funds during their first years of residence. The reason is that as a condition for family reunification, the sponsor's undertaking obliges him to provide financial support for three years from the date the spouse becomes a permanent resident (ten years for children less than twenty-two years of age, Immigration Refugee Protection Regulations, Art. 132(1)).

In Ireland, access to social programmes is not bound to a permanent residence permit but to being a 'habitual resident'. According to Section 246(1) of the Social Welfare Consolidation Act of 2005, a person is considered to be a habitual resident of the State if 'at the date of making the application . . . the person has been present in the State or any part of the Common Travel Area[22] for a continuous period of 2 years ending on that date'. Therefore, immigrants have to fulfil a two-year waiting period to be entitled to non-contributory social programmes.

The United Kingdom is a particular case. As in the United States, permanent residents' access to non-contributory social programmes is very restricted. However, it is linked explicitly neither to being a permanent resident nor to a waiting period; immigrants have to fulfil different conditions to be granted access to welfare programmes. First, they have to be present in the country and be ordinarily resident, that is, be based in the United Kingdom and no other country. Second, immigrants have to pass the habitual residence test, which is not explicitly defined in the regulations, but refers to the 'settled intentions' of foreigners (see Child Poverty Action Group 2008, chapter 58). Alternatively, they may have the right to reside, which, aside from British and Irish nationals, is also granted to Commonwealth citizens and those immigrants with permission to stay under the United Kingdom's immigration rules. Under EC law, all EU citizens have the right to reside in the territory of another EU country for up to three months, which is extended for workers and their family members.[23] Finally, persons should not be subject to immigration controls, such as a 'no public funds' restriction attached to their residence permits, or being 'subject to a formal undertaking' during a period of five years. British citizens, EEA nationals and their family members, and refugees are exempt from these conditions. In other words, while the right to reside mainly aims to restrict the access of inactive EU citizens, the 'subject to immigration control' restriction targets third-country nationals and their family members (Child Poverty Action Group 2008, 1372–74). As a result of combining these three factors, although a permanent residence permit is not a requirement for social benefit entitlement, the corresponding regulation de facto limits access to permanent residents. Immigrants, in principle, can qualify for 'indefinite leave to remain' after five years, though under the condition that they have sufficient financial means for themselves and their family members and that no family member has made use of public funds (Aleinikoff and Klusmeyer 2002; mainly for immigrants in the business or employment category, see IOM 2009, 521).

Second, the Nordic countries, except Denmark, similarly make immigrants' access to social programmes dependent on being in the territory and thus the place of residence, yet without referring explicitly to a length of residence. Moreover, eligible residents are defined in social security laws as those persons who intend to or have stayed in the country for period of at least twelve months (e.g. Sweden and Norway). As a result, immigrants must maintain actual residence in the country. Norwegian legislation further requires the resident to have entered the country lawfully and to be a member of the National Insurance Scheme (National Insurance Act, Art. 2(1)). The Finnish legislation is even more explicit with regard to what is considered as a permanent move. Besides residing lawfully and solely in Finland, immigrants are required to have close ties to Finland, for example, to have previously been a permanent resident or to be of Finnish origin, to be a family member of a permanent resident or to have a Finnish employment contract of at least two years.

Comparing the different approaches defining immigrants' access to non-contributory social programmes across countries, it is immediately apparent that the Nordic countries pursue a less restrictive practice than the Anglo-Saxon countries, where immigrants have to wait for two to five years in order to be entitled to benefits. In contrast, in the Nordic countries, the mere commitment to reside in the country for a period over one year suffices to be entitled to welfare benefits.

Finally, in Continental and Southern European countries, the length and place of residence are less crucial for immigrants as the majority of social programmes in those countries are based on former contributions. Immigrants who have not contributed are simply not entitled to social programmes. Thus, references to immigrants are often not laid down explicitly in laws and regulations. However, if immigrants' access to social programmes is restricted, it is made dependent on a permanent residence permit, which in these countries requires at least five years of residence. The renewal of immigrants' residence permits as well as opportunities for obtaining a permanent residence permit in those countries is contingent on proof of sufficient means for themselves and their families, which is comparable to the United Kingdom (discussed earlier). As a result, although not excluded formally by law, reliance on means-tested benefits such as social assistance can put their legal stay in danger. After having discussed the general principles countries apply with regard to access to social programmes, the following section is devoted to the specific types of social programmes available.

Unemployment Programmes

An overview of the unemployment programmes implemented in nineteen OECD countries is presented in table 3.3 (see first column). Two types of programmes can be distinguished: unemployment insurance and unemployment assistance (programme title in italics). The former exists in all countries except Australia. Because entitlement to unemployment insurance benefits depends on former contributions from employment, all immigration categories are entitled to this benefit as long as they fulfil the respective requirements. Moreover, they have to be in possession of a working permit that allows them to pursue gainful employment. Consequently, the same values have been assigned to all immigration categories, including nationals. Immigration categories that are not allowed to work are coded as 0 (e.g. family members of labour migrants in the United States).

The major difference in unemployment programmes across the countries concerns the required length of contributions, which ranges between 600 working hours in Canada (around fifteen weeks within the past year) and two years of insurance and fifty-two weekly contributions during the past two years in Italy. For most countries, a contribution period between twenty-six and fifty-two weeks is required.

Table 3.3. Immigrants' access to unemployment programmes by immigration category

	Programme title	Condition	Nationals/ family members	Permanent residents/ family members	Labour migrants/ family members
AU	New start allowance	Australian resident and waiting period (2 years)	4	2/3	0
AT	Arbeitslosengeld/ Notstandshilfe (cont. of payment)	Contributory: 52 weeks	1	1	1
BE	Allocation de chômage	Contributory: 52 weeks	1	1	1
CA	Employment Insurance	Contributory: 600 hours	2	2	2
DK	Arbejdsløshedsforsikring	Contributory: 52 weeks	1	1	1
FI	Basic security (perustoimeentuloturva), earnings-related security (ansioperusteinen sosiaaliturva)	Contributory: 43 weeks	2	2	2
	Labour market support (työmarkkinatuki)	Permanent resident (under social security law)	4	4	2[0,4]
FR	Assurance de chômage/ régime de solidarité (cont. of payments)	Contributory: 26 weeks	2	2	2
DE	Arbeitslosenversicherung	Contributory: 52 weeks	1	1	1
	Arbeitslosengeld II	Residence/ work permit (expulsion: 5y)	4	4/1	1
GR	Unemployment insurance	Contributory: 125 days	2	2	2
IE	Unemployment Benefits	Contributory: 39 weeks	2	2	2
	Unemployment Assistance	Habitual residence (2y)	4/2	4/2	2
IT	L'assicurazione contro la disoccupazione	Contributory: 104 weeks	1	1	1
NL	Unemployment Insurance (WW)	Contributory: 26 weeks	2	2	2
NO	Dagpenger	Contributory: 1.5 of basic income	2	2	2

(Continued)

Table 3.3.   Continued

	Programme title	Condition	Nationals/ family members	Permanent residents/ family members	Labour migrants/ family members
PT	Subsídio de desemprego	Contributory: 65 weeks	1	1	1
	Subsídio social de desemprego	Contributory: 26 weeks	2	2	2
ES	Proteccion por desempleo (prestacion)	Contributory: 52 weeks	1	1	1
	Proteccion por desempleo (subsidio)	Contributory: 26 weeks	2	2	2
SE	Inkomstbortfallsförsäkring	Contributory: 52 weeks	1	1	1
	Grundförsäkring	Contributory: 26 weeks	2	2	2
CH	Arbeitslosenversicherung	Contributory: 52 weeks	1	1	1
UK	Contribution-based jobseeker's allowance	Contributory: minimum £2,175	2	2	2
	Income-based jobseeker's allowance	different conditions[a]	4/1	4/1	0
US	Unemployment Insurance (Michigan)	Contributory: 20 weeks, lawful permanent resident	2	2	0

Note: 0 = no access, 1 = contribution period ≥ fifty-two weeks or a waiting period of ≥ five years, 2 = contribution period < fifty-two weeks/partner has to apply for work permit or waiting period < five years, 3 = employment, 4 = full access. Social assistance programmes are highlighted in italic.

[a] These include presence and ordinary residence in the country (habitual residence test), having the right to reside, and not being subject to immigration control (public funds restriction or subject of a formal undertaking).

Source: See appendix table MA.3.

Two additional requirements affecting immigrants in particular should be mentioned. First, legal residence is a condition for being granted unemployment benefits, although not all national social security legislations mention it explicitly (see also Brubaker 1989, 159–60).[24] Second, unemployed persons must reside in the host country. This means that unemployment benefits are hardly ever paid abroad. Although all countries under analysis have signed bilateral social security agreements, they rarely address unemployment insurance and mainly refer to the aggregation of the insurance period paid in the country of origin (e.g. Austria, Belgium, Denmark, Italy, Portugal and Switzerland). EU citizens are a notable exception, as they benefit from the exportability of unemployment payments. Within the European Union, entitlement to benefits can be retained for up to three months under the condition that the EU citizen has sought work and been registered as unemployed in that member state for at least four weeks (Council Regulation (EC) No. 883/2004 of 29 April 2004, Art. 64(1)).

By 2010, this regulation was also extended to TCNs.[25] The residence condition particularly affects temporary migrant workers who lose their right to unemployment benefits upon the expiration of their residence permit. Moreover, unemployment not only endangers the renewal of the permit if the migrant worker cannot find another job during the remaining validity of the residence permit (e.g. in Italy) but also can be a reason for immigrants' expulsion. For example, in Austria, immigrants who are unemployed for more than four months during their first year of residence can be expelled from the country (Fremdenpolizeigesetz 2005, Art. 54(2)). The case of Finland shows that EU citizens are not exempt from this practice. According to Article 160 of the Finnish Aliens Act, an EU citizen maintains his/her status as employed or self-employed for only six months if he/she has worked for fewer than twelve months, or has been employed based on a fixed-term contract for less than one year.

Several countries further provide unemployment assistance programmes that are based on either a reduced contribution period (e.g. Portugal, Spain and Sweden) or continuation of unemployment payments (e.g. Austria and France). As discussed earlier, entitlement to unemployment assistance in those countries depends on having a previous employment record. However, some countries have also implemented unemployment assistance programmes that are granted regardless of former employment and are based on a means test. Here, the access of different immigration categories depends on a permanent residence permit (Australia, Canada and the United Kingdom) or being a resident of the country (Finland and Germany). For example, in Australia, as mentioned earlier, holders of permanent visas are subject to a further two-year waiting period in order to be eligible for the Newstart allowance. This is also the case for their family members, who must be Australian residents. However, in contrast to other immigration categories, their residence period in Australia on the temporary visa for spouses and partners is also counted towards fulfilment of the waiting period. As discussed earlier in the chapter, immigrants' access to non-contributory programmes in the United Kingdom is highly restricted by excluding immigrants from income-based jobseeker's allowance for the first five years. In contrast, entitlement to labour market support in Finland depends only on being a resident with the intent to settle permanently, that is, having a work contract for at least two years or other ties to the country. Germany is a particular case; the respective article in the legislation only requires that immigrants are employable, in other words, that they have a work permit (Sozialgesetzbuch II, Art. 8(2); see also Kingreen 2010). However, reliance on social benefits can be a reason for expulsion (see discussion below). Therefore, although labour migrants are in principle entitled to Arbeitslosengeld II, their access is restricted.

After having compared access by immigration category, how do social rights of immigrants vary across countries and are they related to a country's generosity with their unemployment programmes? Analogously to work rights, an index calculating the mean of four immigration categories has been developed to facilitate a cross-national comparison.[26] Starting with immigrants' access on the horizontal axis, countries that provide traditional unemployment assistance as well as unemployment insurance such as Finland and Ireland are among the most inclusive towards immigrants. In contrast, immigrants' access to unemployment benefits is rather restricted in Continental European and Anglo-Saxon countries. Austria, Belgium and Switzerland rely exclusively on unemployment insurance and thus ban immigrants indirectly from claiming benefits by requiring at least fifty-two weeks of previous social security contributions (see also Denmark and Italy). Anglo-Saxon countries combine requirements such as a permanent residence permit with a waiting period to restrict immigrants' access to unemployment benefits (e.g. Australia and the United Kingdom). It should be mentioned that cross-national variation in the social rights of immigrants is not only relatively low but also rather restrictive. This is mainly due to the prevalence of an unemployment insurance system across countries, which requires a previous contributions period. But figure 3.2 shows that countries also vary regarding the generosity of unemployment programmes; this is evident on the horizontal axis, which is measured as net replacement rates of various household types earning 67 per cent of the average wage (AW) on the vertical axis. On average, 72 per cent of the former income is replaced across countries (*SD* = .11, see appendix table MA.4). Denmark together with Sweden, Portugal and Switzerland is among the countries with the most generous unemployment programmes for low-wage earners. Anglo-Saxon countries together with Greece are among the countries with the least generous unemployment programmes.

As with immigrants' work rights, no clear welfare regime and immigrant incorporation pattern can be identified. Yet, the data indicate a very weak negative relationship between generosity of welfare programmes and immigrant social rights.[27] Denmark is the country with the most generous unemployment programmes but is also among the countries with the most exclusive social rights. The country with the least generous unemployment system, the United Kingdom, clusters together with Greece in the centre field in terms of immigrant access to unemployment programmes. But again, it is not the generosity of the welfare system per se that is expected to affect

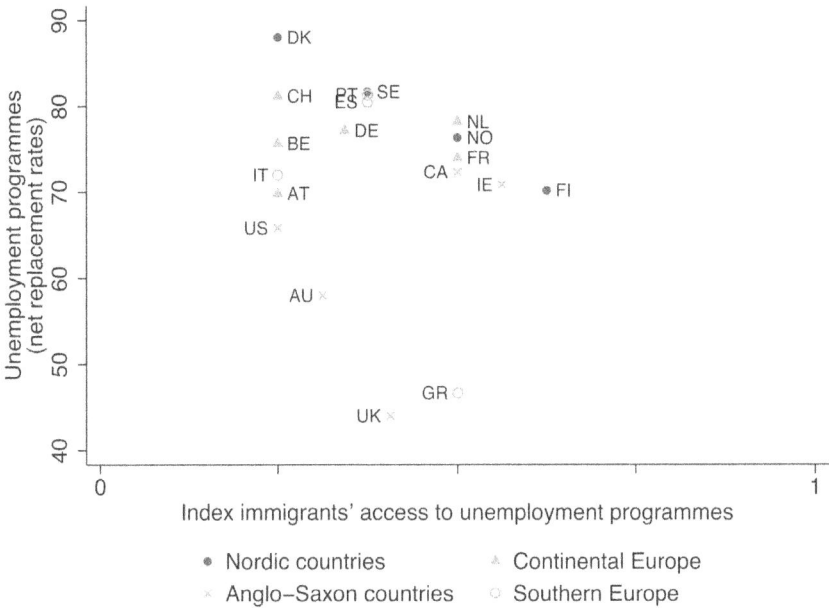

Figure 3.2 Correlation between immigrants' social rights and unemployment programmes. Net replacement rates during initial phase of unemployment for six household types earning 67 per cent of the average wage. *Source*: **OECD (2015c); for social rights, see appendix table MA.3.**

immigrants' poverty. The book's hypothesis is that this poverty-alleviating effect depends on immigrants' access to social programmes. Thus, the impact of unemployment programmes should be larger in countries, such as Finland, granting immigrants easier access compared to countries with more exclusive social rights such as Austria.

Family-Related Programmes

By the end of the 1950s, all countries included in this book had introduced social programmes that addressed the needs of families (Perrin 1969). Two different types can be distinguished: traditional family programmes and dual-earner programmes. They aim to support families in general through child and tax allowances or working parents in particular, for example, maternity and parental leave schemes as well as the provision of childcare. Several countries have also implemented child-raising programmes that compensate for the costs of caring for children. In countries where entitlement is not linked to employment, these specific programmes are included as traditional family benefits.

Dual-Earner Programmes – Maternity/Parental Leave and Childcare

The different social programmes addressing the needs of working parents are presented in table 3.4. Parental benefits are available in all countries except the United States. By 2007, dual-earner support in Australia was confined to childcare benefits.[28] The countries differ as to whether being employed suffices, or whether a specific contribution period should be fulfilled in order to get access. Paid employment is a requirement in five countries, namely Austria, Finland, Germany, Italy and the Netherlands. In the remaining countries, the required contribution period ranges from 120 hours of employment during the past thirteen weeks, as in Denmark, to more than six months in Ireland, Spain, Switzerland and France. Two particular cases are Finland and Sweden, which combine employment-related benefits with flat rate benefits for all inactive residents. For residents in Sweden to receive the contributory parent's cash benefits, they must have been insured for sickness cash benefits above SEK 180 (about €20) for at least 240 consecutive days before confinement. The Finnish social security system requires 180 days of residence in the country and includes self-employed and employed workers not living in Finland but who are entitled to maternity benefits if they have worked for at least four months (MISSOC 2007, Comparative Tables Part 8, 33).

Table 3.4 also includes childcare benefits for working mothers (programme title in italics). These programmes help parents cope with the rising costs of accommodating their children in non-publicly supported or private childcare facilities (e.g. Australia, Finland, France, the Netherlands and Norway). The main condition of entitlement is usually the employment of both parents for a certain number of hours per week. But to be granted childcare benefits in Norway, the lone parent and the child must have resided in the country for at least three years. Several countries – Canada, France and Ireland – also provide universal childcare benefits that allow parents to choose their preferred childcare arrangement regardless of whether or not they are in a position of paid employment (see programme titles marked with an asterisk).

Interestingly, in contrast to unemployment programmes, the respective sections in the social security legislation do not explicitly refer to migrant workers. Exceptions are Canada and Denmark, which make receiving payments dependent on residence in the country. Moreover, some countries also allow immigrant workers under certain conditions to receive their benefits abroad (e.g. Sweden and Italy).

Figure 3.3 shows how immigrants' access to dual-earner programmes and their generosity are related. Starting with immigrants' access (see horizontal axis), Sweden scores the highest by making access to basic parental benefits unrelated to previous employment. The Netherlands and Germany, two Continental European countries, as well as Italy follow where immigrants

Table 3.4.   Immigrants' access to dual-earner programmes by immigration category

	Programme title	Condition	Nationals/ family members	Permanent residents/ family members	Labour migrants/ family members
AU	Child Care Benefit	Employment and Australian resident	3	3	0
AT	Maternity benefits (Wochengeld)	Employment	3	3/2	3/2
BE	Indemnité de maternité	Contributory: 26 weeks	3	3	3
	Congé parental	Contributory: 52 weeks	1	1	1
CA	Maternity benefits, parental care	Contributory: 600 hours	2	2	2
	Universal Child Care Benefit (UCCB)[a]	Permanent residence permit or 18 months of residence	4	4	2
DK	Maternity benefit (dagpenge ved fødsel), parental allowance	Contributory: 120 hours in last 13 weeks	2	2	2
FI	Maternity, parental and paternity allowance (äitiysraha, vanhempainraha, isyysraha)	Employment or permanent resident (incl. 180 days of residence)	4	4	2
	Private childcare allowance (lasten yksityisen hoidon tuki)	Employment and permanent resident	3	3	1.5
FR	Maternal and parental leave (indemnités journalières de maternité et de paternité)	Contributory: 43 weeks	2	2	2
	Complément de libre choix de mode de garde (CMG)	Employment	3	3	3
	Complément de libre choix d'activité (CLCA)	Contributory: 104 weeks	1	1	1
DE	Maternity benefits (Mutterschaftsgeld)	Employment	3	3	3/2
GR	Maternity benefit	Contributory: 200 days	2	2	2
IE	Maternity benefit	Contributory: 39 weeks	2	2	2

(Continued)

Table 3.4. Continued

	Programme title	Condition	Nationals/ family members	Permanent residents/ family members	Labour migrants/ family members
	Family income supplement	employment	3	3/2	3/2
	Early childcare supplement[a]	Habitual residence (y)	4/(2)	4/(2)	2
IT	Congedo di maternità/ paternità	Employment	3	3	3
NL	Maternity leave (Zwangerschaps- en bevallingsverlof)	Employment	3	3	3/2.5
	Kinderopvangtoeslag	Employment	3	3	3/2.5
NO	Parental benefits (foreldrepenger)	Contributory: 26 weeks	2	2	2
	Childcare benefit for single parents (stønad til barnetilsyn)	Employment, legal stay and insured for 3 years	3/2	3/2	2
PT	Protecção da maternidade (e da paternidade)	Contributory: 26 weeks	2	2	2
ES	Prestacion por maternidad	Contributory: 36 weeks	2	2	2
SE	Parental benefits (föräldrapenning)	Legal stay (residence permit) or contributory: 240 days of insurance	4	4	4
CH	Mutterschaftsentschädigung	Contributory: 5 months within 9 months of insurance prior to confinement	2	2	2
UK	Statutory maternity pay and maternity allowance	Contributory: 26 weeks	2	2	2
	Working tax credit	Employment and different conditions[b]	3/(1)	3/(1)	0
US	n.a.				

Note: 0 = no access, 1 = contribution period ≥ fifty-two weeks or a waiting period of ≥ five years, 2 = contribution period < fifty-two weeks/partner has to apply for work permit or waiting period < five years, 3 = employment, 4 = full access. Childcare programmes are emphasised in italic.

[a] Universal benefits leaving the choice of childcare arrangement to the parents regardless whether they are working or not.

[b] For further information see note a in table 3.3.

Source: See appendix table MA.3.

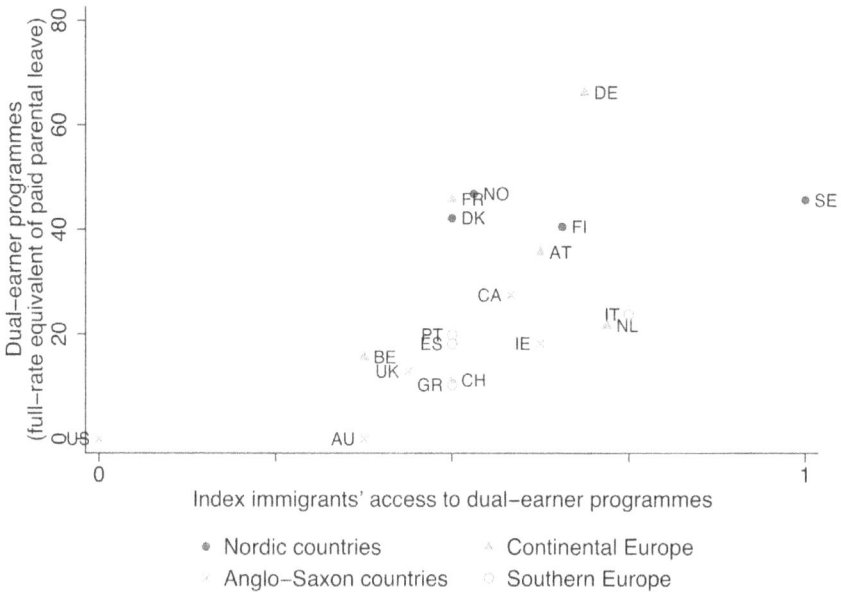

Figure 3.3   Correlation between immigrants' social rights and dual-earner programmes. Full-rate equivalent of paid maternity, paternity and parental leave. *Source*: OECD (2015c); for social rights, see appendix table MA.3.

must just be employed. Australia can be found among the countries with the most exclusive access to dual-earner programmes. Here childcare benefits are available only for employed permanent residents, though without requiring a waiting period. In Belgium, access is also relatively restricted as the parental programme ('congé parental') requires a year of previous insurance payments. The United States scores the lowest as no national parental leave scheme exists. Turning to the generosity of dual-earner programmes (see vertical axis), operationalised as the equivalent of the full-rate of paid parental leave, variation is quite high within the Continental European country group, with Germany being by far the most generous compared to Switzerland and Belgium. However, a clear distinction between generous Nordic countries and Southern European and Anglo-Saxon countries with more basic social protection can be observed. Finally, immigrants' access to and generosity of dual-earner programmes are positively related in figure 3.3.[29] In other words, countries with more generous dual-earner protection are also more inclusive towards immigrants. However, whether more generous social programmes affect poverty of immigrants to a larger extent if they are granted access to these social programmes, for example, if variations in immigrants' access between Sweden and Norway or the Netherlands and Portugal matter when it comes to explaining immigrants' poverty is scrutinised in chapter 4.

Traditional Family Programmes

Table 3.5 provides a summary of traditional family and child programmes implemented across countries. In most of these countries, the programmes are open to citizens and residents on a universal basis, regardless of their former employment record or financial situation. This universal characteristic is also evident when comparing the access of different immigration categories. Any immigrant family legally residing in Austria, Denmark, France, the Netherlands, Norway, Portugal, Sweden or Spain is fully entitled to family benefits. However, in Belgium, Italy and Switzerland, family benefits are linked to employment, while Greece further requires at least fifty days of insurance. Ireland, a particular case, grants immigrant families access to benefits either based on employment or after a two-year waiting period.

In contrast, countries providing means-tested family programmes tend to restrict the access of immigrants by requiring a specific length of residence in the country, which is comparable to unemployment assistance restrictions. Examples are not only the Anglo-Saxon countries (the United Kingdom and the United States) but also Belgium, where a guaranteed family allowance is part of the social assistance system. The person must have resided for at least five years in the country to be entitled to this allowance. Two exceptions are worth mentioning. On the one hand, Canadian labour migrants are eligible for child tax benefits after a residence period of eighteen months. On the other hand, Australian (permanent) residents are entitled to family tax benefits without having to endure a waiting period. In contrast, access to Parenting Payment, an income support programme to help with the costs of raising children, requires two years of residence in Australia. However, as with the Newstart allowance, the length of residence of spouses and partners on a temporary visa is also counted towards the residence requirement (Social Security Act 1991, Art. 729(2)f(v)).[30]

Although family benefits are generally granted to immigrants regardless of their type of residence permit, one major requirement in general must be met in all countries: the eligible person and the child both reside legally in the country. In the case of a child's residence requirement, exceptions are made for migrant workers covered by the bilateral social security agreement (e.g. Austria, Belgium, Germany, Switzerland and the United Kingdom). These workers may also qualify for child benefits even if the child resides abroad as long as the family members abroad do not receive equivalent benefits (for social security treaties at the supra-national level, for example, between the EU and North African countries, see Pennings 2003).

Usually these social security agreements cover basic child allowances but no other types of benefits listed in table 3.5, such as child-raising or single-parent benefits. Concerning child-raising benefits, Austria and Germany

Table 3.5.   Immigrants' access to traditional family programmes by immigration category

	Programme title	Condition	Nationals/ family members	Permanent residents/ family members	Labour migrants/ family members
AU	Family benefits (lump-sum maternity payment, Family Tax Benefit Part A/B)[a]	Australian resident	4	4	0
	Parenting payment (PP)[a]	Australian resident and waiting period (2 years)	4	2/4	0
AT	Family benefits (Familienbeihilfe, Kinderbetreuungsgeld, -absetzungsbetrag, Alleinverdiener- und Alleinerzieherabsetzbetrages)	Legal stay (residence permit)	4	4	4
BE	Allocations familiales	Employment	4	4	4/(2)
	Prestations familiales garanties[a]	residence permit (5 years)	4/(1)	4/(1)	1
CA	Family benefits (Canada child tax benefit)	Permanent residence permit or 18 months of residence	4	4	2
DK	Child and youth benefit (børne- og ungeydelse)	Legal stay (residence permit), liable to taxation	4	4	4
	Child allowance for lone parents (børnetilskud ordinært and ekstra)	Residence requirement: 1/3 (ordinært/ ekstra) years	4/2	4/2	2
	Childcare allowances (by parents, communes)	Residence requirement: 7 years	4/(1)	4/(1)	1
FI	Family benefits (family allowance, child home care allowance [lasten kotihoidon tuki])	Permanent resident	4	4	2
	Partial childcare allowance (osittainen hoitoraha, for parent who reduces working hours to max. 30 hours a week)	Permanent resident and employment	3	3	1.5
FR	Family benefits (allocations familiales, allocation de parent isolé[a])	Legal stay (residence permit)	4	4	4

Table 3.5.   Continued

	Programme title	Condition	Nationals/ family members	Permanent residents/ family members	Labour migrants/ family members
DE	Family benefits (Kindergeld, Elterngeld)	Permanent residence permit or employment	4	4	2[4,0]/ (2[2y])
GR	Child benefit	Contributory: 50 days	2	2	2
IE	Family benefits (child benefit, one-parent family payment)	Habitual residence (2 years)	4/(2)	4/(2)	2
IT	L'assegno per il nucleo familiare	Employment	3	3	3
NL	Algemene Kinderbijslag	Legal stay (residence permit)	4	4	4
NO	Family benefits (child benefit, monthly cash benefit for parents with small children, maternity grant)	Legal stay (residence permit)	4	4	4
	Lone-parent benefit (stønad til enslig mor eller far)	Legal stay (residence permit) and insured for 3 years	4/2	4/2	2
PT	Prestações familiares	Legal stay (residence permit)	4	4	4
ES	Prestaciones por hijo a cargo[a]	Legal stay (residence permit)	4	4	4
SE	Barnbidrag	Legal stay (residence permit)	4	4	4
CH	Kinderzulage	Employment	3	3	3/(2)
UK	Family benefits (child benefit, child tax credit[a])	Different conditions[b]	4/(1)	4/(1)	0
US	Temporary Assistance for Needy Families (TANF)[a]	Lawful permanent resident (5 years)	4/(1)	1	0

Note: 0 = no access, 1 = contribution period ≥ fifty-two weeks or a waiting period of ≥ five years, 2 = contribution period < fifty-two weeks/partner has to apply for work permit (in parentheses) or waiting period < five years, 3 = employment, 4 = full access.

[a]Means-tested programmes.

[b]For further information, see note a in table 3.3.

Source: See appendix table MA.3.

provide particular social programmes that address inactive mothers who are not entitled to maternity leave ('Kinderbetreuungsgeld' in Austria and 'Elterngeld' in Germany).[31] In addition, separate family programmes that address the needs of a lone parent are available in not only Australia but also France, Ireland and Norway. The entitlement conditions for immigrants are comparable to those of child benefits. However, some countries further require that the eligible parent has spent a certain period in the country (e.g. three years for lone-parent benefits in Norway, one to seven years for special child allowances and childcare benefits in Denmark) or have a residence permit that allows him/her to work (e.g. child-raising benefits 'Elternzeit' and 'Elterngeld' in Germany). Despite these minor exceptions, traditional family programmes tend to cover all residents regardless of type of residence permit or employment record.

Figure 3.4 presents the relation between immigrants' access to traditional family benefits and their generosity. In general, Anglo-Saxon countries tend to restrict immigrant families' access to benefits more compared to Nordic and Continental European and also Southern European countries. The front-runner Sweden is now joined by Austria, France and the Netherlands as

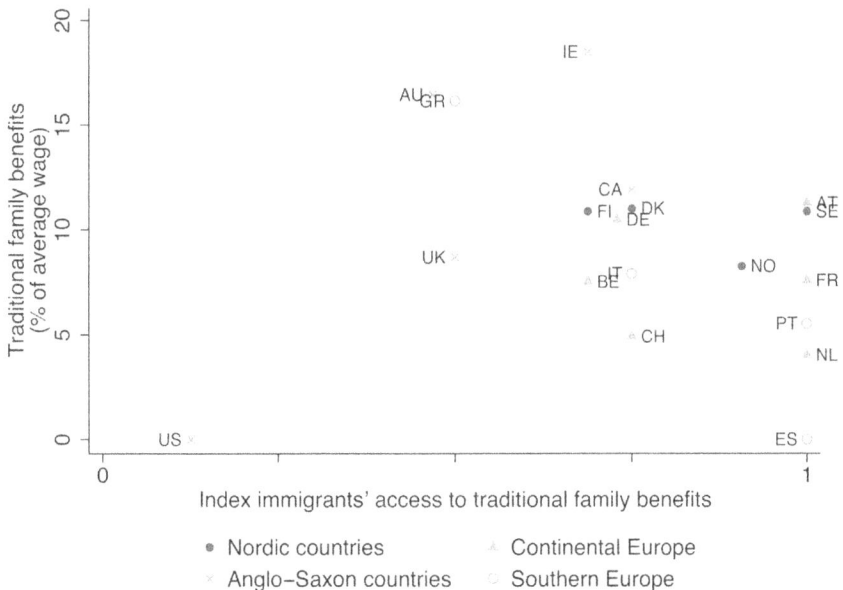

Figure 3.4 Correlation between immigrants' social rights and traditional family benefits. Average traditional family benefits for three different family types earning 67 per cent and 134 per cent, respectively, in percentage of the AW. *Source*: **OECD (2007b); for social rights, see appendix table MA.3.**

well as Portugal and Spain,[32] where legal stay (residence permit) is the only qualifying condition. The welfare clustering is less visible when focusing on the generosity of traditional family benefits, measured as a percentage of the AW of three family types (lone parents, one- and two-earner couples earning 67 per cent and 134 per cent, respectively). Family support is more generous in Ireland, Australia and Greece compared to the United States and Spain, where entitlement is based on a means test, thus excluding even low-wage earners. But family support is also relatively low in the Netherlands and Switzerland. Finally, generosity of traditional family benefits and immigrants access appears to be negatively associated, even more so if the United States is excluded.[33]

Social Assistance Programmes

Compared to the social programmes discussed so far, immigrants' access to social assistance varies most between the countries (see table 3.6). In general, three different practices can be distinguished across countries. First, entitlement to means-tested benefits depends on having a *permanent residence permit*. For example, immigrants and their family members living in Austria's capital Vienna should be in the possession of a residence permit 'Daueraufenthalt-EG' or 'Daueraufenthalt-Angehöriger', which is granted after five years under the condition that they have complied with the integration agreement referring to the acquisition of knowledge of the German language (IOM 2009, 143). In addition, Belgian social security legislation also requires a permanent residence permit. The latter refers rather indirectly to this condition by demanding that the foreigner be inscribed in the population register (Law of 26 May 2002 on the Right to Social Integration, Art. 3(3)), which is for only permanent residents or citizens.

The second group of countries allows access to social assistance benefits *after a specific waiting period*. This condition is applied in most Anglo-Saxon countries discussed earlier, namely Australia, Ireland, the United Kingdom and the United States. Moreover, European countries such as France and Denmark also pursue this practice, where applicants have to prove five or seven years of residence, respectively.[34] De facto, this is the same period as required to apply for a permanent residence permit. According to Spanish national legislation, a residence period of at least one year is required. But since Spanish communities are responsible for social assistance, they can raise the required time of residence, usually to between three and five years (see MISSOC 2007, Comparative Tables Part 2, 112). In the case of Madrid, the residence requirement is limited to having lived in the municipality for one year.

In the last group of countries, access to social and unemployment assistance is granted if the applicants have a *legal residence permit*. Countries following this practice include the three Nordic countries as well as the Netherlands,

Table 3.6. Immigrants' access to social assistance programmes by immigration category

	Programme title	Condition	Nationals/ family members	Permanent residents/ family members	Labour migrants/ family members
AU	Special Benefit	Australian resident and waiting period (2 years)	4	2/3	0
AT	Sozialhilfe	Residence permit (expulsion: 5 years)	4	4/1	0
BE	Revenue d'intégration	Permanent residence permit	4	4	0
CA	Basic financial assistance (Ontario Works)	Permanent residence permit	4/2	4/2	0
DK	Kontanthjælp (Social Bistand)	Residence permit (expulsion: 7 years)	4/1	4/1	0
FI	Living Allowance (toimeentulotuki)	Permanent resident (communes)	4	4	2[0,4]
FR	Droit a l'integration sociale (former: Revenu Minimum d'Insertion)	Residence permit and waiting period (5 years)	4	4/1	1
DE	Sozialhilfe	Residence permit (expulsion: 5 years)	4	4/1	1
GR	n.a.				
IE	Supplementary Welfare Allowance	Habitual residence (2 years)	4/2	4/2	2
IT	Minimo vitale; reddito minimo	Residence permit (valid: 1 year)	4	4	4
NL	Algemene Bijstand	Residence permit	4	4	4
NO	Stønad til livsopphold (sosialhjelp)	Legal stay (residence permit)	4	4	4
PT	Rendimento social de inserção	Legal stay (residence permit)	4	4	4
ES	Renta Mínima de Inserción	Residence requirement (1 year)	4	4/2	2
SE	Ekonomiskt bistånd (socialbidrag)	Legal stay (residence permit)	4	4	4
CH	Sozialhilfe	Residence permit (expulsion: no limit)	4	1	1
UK	Income support	Different conditions[a]	4/1	4/1	0
US	Supplemental Security Income (SSI)	Lawful permanent residents (5 years and 40 quarters of work)	4/1	1	0

Note: 0 = no access, 1 = contribution period ≥ fifty-two weeks or a waiting period of ≥ five years, 2 = contribution period < fifty-two weeks/partner has to apply for work permit or waiting period < five years, 3 = employment, 4 = full access.

[a] For further information, see note a in table 3.3.

Source: See appendix table MA.3.

Portugal and Italy. The latter just requires, according to the national legislation, that the residence permit be valid for at least one year (Decree-Law
No. 286 of 25 July 1998, Art. 41).[35] Also, the social assistance legislation of
Germany and Switzerland, here the canton Zurich, does not explicitly refer
to a specific type of residence permit. However, in both countries, as well
as in Austria, welfare dependency can be a reason for expulsion (see also
Koopmans, Michalowski and Waibel 2012). While in Germany it is a discretionary practice during the first eight years (five years in Austria), permanent
and temporary residents living in Switzerland can be expelled if they rely on
social assistance, regardless of how long they have lived in the country. Since
the revised Aliens Act, which came into force on 1 January 2008, welfare
dependency is no longer a reason to revoke a permanent residence permit but
only after fifteen years of residence in the country (Ausländergesetz, AuG
Art. 63(2)).

   Finally, it should be mentioned that EU member states are free to grant EU
citizens access to social assistance during the first three months. EU citizens
maintain their right to decide 'as long as they do not become an unreasonable
burden on the social assistance system of the host Member State' (2004/38/
EC Art. 14(1)). But once EU citizens reside legally for five years in a member
state, reliance on social assistance is no longer a reason for expulsion (see
also Kingreen 2010, 36–38). However, reliance on means-tested benefits can
be critical for the legal stay of EU citizens and their family members residing
for more than three months but less than five years in another EU country.
After the three-month period, only those who have a right to reside, that is,
workers and their family members, and inactive persons who have sufficient
income to maintain themselves, can claim social assistance, which in turn
puts their right to reside at risk.

   The relation between immigrants' social assistance rights and their generosity among countries is presented in figure 3.5. Concerning immigrants'
social rights, welfare regime typology provides a good starting point; Nordic
countries are among the most inclusive, followed by Southern and Continental European countries. In contrast, immigrants in Anglo-Saxon countries are
confronted with the highest barriers regarding access to guaranteed minimum
assistance. However, as mentioned earlier, several countries deviate from
the expectations of the internal exclusion form of welfare chauvinism. On
the one hand, Italy and Portugal together with the Netherlands stand out
in granting permanent residents and labour migrants full access to social
benefits. Denmark, on the other hand, restricts immigrants' access to social
assistance programmes through a residence requirement of seven years, while
immigrants living in Austria and Switzerland on welfare dependence risk
being expelled within the first years after arrival. The welfare regime pattern
is less evident when turning to the generosity of social assistance, which is
measured through average replacement rates of minimum income protection

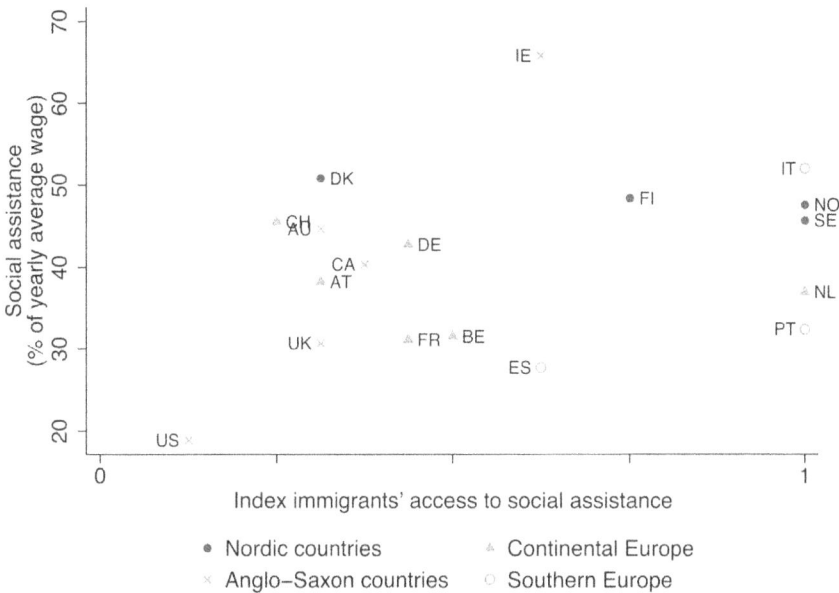

Figure 3.5 Correlation between immigrants' social rights and social assistance. Average minimum income replacement rates for three different household types (single-, lone- and two-parent family), in percentage of yearly AW. *Source*: OECD (2007b); for social rights, see appendix table MA.3.

in percentage of the AW of three different household types (single-, lone and two-parent family, see Nelson 2007). Ireland and Italy together with the Nordic countries have the most generous system, while the most marginal benefits can be found in the United States, followed by Spain, the United Kingdom and Belgium (around 30 per cent). Turning to the relationship between immigrants' access to and generosity of social rights, it is slightly positive.[36] Nonetheless, countries with comparable social assistance replacement rates vary greatly regarding the social rights they grant immigrants, for example, Switzerland and Sweden. Whether cross-national differences in immigrants' social rights might explain observed variations in immigrants' poverty, even after controlling for household characteristics as well as factors at the country-level related to the economy and the immigrant population, is examined in more detail in chapter 4.

THE WELFARE CHAUVINISM THESIS REVISITED: INTERNAL EXCLUSION

Is the 'classic' welfare chauvinism claim that generous welfare states can be maintained only if immigrants' access to social programmes is reflected in social laws and regulations correct? Or can we observe that countries choose a more nuanced form of welfare chauvinism as proposed by Banting (2000)? To start off with, the findings discussed so far partly corroborate Banting's (2000) internal exclusion form of welfare chauvinism. Generally speaking, Nordic welfare states provide immigrants with inclusive access to a variety of social programmes, albeit to a lower extent in Denmark, while Anglo-Saxon countries such as the United States and the United Kingdom tend to restrict immigrants claiming benefits. Thus, the analysis shows that the prevailing type of welfare system indeed matters (see also Sainsbury 2012); welfare states with 'weaker social commitments' tend to restrict immigrants' access to social programmes such as in the Anglo-Saxon countries, while encompassing welfare states do not exclude immigrants internally such as in the Nordic countries (Banting 2000, 23). Between these two poles lie welfare states that rely on a social security system and thus on an indirect ban which limits immigrants' access to social programmes by linking it to employment and former contributions (e.g. Austria, France and Germany).

But as described earlier, several countries do not neatly fit this welfare regime pattern. Considering the Continental European countries, the Netherlands is closer to the three Nordic countries, while immigrants' access to social programmes is relatively restricted in Belgium and Switzerland. Two broader explanations can be put forward: the first relates to the social programme's basis of entitlement of redistribution (based on need, work, residence/citizenship) and the second to a country's (immigration) history as well as the salience of immigration and welfare dependency in the political debate.

First, it is the basis of entitlement to specific social programmes that matters. This argument follows the literature, which argues that social programmes that have been traditionally granted on a universal basis to all citizens are more difficult to restrict to newcomers than social programmes that are based on need and means testing (see Banting 2000, 22–23; Mahnig and Wimmer 2000; Römer 2017).[37] Reasons put forward are not only the ethical principle of equality and equal treatment as a central element of the comprehensive and universal Nordic welfare state model but also more practical concerns such as introducing a specific administration to identify entitled recipients (Rothstein 1998). Thus, to maintain the inherent logic of the welfare state, legal newcomers have to be integrated and included into the welfare community (see also Brochmann 2014).[38] However, as the analysis suggests, it is not the welfare state per se but the social programmes prevalent in the individual countries. The case of universally available traditional family programmes in Austria and France allows that all immigrant families, regardless of the immigration category, are entitled. In contrast, social programmes that target a specific section of the population, for example, benefits for lone-parents in Australia and Norway or poor families in Belgium, require a waiting period as well as a means test. These social programmes are thus comparable to social assistance, where the majority of the countries make access dependent on a permanent residence permit or a certain number of years of residence in the host country. Consequently, the congruence between the basis of entitlement to social programmes and immigrants' access to these programmes partly accounts for the unexpected pattern observed in the Nordic, Continental European and Anglo-Saxon countries.

Second, with a country's immigration tradition in mind, the deviant patterns of those countries that, despite the basis of entitlement, grant legally admitted immigrants full access to social assistance – that is, the Netherlands, Italy, Portugal and to some extent also Spain – can be explained. For Southern European countries, the explanation relates not only to their relatively recent experience regarding immigration and democratisation, compared to other advanced industrialised countries, but also to their 'deeply rooted socialist/communist subculture' (Ferrera 1996, 18), which is echoed in the endeavour to treat all residents equally, including immigrants. In this context, it should be noted that Spanish immigration law mentions immigrants' social rights referring to health care, housing assistance, social security and social services among the first articles following basic rights and thus explicitly puts immigrants on par with nationals (Ley Organica 4/2000 de 11 de enero, Art. 12–14). However, the inclusiveness of immigrants to means-tested and universal social programmes in those countries should be put into perspective in terms of the existence and generosity of these benefits. As welfare state literature indicates, while Southern European countries provide generous protection for their core labour force (e.g. pension), the minimum income protection schemes in Southern European countries remain among the least developed across advanced industrialised countries (see Ferrera 1996).

Concerning the Netherlands, its inclusive approach to extend social rights to immigrants regardless of their immigration category and residence status is closer to the practice observed in Scandinavian countries, such as Sweden and Norway, than in other Continental European countries. Comparable to the Nordic logic based on equal treatment mentioned earlier, one reason to maintain inclusive social rights has been to prevent the establishment of an ethnic underclass (see Hollifield, Martin and Orrenius 2014).[39] Since the 1980s when the Netherlands officially recognised that it had become an immigration country, a range of policies were introduced to promote the integration of ethnic minorities, such as allowing them access to public service employment as well as subsidising immigrant associations (Mahnig and Wimmer 2000; Bloemraad 2014; Maas 2014). In the late 1980s, the policy focus shifted more strongly to labour market integration providing programmes to ameliorate education and increase incentives to learn Dutch (Mahnig and Wimmer 2000). However, while in the past decade, the Netherlands has been moving from civic integration policies to cultural assimilation policies (Joppke 2007a; see also data in the Multicultural Policy Index 2011), for example, requiring a citizenship test for immigrants applying for a residence permit except applicants from specific industrialised countries[40] (Maas 2014, 271), a concomitant shift, at least concerning their social rights, cannot yet be observed.

At this point, it is important to point out that immigrants' social rights are not set in stone but also depend on the salience of immigration in political debates. These factors partly explain the restrictive shift in Dutch immigration-related policies and also why Denmark – primarily concerning social assistance – deviates from the inclusive approach of its Nordic counterparts towards immigrants. However, at least in Scandinavian countries, welfare state and immigration issues have been linked to each other in the public debate, though it was most pronounced and harsh in Denmark (Brochmann 2014). Partly as a result thereof, Denmark put more emphasis on duties – that is, work and employment – than Sweden and Norway and implemented the already mentioned requirement of seven years of residency to receive full social assistance benefits 'as a way to spur employment among immigrants' (Brochmann 2014, 293). The resulting change of government after the Danish election in 2001 from a social democratic one to a coalition between the liberals and conservatives, supported by the Danish People's Party, preceded the aforementioned reforms. The measures included, among others, a reduction in the level of introduction allowance – the alternative social programmes for immigrants and Danish citizens who have lived abroad – below the level of social assistance, restricting family reunification by abolishing family reunion right for immigrants' parents and tightening conditions for spouses, and increasing the residence requirement for a permanent residence permit to seven years (Brochmann and Hagelund 2011; Sainsbury 2012, 233). However, as soon as the Social Democrats returned to government after the 2011 election, the seven-year condition for claiming social assistance was revoked (Brochmann 2014).

SUMMARY OF FINDINGS

The analysis of this chapter supports contributions from migration and welfare state literature as follows. First, as migration and citizenship literature claims, the main division is not between citizens and immigrants but between different types of immigration categories, in particular residents with permanent and temporary residence permits (Brubaker 1989, 156; Hammar 1990; Sainsbury 2006). Permanent residents that have spent up to five years legally in the host country enjoy not only full access to paid employment but also to non-contributory and means-tested social programmes. Second, related to welfare state literature in general and the internal exclusion form of welfare chauvinism in particular, a certain congruence between the type of welfare state and the inclusiveness of access to social programmes can be observed: Nordic countries are more inclusive than Anglo-Saxon countries, with Continental countries in the middle restricting immigrants' access indirectly by requiring a previous contribution record. However, the analysis also suggests that the basis of entitlement of specific social programmes as well as the country's immigration tradition and political debate should be considered.

Chapter 4

Explaining Cross-National Variations in Immigrants' Poverty

This chapter tests the hypothesis of whether immigrants' access to the labour market and social programmes moderates the impact of the labour market and welfare system on immigrants' poverty. The analysis is done separately for the impact of labour market institutions, on the one hand, and welfare state institutions, on the other hand, on immigrants' poverty. Both sections are structured as follows: first the impact of the labour market and the welfare system on immigrants' poverty is tested. However, as argued in chapter 1, a direct impact is not expected since citizens' and immigrants' social rights differ across countries. Then immigrants' social rights are included as a moderating variable. The findings show, first, that the labour market and the welfare system cannot explain cross-national variations and, second, that immigrants' social rights matter. This is the case for not only the role of regulated minimum wage setting but also traditional family benefits. Thus, the prevailing assumption of welfare state literature concerned with immi-grant poverty (e.g. Hooijer and Picot 2015; Kesler 2015) – that citizens' and immigrants' social rights hardly differ and thus can be disregarded – has to be revised, at least when immigrants' socio-economic outcomes are considered. Finally, neither immigration policies, measured by rude proxies referring to the immigrant population and residence permits issued (except permits issued for humanitarian reasons), nor alternative explanations of poverty in the eco-nomic context have a substantial impact on immigrants' poverty. The remain-der of this chapter critically discusses the results and possible explanations.[1]

DO IMMIGRANTS' SOCIAL RIGHTS OF CITIZENSHIP MATTER?

Before testing the impact of country-level determinants, the analysis begins with household-level predictors. This is central to ensure that variations between countries (i.e. level-2 units) are not simply due to cross-national variations in the composition of immigrant groups, for example, that the high poverty incidence of immigrants in a country is not mainly due to a high share of low-skilled immigrants who tend to be exposed to higher poverty risks. Table 4.1 presents the results for both dependent variables, namely poverty based on market and poverty reduction.[2] Model 0, or the null model, serves as a benchmark to assess how much of the variance can be attributed to variance

Table 4.1. Determinants of immigrants' poverty at the household level

	Poverty (market income)		Poverty reduction	
	Model 0	*Model 1*	*Model 0*	*Model 1*
Ref. Low education				
Medium		−.650***		.101
		(.07)		(.08)
High		−1.266***		−.364***
		(.08)		(.10)
Mixed, low		−.268***		.111
		(.08)		(.11)
Mixed		−.501***		−.007
		(.12)		(.16)
Mixed, high		−.720***		−.211
		(.10)		(.14)
Ref. low-service functionaries				
Blue-collar workers		−.490***		−.234*
		(.07)		(.10)
Mixed service functionaries		−.742***		−.141
		(.11)		(.14)
Socio-cultural professionals		−.869***		−.253*
		(.10)		(.13)
Capital accumulators		−1.447***		−.539***
		(.11)		(.15)
Mixed skills, low		−.390***		.060
		(.09)		(.13)
Mixed skills		−.801***		−.093
		(.10)		(.14)
Mixed skills, high		−1.551***		−.436
		(.25)		(.31)
Other		−.171		−.196
		(.13)		(.12)
Ref. no one employed				
One employed		−3.966***		−1.807***
		(.12)		(.10)
Multiple earners		−5.706***		−3.200***
		(.13)		(.13)
Ref. no one employed atypically				
At least one person		.865***		.426***

(Continued)

Table 4.1. Continued

	Poverty (market income)		Poverty reduction	
	Model 0	*Model 1*	*Model 0*	*Model 1*
		(.08)		(.09)
All		1.471***		.945***
		(.06)		(.08)
Ref. no one self-employed				
At least one person		.370**		.068
		(.12)		(.20)
All		.628***		−.266†
		(.09)		(.15)
Number of children, aged ≤2		.567***		.303***
		(.05)		(.07)
Number of children, aged 3–5		.517***		.171*
		(.05)		(.07)
Number of children, aged 6–12		.447***		.260***
		(.03)		(.04)
Number of children, aged 13–17		.564***		.177***
		(.04)		(.05)
Number of persons, aged ≥65		.188*		.726***
		(.08)		(.09)
Constant	−.829***	2.744***	−1.869***	−.664***
	(.09)	(.18)	(.16)	(.18)
Intercept	−.984***	−.606***	−.378*	−.468**
	(.18)	(.17)	(.17)	(.18)
Var (countries)	.140	.298	.470	.392
Intra-class correlation	.041	.083	.125	.107
Log-likelihood	−9,144.695	−5,767.583	−4,455.930	−3,717.778
LR test	182.365	564.767	599.875	286.648
N (households)	15,150	15,150	15,150	15,150
N (countries)	19	19	19	19

Note: Coefficients (log odds) of random intercept logit models, standard errors in parentheses.

† $p < .10$, * $p < .05$, ** $p < .01$, *** $p < .001$.

between countries. As the intra-class correlation for the pre-tax and transfer model suggests, only 4.1 per cent of the variance in poverty based on market income is at the country level, which is quite low, while about 12.5 per cent of the variance in poverty reduction is explained by between country variance.

In the second stage of analysis, household-level factors are added as controls to the benchmark model. Empirical research on poverty shows that structural (or socio-demographic) factors at the individual level play a major role (e.g. Lohmann 2009; Graaf-Zijl and Nolan 2011; Kesler 2015). But just as importantly, this approach addresses the 'methodological nationalism' critique (Wimmer and Glick Schiller 2003, 584), on comparing immigrants' outcomes with the native mean without considering the heterogeneity within immigrant groups, by taking specific socio-demographic characteristics of immigrant households into account. On the one hand, *skills and education* have become more important as structural change related to technical innovations, deindustrialisation and globalisation has increased the demand for workers with different skills. While automatisation has made jobs for medium-skilled workers in routine tasks redundant, the relative demand for low-skilled workers in non-routine tasks has increased as they are more difficult to replace with machine labour. The rising gap in education requirements between newly emerging less-well-paid service occupations and demanding technology-driven jobs exacerbates the situation of low-skilled and inexperienced individuals when it comes to finding adequately paid employment (for the trilemma of the service economy, see Iversen and Wren 1998; for empirical evidence, see Häusermann and Schwander 2009; Whelan and Maître 2010). On the other hand, *working patterns* of household members in general are central. Nowadays, a single wage no longer suffices to provide for a family. In the mid- to late 2000s, poverty rates of dual-earner families were considerably lower than in single-earner families (Fritzell and Ritakallio 2010; OECD 2011, Table 1.3, 41). This is particularly the case for single-parent households because they not only have to rely on a single income but at the same time also have facilitate childcare (Gornick and Jäntti 2012). In addition, employment conditions might also affect poverty, for example, whether a person pursues atypical employment such as part-time or temporary employment, as these employment characteristics tend to be related to lower wages (see Häusermann and Schwander 2009, 2012). Indeed, one might argue that if a family member is employed atypically, this does not mean that the household is exposed to higher poverty risks as long as other family members work, for example, the male insider, and contribute to the household income. Hence, the following socio-demographic variables at the household level are considered: educational attainment, occupation and employment situation of household members and the number of children and elderly persons living in the household.

The results in table 4.1 (see model 1) support the general findings in poverty research (e.g. Misra, Moller and Budig 2007; Brady, Fullerton and Cross 2009; Lohmann 2009). Concerning *immigrants' poverty before taxes and transfers* (left panel), higher education and skills go along with lower poverty risks. For example, immigrant households with medium educational attainments (i.e. upper secondary or post-secondary education) are almost two times less likely to end up in poverty when compared to the reference category, here households with members that have finished at most lower secondary education $(1/\exp(-.650) = 1.91, p < .001)$. Also households with mixed educational attainments (i.e. different combinations of educational

levels within a household) experience lower poverty risks than households with low educational attainment. Turning to occupation,[3] households
employed in low-service-sector jobs, the reference category, have a higher
probability of being poor than households including blue-collar and lower-
level white-collar workers. Mixed service functionaries are less likely to fall
into poverty than blue-collar workers, and socio-cultural professionals and
capital accumulators even less so.

Households' labour market participation, unsurprisingly, is the strongest
predictor of immigrants' pre-tax and transfer poverty. To a lower extent,
the employment type also influences poverty. Immigrant households with at
least one atypically or self-employed adult face significantly higher poverty
risks compared to households with individuals in standard employment, that
is, open-ended and full-time positions (reference category). Households with
children, regardless of age, and elderly persons experience higher poverty.[4]
In sum, these findings confirm the hypothesis that socio-demographic factors,
more precisely skills, education and employment arrangements of households, are important for explaining immigrants' poverty.

When turning to *immigrants' poverty reduction* (right panel), the effect of
household-level determinants is less pronounced, in particular regarding education, employment and the number of children. Immigrant households' education compositions and occupations have little impact on poverty reduction.
Only more highly educated households, blue-collar workers, socio-cultural
professionals and capital accumulators are less likely to be lifted out of poverty when compared to lower-educated households. The effect of employment
of household members has reduced in importance but still remains the most
important determinant of poverty reduction, though in the opposite direction.
Households with at least one employed person are six times less likely to be
taken out of poverty ($1/\exp(-1.807) = 6.09$, $p < .001$). The share of children
and elderly persons both reduce immigrant households' risk of ending up
in poverty, which might be ascribed to supplementary income from family
benefits and/or tax reduction as well as income from pensions. However, the
effect of children living in a household declines with the age of the children.
Nevertheless, self-employed immigrant households still have a higher risk of
ending up in poverty even after taking taxes and transfers into account. One
explanation could be that self-employed persons in a number of countries are
covered by separate social insurance schemes (see MISSOC 2007; SSA 2006,
2007). Generally speaking, the results indicate that welfare states address the
need of families and help them out of poverty.

As has been argued earlier, the inclusion of household-level factors into
the model aims to control for compositional effects of immigrant households
between countries and thus is expected to reduce variance between countries.
However, as the intra-class correlations of both extended models show, a

considerable share of variance remains unexplained by household-level characteristics, namely around 8 per cent in the pre-tax and transfer model and
11 per cent in the post-tax and transfer model. The next sections test whether
country-level determinants can account for the remaining variance between
countries.

The Labour Market and Immigrants' Poverty

Table 4.2 summarises the results testing the impact of different labour market institutions and immigrants' access to paid employment. Models 1a and
1b estimate the impact of wage-setting institutions. As evident in model 1a,
the coefficient referring to Kenworthy's index of wage bargaining is negative, indicating that the higher the level of bargaining coordination, ranging
from economy-wide to industry-level to firm-level to no coordination, the
less poverty risk is based on market income. However, the coefficient is not

Table 4.2. Determinants of immigrants' poverty based on market income – labour market institutions and immigrants' access to paid employment

	Model 1a	*Model 1b*	*Model 2a*	*Model 2b*	*Model 3*
Wage bargaining coordination	−.097				
	(.11)				
Government intervention		−.183			
		(.11)			
Minimum wage setting			.040		
			(.04)		
Minimum wage (% of median)				−.000	
				(.01)	
Index labour market (paid employment)					−.337
					(1.17)
Constant	−2.364***	−2.367***	−2.362***	−2.362***	−2.363***
	(.15)	(.14)	(.15)	(.15)	(.15)
Intercept	−.633***	−.678***	−.635***	−.606***	−.609***
	(.17)	(.18)	(.18)	(.17)	(.17)
Var (countries)	.282	.258	.281	.298	.296
Intra-class correlation	.079	.073	.079	.083	.083
Log-likelihood	−5,767.184	−5,766.394	−5,767.197	−5,767.582	−5,767.542
N (households)	15,150	15,150	15,150	15,150	15,150
N (countries)	19	19	19	19	19

Note: Coefficients (log odds) of random intercept logit models, standard errors in parentheses. All models
are estimated including household-level variables (not shown).

† $p < .10$, * $p < .05$, ** $p < .01$, *** $p < .001$.

significant. The same is also the case for government intervention in wage bargaining (see model 1b). Again, the coefficient is negative but not significant. Although the literature suggests that the level of centralisation and coordination of wage bargaining tends to reduce wage inequalities, especially at the bottom of the wage distribution (e.g. Pontusson, Rueda and Way 2002), this does not directly translate into lower immigrant poverty levels.

Models 2a and 2b estimate the impact of minimum wage policies. Neither the index measuring minimum wage setting nor the level of minimum wages as percentage of the median wage has a significant impact on immigrant poverty. Moreover, the sign of the coefficient referring to the minimum wage setting is positive, indicating that stronger involvement by governments increases immigrant poverty levels. Finally, model 3 shows that the index on immigrants' access to paid employment, introduced in the previous chapter, alone cannot explain their poverty (see model 3). Also, the inclusion of the more differentiated index by immigration category, namely family members of permanent residents as well as labour migrants and their family members, does not have an effect on immigrants' poverty (models not shown).

In sum, these results show that labour market institutions on their own do not contribute to explaining cross-national variations in immigrants' poverty based on market income. However, as discussed in the theoretical chapter, this book postulates that the impact of national labour market institutions on immigrants' poverty is moderated by immigrants' access to paid employment.

The Moderating Effect of Immigrants' Access to the Labour Market

In order to test the labour market hypothesis related to wage-setting systems and minimum wage laws, the models are re-estimated interacting each labour market policy indicator with the index on immigrants' access to paid employment (see table 4.3). It should be noted that, besides the household-level characteristics, two control variables at the country level are included: GDP growth and percentage of foreign-born residents from industrialised countries.

Concerning the former, traditional poverty research emphasises the importance of a country's economic development on poverty, namely that 'a rising tide of economic progress lifts all boats' (Sorensen 2008, 227).[5] Simplifying the argument, the whole of society benefits from increased affluence or is adversely affected by economic downturns (e.g. Gundersen and Ziliak 2004; Bäckman 2009; Brady 2009), though not necessarily to the same extent. This point might be even more relevant for immigrants' socio-economic outcomes as the economic situation also affects poverty indirectly through the risk of unemployment. Immigrants are often among the first to be fired and the last to be employed (for Germany, see Kogan 2004). Further evidence comes from the international migration outlook (OECD 2013b). The study shows that foreign-born immigrants have been hit more severely by the recent economic crisis compared to native-born individuals. In more detail, the international migration outlook further suggests that employment outcomes vary across migrant groups, with those who are younger and lower skilled being more affected compared to female and high-skilled workers (ibid.). Thus, a country's economic situation might be especially important for immigrant outcomes. For this reason, the effect of various economy-related indicators – such as the GDP per capita, employment growth, size of the shadow economy as well as the unemployment rate for the whole population and the immigrant population alone – has been tested (for sources and operationalisation, see methodological appendix). None of these indicators are related to cross-national variations in immigrants' poverty.[6] Concerning more migration-specific indicators, the percentage of permits issued for humanitarian and family-related reasons was the only significant indicator related positively to immigrants' poverty (results not shown).[7] Because the data on permits issued to immigrants are missing for Greece, the following models have been estimated including the share of foreign-born population from industrialised countries. Overall, the findings provide little support for the hypothesis that a country's economic situation, or the composition of the immigrant population and residence permits issued, has an impact on immigrants' poverty.

Models 1a and 1b in table 4.3 refer to the interaction between wage-setting institutions and immigrants' access to paid employment on immigrants' poverty. As both models show, immigrants' work rights moderated neither the effect of wage bargaining coordination nor government involvement in the wage-bargaining process on immigrants' poverty. Although at least the government intervention coefficient is negative as expected, both coefficients are not significant at the 5 per cent level.[8] Based on the data used in this book, it is not possible to support the hypothesis that the poverty-reducing effect of wage-bargaining capacity between employers, employees and the government depends on immigrants' access to paid employment.

In models 2a and 2b, the interaction with minimum wage regulations is estimated. Concerning the impact of government involvement in the minimum wage setting in model 2a, the negative and significant coefficient suggests that the inclusiveness of access to paid employment is important. More specifically, the marginal effect of minimum wage setting on immigrants' poverty is stronger in countries where immigrants are more easily granted access to paid employment. However, disaggregating the immigrants' access to paid employment index by immigration category shows that this poverty-reducing effect can only be found regarding labour migrants (see model 2a [labour migrants]), but not for the access of family members of permanent residents and temporary migrants to paid employment (results not shown).

Table 4.3. Determinants of immigrants' poverty based on market income – the moderating effect of access to paid employment

	Model 1a	Model 1b	Model 2a	Model 2a (labour migrants)	Model 2b	Model 2b (labour migrants)
GDP growth (5-year average)	.193	.209	.074	.129	.150	.220
	(.15)	(.15)	(.15)	(.16)	(.17)	(.14)
Industrialised countries, % foreign-born	-.001	-.011	-.003	-.008	-.012	-.017[+]
	(.01)	(.01)	(.01)	(.01)	(.01)	(.01)
Index labour market (paid employment)	.232	-.219	.299	-.589	-.299	-.706
	(1.10)	(1.17)	(.98)	(.66)	(1.06)	(.69)
Wage bargaining coordination	-.053					
	(.11)					
Wage bargaining coordination X access (emp.)	1.489					
	(.92)					
Government intervention		-.179				
		(.12)				
Government intervention X access (emp.)		-.881				
		(1.38)				
Minimum wage setting			.030	.022		
			(.04)	(.04)		
Minimum wage setting X access (emp.)			-.833*	-.567*		
			(.34)	(.25)		
Minimum wage (% of median)					.001	.001
					(.01)	(.00)
Minimum wage X access (emp.)					-.076	-.064*
					(.05)	(.03)
Constant	-2.336***	-2.350***	-2.364***	-2.327***	-2.329***	-2.274***
	(.14)	(.14)	(.13)	(.13)	(.14)	(.13)

Intercept	−.768***	−.751***	−.852***	−.852***	−.759***	−.759***
	(.18)	(.18)	(.18)	(.18)	(.18)	(.18)
Var (countries)	.215	.223	.182	.182	.219	.219
Intra-class correlation	.061	.063	.052	.052	.063	.063
Log-likelihood	−5,764.945	−5,765.157	−5,763.534	−5,763.534	−5,765.026	−5,765.026
N (households)	15,150	15,150	15,150	15,150	15,150	15,150
N (countries)	19	19	19	19	19	19

Note: Coefficients (log odds) of random intercept logit models, standard errors in parentheses. All models are estimated including household-level variables (not shown).

† $p < .10$, * $p < .05$, ** $p < .01$, *** $p < .001$.

Source: Eugster, Immigrants and Poverty, and Conditionality of Immigrants' Social Rights, *Journal of European Social Policy* (forthcoming) pp. 12, Table 1. Copyright © [2018] (Beatrice Eugster). Reprinted by permission of SAGE Publications.

The marginal effect of minimum wage setting is plotted in order to investigate the range of values on the immigration access index at which the interaction effect is significant. As evident in figure 4.1, more regulated minimum wage setting raises immigrants' poverty if access to paid employment is rather restricted (see left-hand side of the graph). However, as immigrants' access to the labour market becomes more inclusive, this effect diminishes. As the figure also indicates, minimum wage setting would actually have a reductive effect on immigrants' poverty if all immigrants, that is, immigration categories, were granted full access to paid employment (right-hand side of the graph; for the descriptive statistics, see appendix table MA.4 in the methodological appendix). However, a regulated minimum wage setting only draws a distinction in countries where immigrants face high barriers to entering the labour market, namely by increasing their poverty levels (see also figure 4.2 for labour migrants).

Accordingly, the results in model 2b, when including the level of minimum wage as a percentage of the median wage, indicate that higher minimum wages have a stronger effect on immigrants' poverty when combined with inclusive access to paid employment ($b = -.076$, $p = .11$). The separate

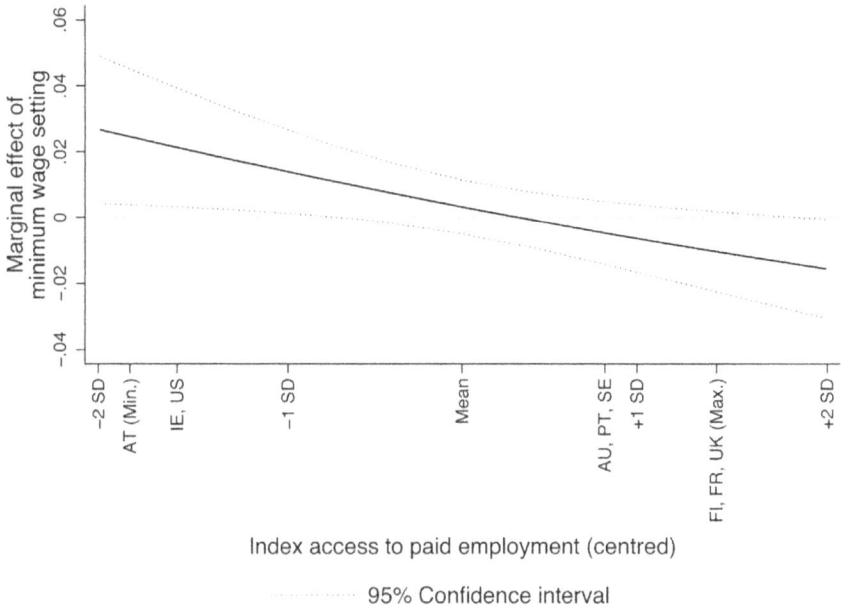

Figure 4.1   **Marginal effect of minimum wage setting on immigrants' poverty based on market income.** *Source*: **Eugster, Immigrants and Poverty, and Conditionality of Immigrants' Social Rights,** *Journal of European Social Policy* **(forthcoming) p. 13, Figure 4. Copyright © [2018] (Beatrice Eugster). Reprinted by permission of SAGE Publications.**

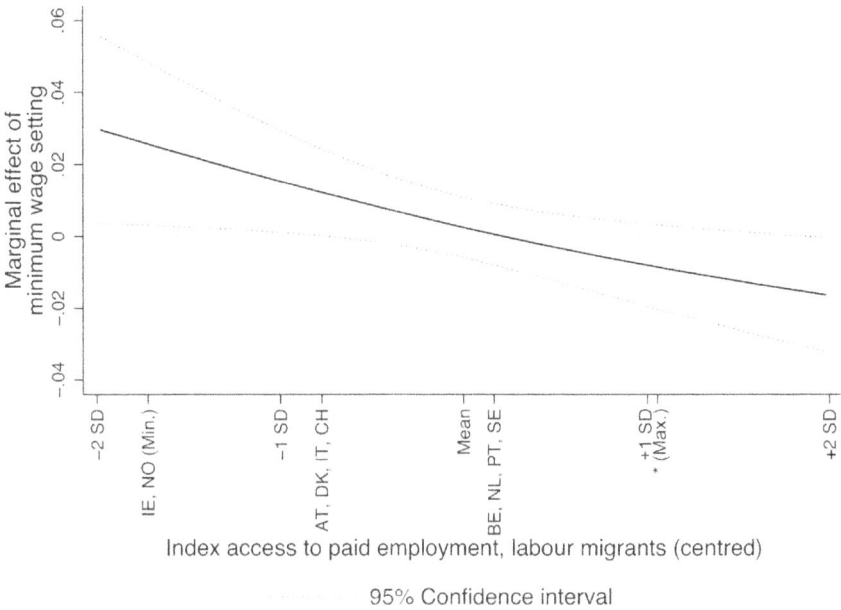

Figure 4.2   **Marginal effect of minimum wage setting on immigrants' poverty based on market income (labour migrants). * Includes Australia, Finland, France, Germany, Greece, Spain and the United Kingdom. *Source*: See methodological appendix.**

analysis by immigration category shows that access to paid employment is particularly important when considering labour migrants (model 2b [labour migrants]). The same pattern can be found, namely that higher minimum wages have a poverty increasing effect but only when the access of labour migrants to paid employment is rather restricted.

Broadly speaking, the findings from model 2a and 2b suggest that immigrants living in countries where minimum wage setting is regulated and their access to paid employment is rather restricted are exposed to a higher poverty risk. These results suggest that immigrants are doubly punished if high barriers to changing one's job (work rights) are combined with more strongly regulated minimum wage legislation. Concerning the poverty-increasing effect of the latter, traditional research refers to its adverse effect on employment by destroying low-paid jobs and hindering the creation of new jobs (e.g. OECD 1998). Low-skilled immigrants with residence permits that make it more difficult to change their employer might be particularly affected. A higher poverty risk would thus result either from the loss of a job without the possibility to find an adequate replacement or by pushing them into irregular employment in the shadow economy where they are paid wages lower than the minimum wage. However, the findings also indicate that more strongly regulated minimum wages do not increase immigrants' poverty risk per se. As the access of immigrants to paid employment becomes more inclusive, higher minimum wages would actually have a poverty-alleviating effect, therefore giving support to those scholars pointing to the positive effect of these regulations (e.g. Fortin and Lemieux 1997).

Concerning the effect of economic factors and the composition of the immigrant population, neither GDP growth nor the share of immigrants from industrialised countries is significant. In sum, the findings so far provide empirical support that the impact of minimum wage policies on immigrants' poverty is moderated by immigrants' access to paid employment, though mainly for labour migrants.

The Welfare System and Immigrants' Poverty

In table 4.4, each social programme is included. In general, the results do not suggest, as comparative welfare state research would expect, that the welfare system has a direct impact on immigrants' poverty. Model 1 refers to unemployment generosity measured as the net replacement rate of workers earning 67 per cent of the AW. Although the coefficient is positive, indicating that more generous unemployment programmes are related to higher poverty reduction, the coefficient is not significant.

The effect of family-related programmes is tested in models 2a and 2b, respectively. When dual-earner support, which refers to the involvement of welfare states supporting the employment of parents, is introduced in model 2a, this factor has a positive and significant effect on immigrants' poverty reduction. The generosity of traditional family benefits in model 2b also has a positive but non-significant effect on taking immigrant households out of poverty. Finally, model 3 estimates the effect of social assistance programmes, measured as the minimum income benefits as percentage of the AW (see Nelson 2010). The coefficient points in the expected direction, but again it is not significant. In sum, these results suggest that the generosity of social programmes per se does not affect immigrants' poverty directly.

Turning to the impact of the indices concerning immigrants' access to social programmes (see models 4–6), only the one related to unemployment insurance has a positive and significant impact. Exploring whether the insurance or the assistance component of the index makes the difference in more detail reveals that immigrants' access to unemployment insurance matters (results not shown), although primarily for temporary migrants and their family members. Considering that entitlement to social insurance programmes in principle does not depend on their immigration category – of course, they should be allowed to pursue paid employment and thus may be excluded

Table 4.4. Determinants of immigrants' poverty reduction – social programmes and immigrants' access

	Model 1	Model 2a	Model 2b	Model 3	Model 4	Model 5a	Model 5b	Model 6
Unemployment programmes (generosity)	1.203 (1.33)							
Dual-earner programmes (generosity)		.021** (.01)						
Traditional family benefits (generosity)			.046 (.03)					
Social assistance (generosity)				.020 (.01)				
Index access (unemployment)					2.874** (1.05)			
Index access (dual-earner)						.923 (.60)		
Index access (traditional family benefits)							.712 (.62)	
Index access (social assistance)								.496 (.46)
Constant	-2.602***	-2.604***	-2.604***	-2.581***	-2.596***	-2.603***	-2.599***	-2.599***
	(.18)	(.16)	(.17)	(.18)	(.16)	(.17)	(.17)	(.18)
Intercept	-.491**	-.684***	-.539**	-.517**	-.661***	-.538**	-.511**	-.506**
	(.18)	(.19)	(.18)	(.18)	(.19)	(.18)	(.18)	(.18)
Var (countries)	.374	.254	.341	.355	.267	.341	.360	.363
Intra-class correlation	.102	.072	.094	.098	.075	.094	.099	.099
Log-likelihood	-3,717.377	-3,714.111	-3,716.583	-3,666.459	-3,714.683	-3,716.670	-3,717.145	-3,717.222
N (households)	15,150	15,150	15,150	15,150	15,150	15,150	15,150	15,150
N (countries)	19	19	19	18	19	19	19	19

Note: Coefficients (log odds) of random intercept logit models, standard errors in parentheses. All models are estimated including household-level variables (not shown).

† $p < .10$, * $p < .05$, ** $p < .01$, *** $p < .001$.

indirectly – the results indicate that lower barriers to unemployment compensation in terms of contribution period reduce immigrants' poverty levels,
regardless of the generosity of these programmes.

The Moderating Effect of Immigrants' Access to Social Programmes

As for the analysis of immigrants' poverty based on market income, the effect
of different economic and migration-related macro-level variables has been
tested (results not shown). In sum, the results concerning economic factors
such as GDP and employment growth, as well as a country's general and
immigrants' unemployment rates, are not significant at the 5 per cent level.
Moreover, a country's redistributive effort, measured as social expenditure
in percentage of GDP, is not related to immigrants' poverty either. Only
employment differences between foreign- and native-born residents have
a significant, though negative, effect on poverty reduction. Turning to the
composition of the immigrant population, only the share of humanitarian-
based permits is significant and positive, suggesting that immigrants' poverty reduction is greater in countries with higher percentages of immigrants
migrating for political and humanitarian reasons. In order to include all
countries, GDP growth and the percentage of foreign-born residents from
industrialised countries are included in the models as control variables.

Overall, the findings in table 4.5 do not support the hypothesis that the
poverty-alleviating effect of more generous social programmes on immigrants' poverty is contingent on the immigrants' access to these specific programmes. The only exception is the moderating effect of access to traditional
family benefits.

Starting with model 1, the interaction between the generosity of unemployment benefits and the inclusiveness of unemployment programmes towards
immigrants is measured. In contrast to the interaction coefficient, the one
referring to the lower-order term index on immigrants' access is positive and
significant ($b = 3.233$, $p < .01$). Because it is included together with the interaction term, it can only be interpreted in relation to the particular case where
the unemployment generosity is set at zero. Here M as a variable has been
centred, which represents countries such as Ireland and Italy with unemployment replacement rates of 70 per cent for low-wage workers (earning 67 per
cent of the AW). It should be noted that these (non-)findings are in line with
previous studies. For example, Scruggs and Allan's (2006, 899) results also
indicate that unemployment insurance programmes have no significant effect
on the relative poverty of the working-age population (see also Moller et al.
2003). Additionally, the separate analysis by immigration category does not
alter the results.

When testing interaction models including family-related programmes,
the results only provide support for the effect of traditional family benefits

Table 4.5. Determinants of immigrants' poverty reduction – the moderating effect of access to social programmes

	Model 1	Model 2a	Model 2b	Model 2b (permanent residents)	Model 3
GDP growth (5-year average)	−.071	.266†	.157	.271†	.346
	(.19)	(.16)	(.18)	(.15)	(.24)
Industrialised countries, % foreign-born	.007	.006	−.004	−.022*	−.019
	(.01)	(.01)	(.01)	(.01)	(.02)
Index access (unemployment)	3.233**				
	(1.08)				
Unemployment programmes (generosity)	1.558				
	(1.22)				
Unemployment programmes X access (progr.)	−3.671 (12.83)				
Index access (dual-earner)		−.326			
		(.62)			
Dual-earner programmes (generosity)		.029***			
		(.01)			
Dual-earner programmes X access (progr.)		−.000			
		(.03)			
Index access (traditional family benefits)			1.770* (.70)	3.076*** (.74)	
Traditional family benefits (generosity)			.074*	.053*	
			(.03)	(.03)	
Traditional family benefits X access (progr.)			.203*	.218*	
			(.10)	(.08)	
Index access (social assistance)					.144
					(.52)

(Continued)

Table 4.5.   Continued

	Model 1	Model 2a	Model 2b	Model 2b (permanent residents)	Model 3
Social assistance (generosity)					.025
					(.02)
Social assistance X access (progr.)					−.060
					(.05)
Constant	−2.597***	−2.608***	−2.581***	−2.642***	−2.483***
	(.16)	(.16)	(.16)	(.14)	(.18)
Intercept	−.753***	−.859***	−.714***	−.911***	−.592**
	(.19)	(.20)	(.19)	(.20)	(.19)
Var (countries)	.222	.179	.240	.162	.306
Intra-class correlation	.063	.052	.068	.047	.085
Log-likelihood	−3,713.109	−3,711.382	−3,713.701	−3,710.343	−3,665.220
N (households)	15,150	15,150	15,150	15,150	14,891
N (countries)	19	19	19	19	18

Note: Coefficients (log odds) of random intercept logit models, standard errors in parentheses. All models are estimated including household-level variables (not shown).

$^{\dagger} p < .10$, $^{*} p < .05$, $^{**} p < .01$, $^{***} p < .001$.

Source: Eugster, Immigrants and Poverty, and Conditionality of Immigrants' Social Rights, *Journal of European Social Policy* (forthcoming) p. 14, Table 2. Copyright © [2018] (Beatrice Eugster). Reprinted by permission of SAGE Publications.

on immigrants' poverty depending on the inclusiveness of access to these programmes but not for the dual-earner support model. Model 2b displays the results of interaction between immigrants' access to traditional family benefits and the generosity of these particular social programmes. The interaction coefficient is positive and significant at the 5 per cent significance level ($b = .203$, $p < .05$). Figure 4.3 shows, as expected, that generous traditional family benefits have a poverty-reducing effect when immigrants' access to traditional family benefits is more inclusive. This poverty-reducing effect diminishes as immigrants' access to these social programmes becomes more exclusive.

Scrutinising the results by immigration category reveals that the poverty-reducing effect can primarily be supported when access of permanent residents is considered (see model 2b [permanent residents]). For the three remaining immigration categories no moderating effect could be found (models not shown).

Finally, when adding the interaction between minimum income protection and immigrants' access to social assistance in model 3, the hypothesis cannot be supported. Immigrants' probability of moving out of poverty does not depend on whether they are granted access to minimum income benefits

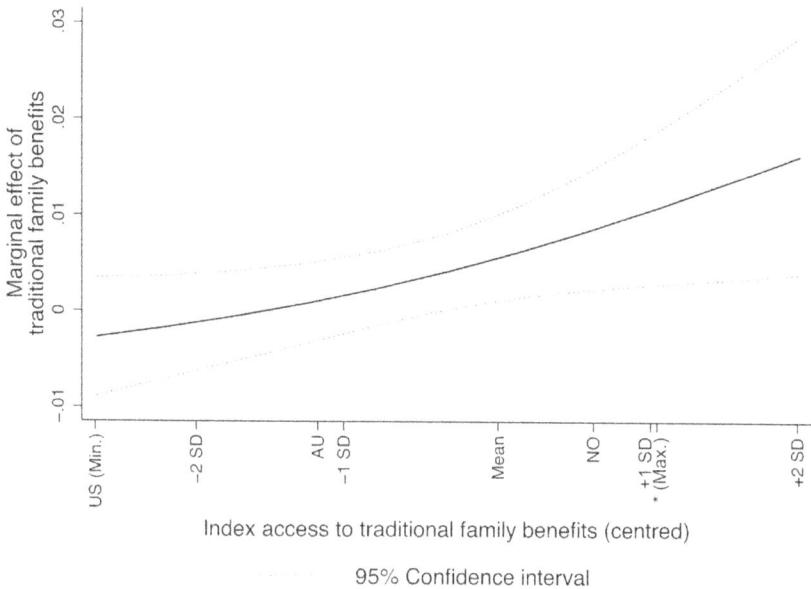

Figure 4.3   **Marginal effect of traditional family benefits on immigrants' poverty reduction. *Includes Austria, France, the Netherlands, Portugal, Spain and Sweden. *Source*: Eugster, Immigrants and Poverty, and Conditionality of Immigrants' Social Rights, *Journal of European Social Policy* (forthcoming) pp. n.a., Figure 5. Copyright © [2018] (Beatrice Eugster). Reprinted by permission of SAGE Publications.**

or not. Moreover, the interaction coefficient is negative, indicating that the poverty-reducing effect of generous social programmes is stronger in countries with more exclusive access for immigrants to social programmes. These results are at odds with the hypothesis formulated in the previous chapter that immigrants' inclusive access to social programmes moderates the impact of social programmes on immigrants' poverty. One reason for the finding put forward in welfare state literature is that social assistance benefits are just too low to lift poor individuals and households out of poverty (Nelson 2004). A more specific immigrant-related explanation, on the other hand, points to the negative effects that welfare dependency may have on immigrants' residence permits and their renewals (e.g. in Switzerland and Germany). Therefore, even if immigrants may be formally granted access to social assistance, it may have no effect on their poverty risk as they refrain from claiming benefits, at least as long as they have not obtained permanent residence status.

Supplementary Analyses: How Robust Are These Results?

So far, the results provide partial support for the hypothesis that immigrants' social rights affect their socio-economic outcomes. However, as previous research shows, poverty measures are sensitive to the poverty threshold, here 50 per cent of the median, and the equivalence scale used (e.g. Mitchell 1991; Buhmann et al. 1998). Thus, the main results have been re-estimated using alternative dependent variables that vary regarding the poverty threshold, that is, 40 per cent and 60 per cent (the official EU poverty line) of median income, and the equivalence scale, that is, the square root scale.[9]

Overall, the results are quite robust (see tables in this chapter's appendix). Concerning the conditional impact of immigrants' work rights and minimum wage-setting institutions on immigrants' poverty, the results corroborate the findings discussed above regardless of the threshold or equivalence scale chosen. This is also the case for the minimum income level (in percentage of median income), which affects immigrants' poverty, though primarily for the models testing the work rights of labour migrants. When turning to the conditional impact of immigrants' social rights and traditional family benefits on immigrants' poverty, the analysis provides support for the findings, but only if 50 per cent or 40 per cent of the median income is chosen as the poverty threshold.

In addition, the explanatory potential of alternative determinants of poverty has been estimated, including, among others, the classical poverty model – controlling for GDP growth along unemployment (see Brady 2009), the estimated size of the shadow economy and, as a crude proxy for labour market discrimination, the difference between immigrant and non-immigrant employment rates.[10] Regardless of the model specification, the effect of minimum wage setting on immigrants' poverty is robust for the index on work rights and the more specific one referring to labour migrants. Again, the results are less robust for the traditional family benefit model, though only when considering the overall index. In contrast, permanent residents' access to traditional family benefits affects immigrants' poverty regardless of which alternative factors are controlled for.

Finally, the sensitivity of the results regarding the impact of individual countries has been tested. As the descriptive analysis has shown, the United States, for instance, is an extreme case (see also Alesina and Glaeser 2004).[11] The rate of immigrant poverty in the United States is considerably higher than in other advanced industrialised countries and immigrants' social rights in terms of access to different social programmes is among the most exclusive. Moreover, the sample of immigrant observations is highly uneven across countries and relatively low in certain countries (see methodological appendix). The American cases make up almost 50 per cent of all cases ($N = 7,659$), while the respective number for Denmark, Finland and Portugal is below 200. Despite this problem, this book relies on multilevel analysis because the preliminary multilevel simulations carried out by Maas and Hox (2005, 86) indicate that extreme imbalance between data elements does not have a strong influence on multilevel maximum likelihood estimates or their standard errors.[12] Therefore, the models discussed earlier in the chapter have been re-estimated excluding the United States and using the jackknife method. However, the results do not turn out to be robust. If the United States is excluded, the conditional effect of immigrants' social rights, including access to paid employment as well as social programmes, disappears. This also applies to the results of the jackknife estimations.[13] In other words, although the analysis in this chapter has shown that there is some partial support for the importance of immigrants' social rights, the findings seem to be sensitive to the immigrant sample and the countries included.[14]

Some final remarks on the data sources used for the analysis: besides the rather small immigrant sample size for a number of countries, income surveys do not provide enough information on the immigrant background of the respondents, such as years since arrival in the host country, language proficiency and reasons for immigration. These are all factors that affect immigrants' poverty, though sometimes indirectly. This effect is partly addressed by controlling for the composition of the immigrant population at the macro-level, but only scant empirical evidence was found that the percentage of permits issued for humanitarian issues matters. Second, more problematic is that not being able to control for the type of residence permits immigrants have been granted. As argued in chapter 1, depending on the type of residence permit, immigrants are granted access to paid employment and social programmes to varying degrees.[15] This is an important point that should be addressed in future research.[16] Another critical point is the aggregation of immigrants originating from EU member countries and non-EU countries, which was done for the European countries, due to the low number of immigrant observations. As the descriptive analysis shows, the social rights of TCNs differ from those of Union citizens and their family members, who are granted almost equal access to the labour market and the welfare state as nationals. This neglects not only that the impact of the labour market and welfare systems might differ between EU citizens and TCNs but also that the immigrant composition related to the country of origin varies across countries.[17]

DISCUSSION

The results so far provide partial support that the impact of the labour market and welfare system on immigrants' poverty depends on their social rights in terms of access to paid employment and social programmes. The three main findings can be summarised as follows. First, the labour market and welfare system per se cannot explain cross-national variations in immigrants' poverty, the generosity of parental leave being the only exception. Moreover, the moderating effect of immigrants' social rights has to be considered. The results indicate that the poverty-reducing effect of the labour market and welfare system is moderated by immigrants' access to paid employment and these social programmes. For instance, more inclusive work rights have a stronger reductive effect on immigrants' poverty in countries where governments are more involved in a minimum wage setting. This is primarily the case when the work rights of labour migrants are considered. For this particular immigration category, the amount of the minimum wage in relation to the median wage also matters. Thus, the results indicate that labour market policies that affect households' earnings more directly have an alleviating impact on poverty. Turning to the impact of the traditional welfare state on poverty, the findings indicate that more generous social programmes have a poverty-reducing effect if the social rights of immigrants are more inclusive in terms of access to social programmes, though only when traditional family benefits are considered. In general, the analysis corroborates the findings from other studies emphasising the central role of the institutional context on immigrants' socio-economic outcomes (e.g. labour market participation; see Lewin-Epstein et al. 2003; Kogan 2006; Barrett and McCarty 2008). Moreover, the results question the prevailing approach of comparative welfare state literature to equate immigrants' and citizens' social rights. Citizens' and immigrants' social rights, as shown in chapter 3, not only differ but also have an impact on immigrants' socio-economic outcomes and thus affect their integration into the host country in general.

The second major finding is that alternative explanations for poverty at the macro-level related to the economic context do not substantively account for the observed cross-national variations in immigrants' poverty. This finding is at odds with orthodox economics, which argues that everyone benefits from economic prosperity (for a critical discussion, see Zweimüller 2000). However, the findings are in line with more recent studies. While the inverse relationship between economic growth and poverty, primarily for the United States, at least in the 1960s and 1970s as well as during the economic boom in the late 1990s (e.g. Freeman 2001; Gundersen and Ziliak 2004), could be supported empirically, this traditional interpretation of the efficiency-equity trade-off was called into question in the 1980s, when economic expansion in the United States did not coincide with the expected reduction in poverty. The main reason put forward was that the effect of economic growth was partly blunted by the concomitant rise in income inequality (Blank 1993).[18] The more recent empirical evidence for Europe is mixed. For example, Brady (2009) and Bäckman (2009) show that economic growth reduces poverty, while Scruggs and Allan (2006) find no statistically significant effect. Moreover, these studies show that the explanatory potential of economic growth is minimal once additional variables, such as welfare state effort, are included in the models. But the analysis also shows that more immigration-specific factors, such as a country's immigrant population composition, cannot explain immigrants' poverty. For instance, only the percentage of permits issued for humanitarian reasons has a positive significant impact at the 5 per cent level on both pre-tax and transfer poverty and poverty reduction, while the latter is further negatively affected by the employment differences between foreign- and native-born residents.

Finally, a household's socio-demographic characteristics play a substantial role in explaining immigrants' poverty, at least when pre-tax and transfer poverty is considered. Among the strongest predictors are employment patterns of households and type of employment pursued by their members (e.g. atypical or self-employment). Broadly speaking, immigrant households with lower labour market attachment, lower educational attainment and skills, higher numbers employed in atypical occupations and those with higher numbers of non-active household members (children and the elderly) are exposed to higher poverty risks. Regarding poverty reduction, both education and skills are less-decisive explanations, while the number of young and older dependent household members along with the number of (atypically) employed household members remains significant determinants.

So how can these partial findings be explained? Or, how could the analytical framework and its empirical implementation be improved to better explain immigrants' poverty? The remainder of this chapter discusses different possibilities that are related to the labour market and welfare system, immigrants' social rights and immigration policies.

First, concerning the role of *the labour market and welfare system*, the point of departure and a central assumption of the analytical framework is that countries with more regulated and generous labour market and welfare systems feature lower poverty as a general rule. However, poverty reduction is only one of the goals of welfare states alongside others, such as diminishing inequality, facilitating societal integration[19] and increasing participation (in Marshall's sense [1950]). It may simply be that the labour market policies and social programmes addressed in this book do not affect immigrants' (and non-immigrants') poverty.

Focusing on labour market institutions, and wage-setting institutions in particular, one reason why their effect on poverty is not dependent on immigrants' access to paid employment could be that they do not have the same impact on all workers. Different studies show that low-skilled workers benefit most from centralised bargaining systems (e.g. Pontusson, Rueda and Way 2002; Lohmann 2009). This is the case for workers who are actually protected by centralised wage bargaining, namely low-skilled insiders. However, as the new social risk and dualisation literature suggests, certain groups (e.g. women, young workers and low-skilled workers, but also immigrants) tend to work in sectors or be employed by work contracts that are not covered by those regulations (Bonoli 2007; Emmenegger et al. 2012). As Eichhorst and Marx (2012, 76) show, Bismarckian (or Continental European) countries managed to create non-standard employment without altering the institutional core of the labour market system by simply bypassing or converting existing regulations (e.g. partial deregulation of employment protection; see also Ochel 2008). Consequently, even if countries put immigrants on par with non-immigrants with regard to labour market access, as long as immigrants are overrepresented among these excluded groups, they are barred from the beneficial effects of wage bargaining on poverty. Therefore, the quality of employment, that is, the extent to which they are protected by labour market policies (e.g. job security or pay), needs further scrutiny.

When turning to the welfare system, the results are more intriguing as the generosity of specific social programmes such as unemployment compensation, parental leave and social assistance does not interact with immigrants' access to these social programmes. The analysis, thus, does not corroborate findings of previous studies showing that the generosity of social programmes has a direct impact on poverty, at least when all residents of a country are considered (e.g. Moller et al. 2003; Misra, Moller and Budig 2007; Bäckman 2009; Lohmann 2009). Two reasons can be put forward, both of which are related to the retrenchment and restructuring of welfare states over the past few decades.

On the one hand, it may be that the social programmes analysed in this book are just not generous enough to lift households out of poverty, here defined as 50 per cent of the median income. The robustness tests using 60 per cent of the median income support this claim and show that the moderating effect of immigrants' access to traditional family benefits fades away (see appendix tables 4A.4 and 4A.8). Nelson's (2011, 7) estimations of social assistance adequacy rates, measured as equalised net social assistance benefits divided by the equalised median disposable income, suggest that they are far from reducing poverty effectively. Adequacy rates in European countries in 2008 are on average around 40 per cent of the median income, too low to lift individuals and households out of poverty. Germany and Switzerland are the two countries with adequacy rates above 50 per cent, while the Nordic countries, as well as the Netherlands and Ireland, range between 40 and 50 per cent. Moreover, since the mid-1990s, these social assistance adequacy rates have declined, though this is most pronounced in the Nordic countries and the British Isles and to a lesser extent in Continental European countries. As the literature shows, this has gone hand in hand with restricting eligibility and toughening conditions to obtain social benefits, which mainly affect those individuals with lower skills and rather sporadic employment histories (Emmenegger and Careja 2012). Although these reforms address all residents in general, immigrants can be more strongly affected because they tend to be overrepresented among those with a weak labour market attachment (Causa and Jean 2007).[20] Taking these considerations into account, one possibility to further explore variations in the generosity of these social programmes could be to consider alternative measures of poverty that are better suited to assess the 'life of a civilised being according to the standards prevailing the society' (Marshall 1950, 11). Measures based on consumption (expenditure) rather than income are better suited to capturing permanent income, as they are less prone to temporary fluctuations in earning, for example, due to unemployment, especially for those at the bottom of the wage distribution (see Meyer and Sullivan 2013). Material deprivation, for instance, is a non-monetary indicator of poverty that assesses different items related to the basic needs of a household (e.g. affording a phone or holidays every year; see Whelan and Maître 2007; Nolan and Whelan 2010). The change from a binary poverty measure to a more differentiated indicator could uncover the poverty-alleviating effect of these social programmes taking place below the poverty threshold.[21]

On the other hand, new poverty-alleviating programmes focusing on the labour market (re)integration of those individuals at the margins of the society could have supplemented more 'traditional' income replacing benefits. As the literature indicates, a shift from welfare to work has taken place since the 1970s, though the origin of this shift in practice and perspective dates back to 1950s Sweden. This development can be traced back to socio-economic transformations related to deindustrialisation, destandardisation of employment and changes in family structure with which welfare states were confronted during the past few decades; this was also a time beset by economic downturn and retrenchment (Bonoli 2007). Although welfare states adapted to varying extents and timing to these new challenges, they ultimately moved from passive to active social programmes linking entitlement more closely to employment, for example, making receipt of benefits contingent on the effort that is made by beneficiaries towards finding employment (see contributions in Morel, Palier and Palme 2012). While the main focus of this book has been on traditional job and income protection, this alternative type of labour market policy, which aims to facilitate the labour market participation of the inactive population or workers with obsolete skills, might provide an alternative explanation for cross-national variations in immigrants' poverty. As Nelson's (2011) results demonstrate, cuts in social assistance adequacy rates have been accompanied by increasing expenditure in active labour market policies (ALMPs, as a percentage of GDP per capita). Therefore, efforts of countries to actively promote labour market entry of school leavers and those not participating in the labour market might have positive effects not only on non-immigrants' socio-economic outcomes but also on those of immigrants as these programmes usually target individuals regardless of their background. As the findings of this chapter show, labour market participation is a central determinant of immigrants' poverty. Moreover, research indicates that

ALMPs are related to not only work incentives, benefit conditionality and sanctions for putting individuals back to work (known as workfare) but also investment in education and further training, and provision of services, such as job search programmes and job subsidies (see Bonoli 2009). Although these programmes are not designed to integrate immigrants, in particular, they could improve their employment chances and thus indirectly reduce their poverty risks. For example, job training might have a positive effect because employers often underestimate immigrants' educational credentials. Although the success of these policies is contested (e.g. Martin and Grubb 2001; contributions in Morel, Palier and Palme 2012), the availability of these programmes could partly explain cross-national variations in immigrants' poverty. In sum, it would be promising to explore the role of active labour market policies in future research.

The second major point refers to *immigrants' social rights*. Although immigrants have full formal social rights in terms of access, they might not match their substantive (or de facto) social rights, that is, the exercise of their rights. This book's measurement of immigrants' social rights has mainly focused on the entitlement of immigrants. Thus, it considers whether immigrants are granted access to various social programmes by law. However, immigrants' social rights may consist of various aspects beyond mere entitlement, comparable to Esping-Andersen's (1990, 49) de-commodification index, which accounts for net replacement rates, disincentives, maximum duration of entitlement and conditions for eligibility based on contributions, work experience or means test. As mentioned in the previous chapters, legal stay and permit renewal of immigrants with temporary residence permits often depend on proof of sufficient means of subsistence for themselves and their families (IOM 2009, Tables B and C). In fact, reliance on means-tested welfare benefits could put the stay of immigrants in several countries at risk, at least de jure (e.g. Switzerland, Austria and the United Kingdom; see Child Poverty Action Group 2008; Koopmans, Michalowski and Waibel 2012). This would in turn explain why immigrants who legally have formal social rights, that is, access to social programmes, may not be able to rely on them and consequently why there is no moderating effect of access to social programmes on immigrants' poverty, in particular, regarding social assistance.[22] Therefore, additional factors of immigrants' social rights referring to the consequences of welfare reliance, such as expulsion and non-renewal of residence permits, should be taken into account too (see also Römer 2017). One way could be to consider three different socio-economic situations that put immigrants and their families' legal stay at risk either through expulsion or non-renewal of the residence permit:[23] reliance on specific social benefits, poverty without welfare reliance (related to the self-sufficiency requirement for immigrants and their family members that is attached to the residence permit) and unemployment.[24]

This point also applies to work rights, which has measured in this book as access to paid employment. But work rights can be understood more broadly than just whether immigrants have the right to freely choose their (paid) employment. This includes not only whether immigrants can take up self-employment but also other work rights that have a more direct impact on earnings and employment opportunities. Examples are whether immigrants have the right to equal pay, to equal treatment regarding employment conditions and protection, or to appeal if employers violate the agreements made in work contracts (see also Ruhs 2011). In this vein, the access of different immigrant categories to public sector employment could also be added (e.g. teachers, judges and police; see Koopmans, Michalowski and Waibel 2012).

This book has focused on social rights that put immigrants on par with citizens, in particular regarding access to social services and the labour market to which citizens, at least average production workers, have full access. In other words, to what extent public policies integrate immigrants has been assessed. According to Hammar (1985), these rights and related policies can be referred to as indirect integration policies, while direct integration policies target only immigrants settled in the country. Future research could focus more on these types of policies, which reveal a country's effort to actively promote the integration of immigrants. Several countries have introduced special measures, which mainly intend to improve immigrants' language skills and knowledge of the society (OECD 2006; Goodman 2010, 2012).[25] Although the primary aim of these integration policies is to facilitate the integration of immigrants into the society by enhancing their familiarity with the country, the language, as well as its social values, these integration policies might also have a spillover effect on their economic integration and their labour market opportunities. Language proficiency, for example, improves their chances of finding a job. Moreover, several countries combine language courses with personal vocational guidance, vocational training and work experience (e.g. Belgium, Canada and Sweden; see OECD 2006 for an overview). Research shows that 'migration histories', such as knowledge of the language of the host country, in addition to years since entry, are important determinants of socio-economic outcomes. Several studies, such as Dustmann and van Soest (2002), provide empirical support for the positive effect of language acquisition on wages. However, more recent studies on language proficiency of male and female immigrants in the Netherlands only find an effect for the latter (Yao and Ours 2015; for a review, see Chiswick and Miller 2015). Therefore, variations in the direct integration policies related to the labour market integration of immigrants could also explain cross-national differences in immigrants' poverty.

The final point refers to the importance of *immigration policies*, which, as the discussion earlier and in the previous chapter has shown, are closely linked to integration policies (e.g. the requirement for family reunification that the sponsor can support his family without relying on welfare benefits). Immigration policies have been only marginally addressed in the analysis and merit further empirical consideration on how they affect immigrants' poverty. The theoretical chapter argued that *immigration policies* regulate the inflow of immigrants and thus (to a certain extent) the composition of a country's immigrant population, which in turn may affect their socio-economic outcomes (see also Helbling et al. 2013). Depending on the motive to migrate, for economic or political reasons, individuals have more time to prepare and invest in the transferability of their skills. Moreover, stricter requirements for labour migrants, at least when concerning their labour marketability (see IOM 2009), ensure that immigrants are employed and can maintain themselves. This is further reinforced by the self-sufficiency conditions related to their legal stay. This argument can be developed further by distinguishing types of immigrants in more detail within the broader immigration categories. An example related to labour migration is whether countries allow mainly low-skilled immigrants to enter the country, as is the case with the United States, or try to attract highly qualified workers. Further differentiation can be made between countries that pursue high-skilled immigration, that is, whether immigration of highly skilled persons with general human capital is promoted (e.g. in Canada), and those that focus instead on the rapid employability of immigrants (e.g. in Australia; see Hawthorne 2008).[26] If immigration policies and thus the selection of immigrants are related to their labour market integration, this could explain cross-national variations in immigrants' poverty.[27] Considering that many immigrants come to stay permanently, it would be promising to look at changes during the past few decades rather than taking a snapshot of immigration policies. As recent reforms of immigration policies show, advanced industrialised countries have shifted their focus more strongly towards skilled immigration (OECD 2008).[28] Moreover, the account of previously implemented immigration policies could also help to explain the socio-economic integration of long-term settled immigrants. Emphasising a country's practices in admitting immigrants and the related conditions that certain immigration categories have to fulfil could therefore shed some light on why immigrants in some countries are better integrated than in others.

In sum, the analytical framework used in this book needs further refinement. The propositions for achieving this include a stronger focus on active labour market policies within the labour market and welfare system, the extension of social rights to include aspects related to consequences of welfare dependence as well as the inclusion of direct integration policies and, finally, a more detailed elaboration on the role of immigration policies in explaining cross-national differences in immigrants' poverty.

Conclusion

Increased immigration has accentuated the ethnic diversity of societies. This development brings with it challenges for nation states to incorporate immigrants into the receiving country, more precisely the society and political system, as well as the labour market and welfare state. This book has focused on the latter and addressed the question of how nation states integrate immigrants into the labour market and welfare state and how this affects the poverty of immigrants.

The incorporation of immigrants into the labour market and welfare state has been a major concern in public and political debate for a long time and has become more salient and relevant with the European refugee crisis in 2015. However, as the case of refugees in Germany today shows, despite a warm initial 'Willkommenskultur', immigrants' labour market integration might not always be smooth and straightforward. While it has been argued (and hoped) that refugees could be a response to the country's 'Fachkräfte-mangel' (i.e. shortage of skilled labour), many refugees turned out to lack the human, financial and social capital necessary for labour market integration. Even skilled refugees face many barriers, for example, related to (non-)recognition of informally acquired qualifications or temporary right to asylum (see Aumüller 2016). Therefore, if refugees' labour market integration is to be part of the solution to the shortage of skilled labour, national administrations, associations and other actors will have to engage in improving and investing in immigrants' qualifications (see practices and recommendations in ibid.). As the German example illustrates, immigrants' socio-economic integration depends on not only their own individual capabilities but also the integration capacity of the receiving country.

The endeavour of this book has been to examine how the institutional structure of the labour market and welfare state in terms of social rights affects socio-economic outcomes of immigrants in terms of poverty. Focusing on immigrants' social rights, the cross-national variations in immigrants' poverty in advanced industrialised countries have been explored. The argument, in brief, is that immigrants' social rights – namely access to paid employment as well as welfare benefits – condition the impact that both the labour market and welfare system have on immigrants' poverty.

This book proposes an analytical framework, which builds on two central assumptions. First, immigrants are not a homogenous group; instead, various forms of immigration can be distinguished, such as family reunification or labour migration with each group entitled to a different range of social rights. Second, immigrants' social rights have to be understood more broadly: on the one hand, as including the '*right to a modicum of economic welfare and security* (Marshall 1950, 11, emphasis added)' that allows workers to maintain an acceptable standard of living when opting out of work and, more generally, prevents individuals and families from being dependent on labour market participation (Esping-Andersen 1990). On the other hand, as including a '*right to work*', or access to paid work (Orloff 1993), which acknowledges that certain groups may be excluded from the labour market either informally, such as women who have to pursue domestic and caring work, or formally, such as immigrants who are simply not allowed to work. As has been argued, both understandings of social rights are essential when explaining immigrants' poverty; the 'right to work' is related to pre-distribution and thus the labour market, while the 'right to a modicum of economic welfare and security' is linked to re-distribution and the welfare state.

By drawing specific attention to the social rights of various immigrant groups, this book contributes to comparative welfare state and migration literature with an analytical framework to explain immigrant poverty that links immigrants' social rights, on the one hand, to a country's prevailing labour market and welfare system and, on the other hand, to immigration policies regulating the inflow of immigrants into the country; thus, the immigration category and residence permits aliens are allotted.

In this chapter, the empirical answers and their theoretical implications to the main research questions guiding the three empirical chapters of this book are presented: What do poverty patterns of immigrants look like, across countries and compared to non-immigrants? How do nation states deal with immigrants, that is, how inclusive are social rights towards immigrants and how are they related to immigration policies and the welfare and labour market system? How do they jointly affect immigrants' poverty? Before elaborating on three practical ways in which nation states and policy-makers could alleviate immigrants' poverty, the possible consequences of the financial and European refugee crisis for the theoretical argument are briefly discussed.

HOW DO IMMIGRANTS FARE? COMPARING POVERTY PATTERNS ACROSS COUNTRIES

The empirical evidence in chapter 2 has shown that immigrants' poverty outcomes vary across countries. In general, immigrants are more often exposed to poverty than non-immigrants, regardless of the poverty measures used, that is, poverty rates, income gaps, intensity and poverty gaps. This is in line with previous findings from poverty research on immigrants (Morissens and Sainsbury 2005; OECD 2012b; Sainsbury 2012; Corrigan 2014; Kesler 2015). Nevertheless, these results have to be put into perspective. Immigrants' poverty levels and gaps diminish not only once taxes and transfers are taken into account but also when socio-demographic characteristics such as education and, most importantly, labour market participation are controlled for. The results, therefore, indicate that labour market integration (via employment) and the welfare system (via redistribution) affect immigrants' finances.

In addition, a closer inspection of immigrants' poverty and poverty gaps between immigrants and non-immigrants did not coincide with the traditional types of welfare state regimes. Conventional approaches of comparative welfare state literature, at least when used to describe poverty patterns of immigrants, thus could not explain why immigrants' poverty outcomes vary considerably across countries. Drawing on Esping-Andersen's (1990) three types of welfare state regimes and adding a Mediterranean type (see Leibfried 1992; Ferrera 1996; Manow, Palier and Schwander 2018), the degree of de-commodification necessary to affect immigrants' poverty and poverty gaps would be expected to be as follows: high levels of immigrant poverty in liberal welfare state regimes and Southern European countries, followed by conservative and social-democratic types of welfare state regimes (see also Morissens and Sainsbury 2005), while poverty gaps between immigrants and non-immigrant would be more pronounced in conservative welfare state regimes (contribution-based) compared to liberal and social-democratic welfare state regimes (based on need and citizenship/residence). Nonetheless, the findings on immigrant poverty rates after taxes and transfer have shown that social-democratic welfare states cluster together with the Mediterranean type around the mean, while high intra-regime variation exists within both the conservative and liberal welfare regime types. Comparably for poverty gaps, Mediterranean and social-democratic welfare states were relatively homogeneous in contrast to liberal and conservative welfare states, which varied considerably within the respective welfare regime. As can be seen, the type of welfare regime per se cannot explain cross-national variations in immigrants' poverty and poverty gaps. Therefore, alternative explanations have to be considered.

Consequently, the first theoretical implication of the book is that we should return to the theoretical concepts that form the basis for traditional welfare regime typology, notably social rights. In particular, the implicit assumption of comparative welfare state literature that immigrants and non-immigrants' social rights hardly differ has to be challenged and further scrutinised. Drawing on international migration literature, the starting point and crucial assumption has been to account for various immigration categories (e.g. labour migration, family reunification and refugees) and their consequent social rights in the analytical framework.

IMMIGRANTS' SOCIAL RIGHTS – WHERE DO ADVANCED INDUSTRIALISED COUNTRIES STAND?

The detailed analysis of immigrants' social rights, the core explanatory factor of immigrants' poverty in the analytical framework, has indicated that the extent to which immigrants are granted access to social programmes depends on two central factors: the immigration category and the basis of entitlement to social programmes (see chapter 3). For the comparison of immigrants' social rights across nineteen advanced industrialised countries, the newly collected data not only differentiate between various immigration categories but also distinguish different types of social programmes that were designed explicitly to tackle the working-age population's poverty risk.

The first major finding is that social and work rights differ between immigrants and non-immigrants. A closer inspection revealed that the extent of such rights depends on the particular immigration category, such as immigrants with permanent or limited residence permits, family migrants, recognised refugees and EU citizens. In line with research from international migration literature (e.g. Brubaker 1989; Hammar 1990; Soysal 1994), permanent residents across countries enjoy almost the same social rights as nationals, that is, full access to employment and different social programmes, without additional restrictions. Preferential treatment in terms of inclusive work and social rights is also granted to recognised refugees and EU citizens. In contrast, major differences arise when comparing the rights of immigrants holding permanent and limited residence permits: permanent residents benefit from more encompassing social rights than immigrants with temporary residence permits. In other words, the inclusiveness of social rights and the security of the residence status related to the respective immigration category tend to go hand in hand.

The second major finding is that there is some evidence for a congruence between type of welfare state regime and immigrants' social incorporation in terms of social rights. This is different from the findings in chapter 2 that immigrants' poverty and poverty gaps vary markedly within (the liberal and conservative) welfare regimes. The Nordic countries, except for Denmark, provide rather inclusive access to welfare programmes and the labour market for immigrants. On the contrary, immigrants' access to the labour market and the welfare state is more restricted in countries with more residual welfare states, such as the United States, the United Kingdom and Switzerland. This suggests that more universal welfare states tend to incorporate immigrants more easily than welfare states where entitlement to social programmes is mainly means tested. Between these two poles lie countries classified as conservative corporatist welfare regimes (e.g. Austria, France and Germany), which indirectly restrict immigrants' access to social programmes by linking access to employment and previous social security contributions. The institutional legacy of the welfare state and the political economy regime is also evident when comparing the right to paid employment across immigration categories. Countries with rather 'conservative' traditions, which in the past discouraged women from working (see Esping-Andersen 1990, 28), also tend to restrict the labour market access of immigrants' family members (e.g. Austria and Germany). In contrast, Nordic countries grant full access to family members of immigrants from the beginning of their stay. This approach reflects the social-democratic commitment to consolidate work and welfare with gender equality by actively promoting women's labour market participation and thus striving for a policy of full employment (Sainsbury 1999).

A detailed analysis of individual social programmes has shown that the basis of entitlement to these social programmes (universal, employment-related and means tested) is decisive, whether or not specific immigration categories are granted access. Generally speaking, universal programmes tend to be less exclusive towards foreigners, regardless whether labour migrants, permanent residents or their family members considered (e.g. traditional family benefits in Austria, France and Portugal are aimed at all immigrant families, regardless of the residence permits of the sponsor or family members). Following Rothstein (1998, 159–61), there are two reasons as to why universal social programmes might be more inclusive towards immigrants. First, as a universal welfare policy comprises all citizens, the welfare community is primarily concerned with how to fairly organise social measures rather than where and how to draw the line between the needy and the non-needy. Consequently, it might be more difficult to politically endorse the exclusion of immigrants from universal social programmes because the distinction between 'us, the citizens' and 'them, the immigrants' runs contrary to the ethical principle of equality. Second, as universal social programmes do not require eligibility tests to decide whether someone is qualified and to what extent, they are easier and cheaper to implement without the need for a cumbersome bureaucratic apparatus. Therefore, extending social rights to immigrants seems a more viable and less expensive alternative than introducing new selective practices and respective administrations.

Contrary to this, access to means-tested benefits in the majority of the countries depends on having resided a number of years in the country of residence (e.g. in Australia and Norway, two and three years, respectively, are required to receive lone-parent benefits) or holding a permanent residence permit (e.g. social assistance), a practice mainly prevalent in Continental European countries, where immigrants have to prove that they have resided in that country for an average of five years. The restriction of immigrants' access to means-tested programmes is more clearly observed in the case of social assistance programmes, where selective systems identifying the needy and non-needy are already in place. Employment-related social programmes are in the middle ground, where beneficiaries have to prove previous labour market participation. In brief, this practice can be found in the majority of advanced industrialised countries; making immigrants' access to social programmes contingent on the basis of entitlement can be observed across advanced industrialised countries, irrespective of immigration category and welfare regime type.

Based on these findings, this book's first theoretical contribution to comparative welfare state literature concerned with social rights is as follows: we should consider the immigration category as an additional socio-structural characteristic that is related to entitlement and exercise of social rights alongside gender, occupation and class. As has been shown, residence per se does not grant immigrants the same social and work rights as citizens. Actually, social rights not only vary between citizens and immigrants in general but between different types of immigration category. As a consequence, we should consider this native/immigrant gap in social rights if we want to understand the socio-economic integration and outcomes of immigrants and, more generally, of the entire population. As feminist and dualisation literature has claimed, the socio-structural environment of an individual not only directly affects employment trajectories and labour market vulnerabilities but also indirectly affects their social rights, for instance, to which they are entitled to as housewives or part-time workers, and so forth, and thus their poverty risk (e.g. Orloff 1993; Häusermann and Schwander 2012). However, for immigrants, the essential question is not whether or how they exercise their social rights but if they even enjoy formal social rights in the first place. In contrast to citizens in general, but also to female, young and low-skilled non-immigrant outsiders in particular, certain immigration categories simply lack social rights in terms of access to paid employment and social programmes. In conclusion, it is not having an immigrant background per se that matters regarding entitlement to social rights but rather the specific immigration category. In other words, whether immigrants have social rights depends on the immigration category, with permanent residents and their family members enjoying more encompassing social rights than immigrants with temporary residence permits.

Second, this book contributes to welfare chauvinism literature, by addressing the question of whether the form of exclusion of immigrants from welfare states depends on the structure and type of welfare system. This differentiated form of welfare chauvinism argues that encompassing welfare states are less restrictive regarding immigrants' social rights compared to more basic welfare states (see Banting 2000); the results of this book suggest that generous welfare states with universal social programmes tend to incorporate immigrants into existing structures. An example is Sweden where universal welfare programmes prevail or complement contribution-based programmes (e.g. parental benefits). At the same time, residual Anglo-Saxon welfare states in general (the United States being a prime example), where means-tested programmes predominate, tend to constrain immigrants' access to social programmes. However, due to a lack of adequate data on immigration policies, there is no conclusive evidence for the external exclusion form of welfare chauvinism, namely that more generous welfare states choose more restrictive immigration control. The preliminary descriptive evidence on permit-based statistics suggests that encompassing welfare states do not choose restrictive immigration policies as an alternative to constrain immigrants' social rights (see section 3.1). Moreover, the most inclusive welfare states towards immigrants, such as the Netherlands, Sweden and Norway, seem at the same time to have the most liberal immigration policies, at least when permits issued for humanitarian reasons are considered (see also Boräng 2015). Nonetheless, encompassing welfare states might opt for other forms of exclusion not addressed in this book. For example, Continental European countries do not explicitly restrict the access of immigrants to means-tested benefits in their social security law (e.g. Germany or Switzerland); instead they link welfare access not only to the renewal of a residence permit but also to the prospects of obtaining a permanent residence permit or citizenship. Other examples of the importance of the residence permit can also be mentioned. If immigrant workers with a limited residence permit become unemployed, this circumstance affects not only the renewal of their residence permits but also their rights to unemployment benefits, which end when the residence permit expires. Consequently, future research is needed to disentangle the interplay between immigration policies, welfare states in general and social programmes in particular, and immigrants' social rights. By and large, the generosity or type of welfare regime provides a good indicator as to whether immigrants' access to welfare programmes is restricted or not, at least at first glance.

However, the basis of entitlement to a particular social programme allows for a more nuanced picture. The empirical findings have indicated that the basis of entitlement is the crucial factor as to whether immigrants are incorporated into the welfare state or not. Most welfare states combine universal, employment-related and means-tested social programmes, as shown in chapter 3. Thus, depending on the research focus, for example, social rights of insiders or benefits for those at the margins, the implications for comparative welfare state research have to be put into perspective: the type of welfare regime and form of immigrants' incorporation into the welfare state do not go hand in hand but rather depend on the social programme's basis of entitlement.

DO IMMIGRANTS' SOCIAL RIGHTS MAKE A DIFFERENCE TO POVERTY ALLEVIATION?

Chapter 4, by means of a multivariate analysis, showed that the usual poverty approaches fail to explain cross-national variations in immigrants' poverty. Moreover, the theoretical argument that immigrants' social rights moderate the impact that both the labour market and welfare system have on immigrants' poverty finds empirical support, though only under specific circumstances.

The first finding is that labour market policies and social programmes per se do not play an important role in immigrants' poverty, even though welfare state generosity is one of the most influential predictors of a country's general poverty level (e.g. Korpi and Palme 1998; Kenworthy 1999). To put it another way, neither more strongly regulated labour market policies nor more generous social programmes have a significant reductive effect on immigrants' poverty. Equally, economic growth and unemployment, which are proposed by economic research approaches as determinants of poverty (e.g. Freeman 2001; Gundersen and Ziliak 2004), fall short when it comes to explaining immigrants' poverty. This is also the case for more immigration-specific explanations such as immigration policies.

In contrast, socio-demographic characteristics at the household level have a consistent effect on immigrants' poverty. Indeed, the greatest percentage of the variance in poverty can be ascribed to the individual level. Generally speaking, households with lower labour market attachment (the most relevant poverty predictor), with more self-employed members or members employed in atypical occupations (e.g. part-time or on temporary contracts), with lower educational attainments and skills and with higher numbers of non-active household members (children and the elderly) are exposed to higher levels of poverty, irrespective of whether poverty is measured before or after taxes and transfers. These findings suggest that the individualist poverty perspective, the 'prevailing social science explanation of poverty' (Brady 2009, 13), should not be neglected but considered together with the institutionalist approach.

In line with this book's theoretical argument, the second major finding is that labour market policies and social programmes that address the needs of individuals within a society affect immigrants' poverty, but only if combined with inclusive immigrants' social rights. In fact, empirical evidence for this effect has been found regarding minimum wage regulations and the generosity of family benefits. More precisely, strictly regulated minimum wages have a stronger reductive impact on immigrants' poverty in countries that grant immigrants access to paid employment than in countries with more restrictive labour market access. Correspondingly, the poverty-reducing effect of generous traditional family benefits on immigrants' poverty was stronger when immigrants' access to these programmes was more inclusive. Moreover, further analysis has shown that immigrants' social rights were particularly relevant in specific immigration categories, that is, for immigrants with temporary residence permits in the case of minimum wage regulations and for permanent residents in the case of traditional family benefits. On the other hand, no empirical evidence has been found that other labour market and social programmes, be they collective wage bargaining, work-related programmes such as unemployment compensation and parental leave or social assistance, affect immigrants' poverty.

Based on these findings, this book's last theoretical contribution is to the literature on international migration and comparative welfare state research. It is essential to take the broader institutional setting of a country into account, into which migration-specific policies are embedded, in order to understand not only various immigrants' outcomes (e.g. poverty, income, job prosperity and political integration) but also socio-structural divides between the native and immigrant population. While comparative welfare state literature neglects the fact that citizens' and immigrants' (categories) social rights differ, as argued earlier in the text, the abundant international immigration research mainly studies migration-specific characteristics and policies without embedding them into a country's broader institutional context (see van Tubergen, Maas and Flap 2004; Koopmans et al. 2005; Adsera and Chiswick 2007; Kesler 2015). This book has proposed and empirically tested an analytical model to explain cross-national variations in immigrants' poverty that details how immigrants' social rights condition the effect of both the labour market and welfare system on immigrants' poverty.

AS TIME GOES BY: CONSEQUENCES OF THE GREAT RECESSION ON IMMIGRANTS' POVERTY

The outbreak of the financial crisis in 2007–2008 and the resulting Great Recession, which affected advanced industrialised countries to varying degrees, has been the main reason to choose a cross-sectional research design using data for the year 2007. Nonetheless, in what follows, some thoughts are presented about how this event in particular, and bringing in a temporal dimension in general, might affect the theoretical argument. This chapter concludes with an outlook on the effects of the European refugee crisis.

First, the most immediate impact of the Great Recession is on the levels of economic growth and unemployment. However, research shows that immigrants were more exposed to the crisis as immigrants' unemployment rates were more strongly affected than those of local workers (OECD 2009, 2010, 2013b; see also Emmenegger and Careja 2012). Alternative explanations have been put forward that are related to structural factors such as discrimination in hiring immigrants last and firing them first during economic downturns; immigrants' overrepresentation in specific sectors such as construction or hotels and restaurants, in less-skilled occupations and in jobs with less-stable work arrangements (e.g. temporary and part-time employment), which are all more strongly affected by economic slowdown (OECD 2009). Even though countries were hit to different extents and at different times by the crisis, the analytical framework suggests the impact of economic and socio-demographic factors to be more pronounced in explaining cross-national variations in immigrants' poverty (OECD 2010). For all that, it should be kept in mind that economic factors did not have a significant effect on immigrant poverty in chapter 4, at least before the outbreak of the crisis.

A second impact of the Great Recession relates to the very structure and organisation of the labour market and welfare system. As discussed in chapter 1, some labour markets and welfare systems are better equipped to handle economic fluctuations than others. One example of such a measure is a shift to short-term work during recessions (see OECD 2010). But the financial and economic crisis has also caused changes and adjustments to labour markets and welfare states in several countries, if not necessarily radical welfare state reforms. In general, academic research has shown that austerity measures, that is, retrenchment and cost containment, were the main response to the Great Recession (for a literature review, see van Kersbergen, Vis and Hemerijck 2014). But at the same time, the Great Recession caused many countries to introduce new or to expand existing social programmes, targeted at the poor. The most prominent example is that of Italy, which finally expanded its unemployment insurance to cover more than just the core insiders (Vis, van Kersbergen and Hylands 2011; van Kersbergen, Vis and Hemerijck 2014; but see, for example, Armingeon 2012). By and large, these developments of welfare state expansion and retrenchment should affect immigrants' poverty in the same way as non-immigrants' poverty, though only if, as has been argued in the previous chapters, immigrants, or more precisely various immigration categories, are granted access to these social programmes.

Nevertheless, immigrants might be more strongly affected by social policy reforms despite non-discriminating social rights if they are overrepresented among the welfare beneficiaries (for this argument, see Emmenegger and Careja 2011, 2012).

Finally, immigration-related policies, in particular immigrants' social rights, have been affected by the Great Recession. Different political and academic arguments have been invoked to explain why social rights of immigrants or particular immigration categories might or might not be restricted. The relative stability of social rights over time can be related to moral norms inherent in the logic of welfare states or social policies and the resulting bureaucratic practices as discussed earlier (Rothstein 1998). In contrast, welfare chauvinism literature presents arguments and political demands that call for the restriction of immigrants' social rights; these political demands, however, have not led to reforms in social policy. However, for instance, Denmark cut welfare benefits for newly arrived immigrants by 50 per cent in 2015 (Handlos, Kristiansen and Norredam 2016), while the United Kingdom reduced support payments for asylum seekers with children by up to 30 per cent (Travis 2015). But for the most part, policy change targeting the rights of immigrants has been rare and mainly concentrated on asylum seekers' access to welfare benefits (see Emmenegger and Careja 2011). This is even more surprising when considering the salience and presence of welfare abuse by immigrants and asylum seekers in public debate and the party agendas of right-wing populist parties (see Bale 2003; Helbling 2012; Reeskens and van Oorschot 2012). Nonetheless, the financial crisis and the following recession have provided a distinctive opportunity for social policy change that restricts not only social rights in general but also those of immigrants in particular, at least in those countries hit hardest by the Great Recession. In Portugal, for example, since 2012, national and EU citizens have to prove at least one year of residence, and TCNs at least three years to get access to social assistance (Decree Law 133/2012, Art. 6). Given these points, the analytical framework would expect any given social policy change relevant to immigrants to have an immediate impact on immigrants' poverty. This is also the case for immigration policy and immigration rates.

Because of the financial crisis and Great Recession, immigration rates changed, if not necessarily immigration policies. Permanent migration flows decreased between 2007 and 2014, though mainly through reduced labour migration, while leaving humanitarian and family reunification inflows unchanged (OECD 2015b). Following this book's theoretical argument, we would expect higher immigrant poverty rates after 2007 as the percentage of foreign workers with higher labour market attachment decreased. Since 2014, however, permanent migration flows into OECD countries have steadily increased from +4 per cent in 2014 to an estimated +10 per cent in 2015. These figures also comprise the 1.65 million new applications for asylum in OECD countries with more than 50 per cent coming from Syrians (24 per cent), Afghans (16 per cent) and Iraqis (12 per cent) (OECD 2016).

The consequences of the recent refugee crisis for this book's framework are most relevant when considering the impact of immigrants' social rights, immigration policies and composition on immigrants' poverty. In contrast to the Great Recession, the sheer number of persons granted refugee or subsidiary protection status, hereafter referred to as refugees, and asylum seeker status is too small to substantially and immediately affect a country's economic growth and unemployment rates or the general structure of the labour market and welfare system (e.g. in 2015, Sweden received the highest number of applications, namely 16,000 per million inhabitants; OECD 2016, 31).

However, the integration of humanitarian newcomers is relevant for different reasons. First, taking the case of the Syrian crisis and conflicts in the Middle East into account, refugees and asylum seekers seem to stay on, if not permanently. Second, research shows that foreigners migrating for humanitarian reasons have lower labour market participation rates compared to other types and groups of immigrants. Reasons are not only insufficient language proficiency and inadequate qualifications but also legal constraints such as a waiting period for asylum seekers to enter the labour market or lack of knowledge among employers that refugees and asylum seekers are allowed to work (see Poptcheva and Stuchlik 2015). Therefore, nation states are required to actively promote and support the long-term integration of refugees and asylum seekers into the society and labour market. The introduction of measures related to language courses, skill assessment and facilitated labour market access can already be observed in those countries most affected by the refugee crisis (e.g. Austria, Finland, Germany, Norway and Sweden; OECD 2016, 11).

Related to the relevance of integrating refugees is also the effect of the refugee crisis on immigrants' social rights. Rather than simply excluding refugees and in particular asylum seekers from welfare benefits, it seems more common that social policy changes consist of benefit cuts, as described earlier, and tightening conditions for entitlement. In Germany, for instance, welfare benefits for asylum seekers have been cut since August 2016, but only if they refuse to attend language and integration courses (Bundesregierung 2016). At the same time, several countries facilitated asylum seekers' access to the labour market by reducing waiting times (OECD 2016). This approach to 'fördern und fordern' (Bundesregierung 2016), that is, not only to promote but also to demand, is reminiscent of welfare to work practices put forward by the new social risks and social investment literature (Pierson

2001; Häusermann 2010; Morel, Palier and Palme 2012). It is not yet clear how these social rights developments might affect the welfare access of other immigration categories. On the one hand, it is plausible to expect no major reforms of social rights due to the earlier mentioned reasons, namely the logic of welfare states and their bureaucratic practices. On the other hand, social policy changes targeting asylum seekers and refugees might serve as precedents leading to similar changes affecting other immigrant groups. However, taking the relatively modest impact of the public debate on 'wanted and unwanted immigration' or 'bogus asylum seekers' into account, uniform social policy changes that would also affect other immigration categories seem rather unlikely.

Given these points and based on this book's framework, the recent refugee crisis should lead to an increase in immigrants' poverty for two reasons. First, immigrants moving for humanitarian reasons encounter more difficulties concerning labour market integration compared to labour migrants. Thus, as their numbers rise, immigrants' poverty should increase, *ceteris paribus*. Second, restricting immigrants' social rights by tightening eligibility conditions would be directly reflected in less capacity for social rights to alleviate immigrants' poverty. Yet the theoretical argument and framework can be further specified. In particular, the role of integration policies, such as the earlier mentioned language courses, recognition of acquired qualifications and further training that go beyond social rights as access to paid employment and welfare benefits, could be explicitly considered (see also discussion in chapter 4). To conclude, the analytical framework presented in this book should provide a good starting point for refinement and complementing a temporal dimension. Nonetheless, future researchers will have to give a conclusive answer as to how the temporal changes, in particular those related to the financial and refugee crisis, affect immigrants' poverty across countries.

THREE WAYS TO ALLEVIATE IMMIGRANTS' POVERTY

With the main conclusion from the descriptive and multivariate analysis in mind – that there is no best practice across countries to reduce immigrants' poverty – this book's analysis bears important political implications. Three different approaches can be identified that make some countries better at alleviating immigrants' poverty than others. *One way* is to combine strict immigration policies with limited access to social programmes. Encouraging 'desired' immigration, that is, labour migration rather than family migration, is pursued through tough requirements, for both border crossing and remaining in the country. Socio-economic integration, once an immigrant has arrived in the host country, mainly takes place through labour market participation rather than through redistribution. A prime example is Switzerland, where the majority of immigrants originate from the surrounding EU15 countries. Restrictive immigration policies are, for example, observed in the case of family reunification, which, as a legal claim, is reserved for permanent residents, while immigrants with limited residence permits have to rely on the discretion of bureaucratic administrations and different conditions (Niessen et al. 2007, 178). In addition, the existing immigration policies allow repatriation of immigrants by simply not renewing residence permits in the case of unemployment or welfare dependency, a practice pursued during the economic crisis in the 1970s (Mahnig and Wimmer 2003, 141).

The findings of the descriptive analysis show that Switzerland is outstanding in terms of poverty rates based on immigrants' market income. It is the country with the lowest proportion of immigrants living below the poverty line. At the same time, the redistributive capacities of the Swiss welfare state in reducing immigrants' poverty are very modest compared to other countries. This can be explained not only by the residual welfare state, even for non-immigrants, but also by the restricted access of immigrants to social programmes, which is mainly dependent on former employment, as the case of traditional family benefits shows. In a nutshell, an immigrant is unlikely to live in poverty in Switzerland. But if immigrants cannot escape poverty on their own, the probability that they will remain poor is relatively high.

As long as a country's economy is prospering, the combination of restrictive immigration policies and mere socio-economic incorporation of immigrants through the labour market might be a viable solution. However, the passive position of nation states in incorporating immigrants could become a burden: on the one hand, most countries have experienced an economic downturn during the past decade and, on the other hand, nation states cannot rely simply on restrictive immigration policies to fully control immigration inflows (e.g. illegal immigration) and outflows. Permanent immigrants, for instance, enjoy a certain security of residence status; the majority of immigrants in advanced industrialised countries have received permanent residence permits. Switzerland is a good example, where over 60 per cent of the immigrant population are permanent residents despite strict conditions and a long waiting period (up to ten years) for obtaining a permanent residence permit (Bundesamt für Statistik 2016). Thus, restrictive immigration practices are complicated not only by normative and humanitarian considerations such as socialisation within the country but also by the legal framework. If the smooth transition of immigrants into the labour market fails, in particular, for the second generation, the restriction of immigrants' access to social programmes only accentuates their disadvantaged position and social exclusion.

As the social riots in French and Swedish suburbs have shown, it might be just a matter of time until further social tensions break out.

Thus, a *second way* to incorporate immigrants would be to grant settled immigrants equal rights as nationals, and thus provide full access to the labour market and social programmes. In this case, socio-economic incorporation in the host country would proceed through labour market participation as well as through redistribution. The latter would ensure that immigrant households that fall through the economic cracks were able to maintain a socially acceptable standard of living. The Netherlands comes closest to this proposed approach. As the descriptive analysis revealed, it is among those countries that grant immigrants, regardless of immigration category, the most inclusive access to the labour market and social programmes. The redistributive effect is further observed in the low poverty rates after taxes and transfers. The Netherlands is also the most effective country in reducing immigrants' poverty. Therefore, from a poverty perspective, the Dutch case is a prime example of a successful socio-economic incorporation of immigrants.

There are different reasons as to why this practice has difficulties in 'travelling' to other countries. The difficulties are related to the institutional legacies concerning the structure of the welfare system and the immigration regime. Moreover, the recent economic crisis has put even tighter constraints on governments' financial budgets (see Armingeon 2012; van Kersbergen, Vis and Hemerijck 2014). But a certain level of social benefit generosity is a precondition for reducing poverty. Also, the extension of full social and work rights to immigrants might not be politically feasible. As Mahnig (2001) has argued, policies that benefit only immigrants are difficult to implement because the national electoral majority perceives this as providing immigrants with undeserved privileges. Finally, recent policy changes in the Netherlands away from multiculturalism, recognising the cultural differences of ethnic groups, and towards civic integration and language acquisition (see Joppke 2007b; Goodman 2012), emphasise the problems related to this approach when it comes to incorporating immigrants into the labour market (Koopmans 2010). This is exemplified in the descriptive chapter by the relatively high pre-tax and transfer poverty of Dutch immigrants. While granting immigrants full social and work rights reduces immigrants' poverty, it is not sufficient to achieve their full socio-economic incorporation.

Therefore, as a *third way*, countries should actively promote immigrants' labour market integration combined with inclusive access to (employment-related) social programmes. The labour market integration of immigrants is possible through specific integration policies for immigrants and active labour market policies. The importance of labour market participation and access to employment-related programmes is also supported by the empirical findings of this book. Labour market participation is a central determinant of poverty, while access to paid employment is particularly important for minimum wage legislation. In light of financial austerity and low prospects of ensuring that immigrants are able to maintain themselves financially by granting them full social rights, this approach is a feasible alternative to the other two approaches. In addition, it is in line with the EU's common basic principles on immigrants' integration policies, which state that employment is 'a key part of the integration process' (Donner, Remkes and Verdonk 2004, 20). Labour market integration not only makes the contribution of immigrants to the host country visible (e.g. addressing manpower shortages in economies or ensuring the viability of the welfare state) but also allows immigrants to pursue a self-determined, self-sufficient and independent life (see also Joppke 2007b, 2–5). The proposition presented here, however, goes one step further in demanding the integrative efforts of not only immigrants but also governments and receiving societies in the implementation and extension of respective policies and programmes for immigrants. A majority of the countries researched in this book already pursue and have further intensified this strategy in light of the European refugee crisis by promoting immigrants' employment through language courses and professional training (see OECD various years). For instance, the Austrian and Swiss governments offer vocational training and language courses to young refugees in regions or sectors where apprentices are scarce. Moreover, the recognition of qualifications and skills has received special attention. In Norway and Sweden, the process has been speeded up and the recognition system streamlined; while Germany, Finland and Denmark already assess the skills of refugees in reception centres (OECD 2016, 77–89). This strategy of pursuing the socio-economic incorporation of immigrants through both the labour market and the welfare state could not only be supported by both the native and immigrant majorities but also allow both groups to pursue a socially acceptable standard of living.

This book has argued and empirically shown that both a country's prevailing institutional structure of the labour market and the welfare state and its migration-specific institutional setting are crucial to understanding why immigrants fare better in terms of poverty in some countries compared to others. With this in mind, merely implementing a regulation that was successful in one country might not yield the desired outcome in another. Moreover, one of the main policy implications of this book is that when formulating immigration-related policies and regulations, such as immigrants' social rights, the interdependencies with a country's broader institutional setting that concerns all residents, immigrants as well as non-immigrants should be considered. The socio-economic incorporation of immigrants through the labour market and welfare system is an essential dimension of immigrants' incorporation into the host country. Yet, it is just one aspect of integration among other dimensions such as the society and the political system, which are equally important. Future research should consider how these different dimensions of immigrants' incorporation – the labour market, welfare state, political system and society – are linked and affect each other, in order to give a comprehensive answer as to why immigrants in some countries, using Marshall's words (1950, 11), can 'live the life of a civilised being according to the standards prevailing the society' compared to immigrants in other countries.

Methodological Appendix: Methodology, Operationalisation and Statistical Methods

This appendix describes the methodological approach, including the selection of cases and the time frame, and provides detailed information on operationalisation and data sources as well as a brief overview of the statistical methods.

METHODOLOGICAL APPROACH

Starting with the case selection and the time frame, this book relies on a cross-sectional quantitative analysis in 2007 to test the hypotheses developed in chapter 1. The case selection is driven by the research question, which aims to explain how nation states cope with immigration, rather than emigration, and the efforts countries make to affect immigrants' socio-economic outcomes. Therefore, advanced industrialised democracies were selected for this sample, which vary not only with respect to labour market and social policy but also with concerning their immigration histories and the respective policies governing the integration of settled immigrants (see section 3.1). The nineteen cases included in the analysis are Australia (AU), Austria (AT), Belgium (BE), Canada (CA), Denmark (DK), Finland (FI), France (FR), Germany (DE), Greece (GR), Ireland (IE), Italy (IT), Netherlands (NL), Norway (NO), Portugal (PT), Spain (ES), Sweden (SE), Switzerland (CH), the United Kingdom (UK) and the United States (US).[1] The year 2007 has been chosen to account for the financial situation of immigrants before the beginning of the financial crisis in 2007–2008, which affected advanced industrialised countries to varying degrees and consequently evoked divergent policy responses (see Marchal, Marx and van Mechelen 2014). Moreover, recent studies have indicated that the crisis has hit immigrants particularly hard (OECD 2009, 2010).

OPERATIONALISATION

The Dependent Variable – Poverty Rates

Following international studies and comparative research on poverty (e.g. Korpi and Palme 1998; Hicks and Kenworthy 2003; Brady, Fullerton and Cross 2009), *poverty rates* are defined in relative terms as the share of households whose income is below the poverty line, here defined as 50 per cent of a country's median income. It should be noted that the poverty line is calculated from the income distribution for the full samples, including individuals of all ages. The analysis, however, is based only on the working-age population, defined as those individuals aged between twenty-one and fifty-nine, because this is the group that is mainly affected by the labour market policies and social programmes analysed in this book (Blume et al. 2007, 380). The size of households is controlled for by using an equivalence scale, which accounts for the fact that economies of scale exist in a household, that is, that the marginal income needed decreases as the household size grows (see also Bradley et al. 2003, 209–10). The modified OECD equivalence scale used in this book adjusts the household income for the size of the family by assigning a value of 1 to the household head, 0.5 to each additional adult member aged fifteen or above, and 0.3 to each child below the age of fifteen (for a critical discussion of different measurements of poverty and equivalence scales, see Buhmann et al. 1988).[2]

The analysis presented in chapters 2 and 4 distinguishes two types of incomes, namely market income and disposable income, and consequently different poverty measures. The main reason for this differentiation is that market income (before taxes and transfers) and disposable income (after taxes and transfers) are expected to be affected by different determinants and mechanisms, namely labour market institutions in the former case and social programmes in the latter case (see also Moller et al. 2003; Lohmann 2009). Poverty measures based on *income before taxes and transfers* include salaries, earnings from self-employment and income from cash property, while poverty measures based on *income after taxes and transfers* consider, besides market income, social transfers, payroll and income taxes (e.g. Bradley et al. 2003; Moller et al. 2003).[3] Because inequality and poverty measures are sensitive to extreme values at the bottom and top of the income distribution, negative values are recoded to zero and the upper threshold is set at ten times the median income.

In addition to poverty rates before and after taxes and transfers, *poverty reduction effectiveness (PRE) scores* were calculated for the analysis in chapter 2, which is simply the difference between a country's poverty rate on market income and disposable income divided by the poverty rate based on market income.[4] Higher PRE score values indicate higher effectiveness of countries in reducing poverty, and vice versa (see Mitchell 1991, 65; Moller et al. 2003, 33; Morissens and Sainsbury 2005). The main advantage of using PRE scores over poverty rates after taxes and transfers is that they take the economic situation of a country into account. If countries already have low poverty rates before taxes and transfers due to other factors in addition to redistribution policies, for example, high demand for labour allowing residents to find well-paid jobs, they score highly on the PRE score indicator only if they can further reduce poverty in relative terms. This poverty measure is also used as a dependent variable in the explanatory analysis in chapter 4, though at the household level. Accordingly, *poverty reduction* is a binary variable that considers whether a household can escape poverty, that is, is defined as poor based on market income but moves out of poverty due to the tax and welfare system (see Lohmann 2009).[5,6]

   However, relative poverty rates as presented earlier have been criticised for several methodological and conceptual reasons.[7] For instance, even though the calculation of poverty rates (or headcounts) is a simple measure, it does not provide insight into the depth of poverty, that is, whether households are close to the selected threshold or not. Different alternative measures have been proposed, such as income gaps, which are based on the average of the difference between the poverty line and income of the poor, with this data being standardised by the poverty line. The main advantage of this measure is that it allows accounting for the average depth of poverty, but in doing so, it ignores the number of individuals living below the poverty threshold. A simple measure to account for both, that is, quantity and depth of poverty, is the intensity measure, which is simply the multiplication of the income gap and the poverty rates. These three measures are also used to describe a country's prevailing level of poverty in chapter 2 (for descriptive statistics, see tables in this chapter's appendix).

Data Sources

The following national household income surveys are used to measure poverty: 'EU Statistics on Income and Living Conditions' (EU-SILC)[8] for sixteen European countries, the 'Household, Income and Labour Dynamics in Australia Survey' (HILDA), the Canadian 'Survey of Labour and Income Dynamic' (SLID) and the 'Current Population Survey' (CPS) for the United States. These surveys provide standardised information on income composition and allow the cross-national comparison of earnings, market income and the disposable income of households. To make the EU-SILC and national household income surveys comparable, the Luxembourg Income Study (LIS) terminology on factor income and disposable household income after taxes and transfers were utilised. Whenever possible, the detailed income components to calculate market and disposable household income were used. However, for Australia and Canada, aggregated income variables were used. The main reason is that these variables could not be replicated using the specific income components, mainly due to top-coding and imputations. Therefore, the Canadian poverty rates, based on market income, include 'other taxable income' and alimonies (replicating the analysis in chapter 4, excluding both components, does not yield different results). An additional caveat should be mentioned regarding the reporting of specific income components (see also Marx, Salanauskaite and Verbist 2013): a few countries in the EU-SILC survey only disclose net income of taxes and social contributions (either for all income components, for example, Greece and Italy, or for only single income components, for example, Spain and Portugal) or net income of social contributions only (e.g. France and the Netherlands). Additionally, the surveys also differ concerning imputation practices, minimum age of respondents (fifteen years in the HILDA and CPS surveys, sixteen years in the SLID and EU-SILC surveys) and household definitions. The definition used in this book is based on the definition provided in the EU-SILC income survey as this data source is used for the majority of the countries. Accordingly, a household is formed by persons living together in a private dwelling and – most importantly – sharing expenditure. Therefore, I choose the income units that come closest to this definition for non-European surveys (e.g. economic families in the SLID survey rather than households).

These household surveys give an insight into the *immigrant background*. In this book, immigrants are identified based on whether respondents are foreign-born or not. The reason why place of birth is used is that there is little information available on immigrants coupled with small sample sizes. Starting with the immigrant information, as immigrants were not the primary focus of these national income surveys, detailed information on immigration histories, such as type of residence permits, and year of arrival, is scarce (see also Poulain and Herm 2010). In the EU-SILC survey, for instance, only two indicators related to the place of birth and citizenship are available. Each of these indicators distinguishes three categories, namely whether the respondent is a citizen of or born in the country of residence, an EU member state, or outside the EU. The Canadian SLID survey has problems as well and only differentiates between whether the person is born in Canada or not. Furthermore, immigration status is available only for persons living in urban areas with 500,000 inhabitants or more for confidentiality reasons.

The second difficulty is that immigrants tend to be underrepresented in the samples. Depending on whether nationality or place of birth is used as an identifier, the number of immigrant respondents is relatively low (for an overview of immigrant households included in the surveys, see appendix table

MA.1). For example, when taking nationality as the criterion, working-age immigrant households represent less than 2 per cent of the survey sample in the Netherlands *(n* = 39), Finland (*n* = 72), Portugal (*n* = 43) and Germany (*n* = 121). The share of respondents exceeds the threshold of 2 per cent when using 'place of birth' as the criterion, with the exception of Finland (*n* = 123), while the number of immigrant households in Portugal is below 100 (*n* = 86). In contrast, the Australian HILDA and the American CPS survey contain not only a reasonable sample of immigrants (*n* = 770 and *n* = 7,659, respectively) but also information on place of birth and nationality by country.[9]

In addition to small immigrant sample size, it can be further argued against using the nationality criterion because countries differ greatly regarding the naturalisation procedure and related conditions such as waiting periods for obtaining citizenship (e.g. three years as permanent resident in Canada versus twelve years in Switzerland; see Bauböck 2006 for an overview of citizenship rules). Thus, place of birth, in contrast to nationality, allows controlling for variations in naturalisation law because place of birth is unique and can be applied in the same way across countries. Finally, in countries that grant citizenship after a short time period, immigrants are underrepresented in the income surveys used for the analysis, as briefly described earlier (for details, see appendix table MA.1). For these reasons, this book relies on the crude proxy of whether the respondent is foreign-born or not to identify immigrant respondents, though this represents a limitation in the data and analysis.

Independent Variables

This book argues that institutions at the national level are important to explain poverty. Institutions are broadly understood as national laws, regulations and policies implemented in particular fields, here referring to the labour market and welfare system as well as to immigration. The focus on institutions and policies means that indicators do not account for how they are applied in practice and experienced by individuals but rather how they exist in law.[10] National immigration, labour and social security laws therefore constitute the main source for operationalising a country's institutional setting. The main reason for looking at institutions and policies is that they mirror the different rights individuals are entitled to and the conditions they have to fulfil to get access to the labour market and social programmes.

Two broader types of national policies are distinguished in this book. The first refers to those policies related to the labour market and welfare system. Here the respective regulations in the domain of the political economy are compared across countries regarding the extent to which they protect individuals through respective regulations within the labour market and the welfare state. The second type of policies concentrate on immigrants' social rights or socio-economic policies directed at immigrants only, namely those regulating their access to paid employment and social programmes. These policies are classified in terms of inclusiveness, that is, immigrants' ease or difficulty of getting access to the labour market and the welfare state.

The Labour Market and Welfare System

Starting with the labour market, two policy areas related to wage-bargaining systems and statutory minimum wages are measured as follows. If not indicated otherwise, the data are taken from Visser's (2013) 'Database on Institutional Characteristics of Trade Unions, Wage Setting, State Intervention and Social Pacts in 34 countries between1960 and 2011' (ICTWSS). First, *wage-bargaining institutions* are measured by Kenworthy's (2001) five-point index of coordination of wage bargaining, which distinguishes between different levels where coordination takes place, higher values indicating more coordinated wage-bargaining systems (see appendix table MA.2 for details). Because Kenworthy's original index also includes government intervention in wage bargaining reported separately in the ICTWSS dataset, a second indicator accounting for the degree of government intervention in wage bargaining is added. This variable distinguishes between five different levels of government participation in wage settlement. Second, for the operationalisation of *statutory minimum wages*, two indicators are used. The first indicator measures minimum wage setting, combining information on different actors participating in wage bargaining as well as the level of application (sectoral or national agreements). The second indicator refers to the share of the minimum wage as percentage of the median wage, available from the OECD.Stat (OECD 2015c). Countries without statutory minimum wages are coded as zero.

Turning to the welfare state, three social programmes are presented that have been identified as being central to the working-age population's fight against poverty: unemployment programmes, social assistance and family-related programmes (Huber and Stephens 2001; Pfeifer 2012). While the former two compensate for loss of income due to either the loss of employment or difficulty entering the labour market, the latter helps families to reduce their poverty risk (e.g. Temporary Assistance for Needy Families [TANF] in the United States).

Drawing on previous contributions on social rights (see Esping-Andersen 1990; Korpi and Palme 1998; Scruggs 2004), the generosity of *unemployment programmes* is used to operationalise unemployment programmes, which is measured as the net replacement rate during the initial phase of unemployment for six different types of households in 2007: single, one-earner and two-earner couples either with or without two children, provided by the OECD (2015b). The unemployment replacement rate for households earning 67 per cent of the AWs is used.[11] Because this book is concerned with explaining poverty, the situation of marginal households with low previous incomes rather than AW households is assessed.

Two forms of family programme generosity are distinguished: dual-earner programmes and traditional family benefits. First, following previous research on employment-related family programmes (Gornick, Meyers and Ross 1997; Korpi 2000; Mandel and Semyonov 2005), *dual-earner programmes* are measured by the full-rate equivalent of paid maternity, paternity and parental leave, available in the OECD Family Database (OECD 2015c). Second, *traditional family benefits* are measured as the average benefits for three household types earning 67 per cent (or 134 per cent) of the AW, that is, a lone-parent family, a single-earner family, and a two-earner family, as a percentage of the AW.[12] Both indicators were calculated using the dataset accompanying the OECD benefits and wages report for 2007.[13] These family benefits include yearly flat rate or lump sum benefits, family tax allowances, as well as child-raising benefits paid to parents looking after their children at home but exclude any benefits or tax reductions for public or private childcare expenditures or the use of particular childcare services (see OECD 2007b).

The data used to operationalise *social assistance* are based on Nelsons' (2007) 'Social Assistance and Minimum Income Protection Interim Data Set' (SaMip), which contains information on yearly minimum income protection across three different family types: single persons, lone-parent and two-parent families. In order to compare the minimum income benefits within and across countries, the indicators are calculated as a percentage of the yearly AW. Analogous to the unemployment replacement rate, the average of these three types of family is used.[14]

Immigrants' Social Rights: Access to Paid Employment and Social Programmes

The second type of policies refers to social rights or socio-economic integration policies that target immigrants once they are settled in the country. Here, four specific immigration categories have been differentiated (see also Aleinikoff and Klusmeyer 2002), which are operationalised based on the type of residence permit issued to immigrants: (1) holders of temporary residence permits issued for the purpose of work (hereafter: labour migrants); (2) family members of labour migrants; (3) holders of permanent residence permits (hereafter: permanent residents) and (4) family members of permanent residents. Nationals and their family members serve as a reference point for the comparison of social rights.

Starting with *immigrants' work rights* in terms of access to paid employment, the operationalisation draws on Cerna's (2008) and Ruhs' (2011, 2013) measures on the openness to labour migration and distinguishes four differ-ent categories or levels of immigrants' access to employment. For labour migrants, these are as follows:

0: employment is *tied to a specific employer*
1: change of employment possible, but requires a *new work permit*
2: workers are allowed to change employment within a *specific sector, occu-pation or region*
3: migrant workers have the same *full access as nationals*

Since most countries usually admit migrant workers under various pro-grammes, which are related to different admission requirements, several subgroups are distinguished drawing on Ruhs' (2013, Table A.3, 203) clas-sification of labour immigration programmes (excluding programmes lasting less than twelve months, such as seasonal worker programmes, working holi-day programmes, etc.). Accordingly, the access to paid employment of family members of each programme has been coded separately. These categories, as for permanent immigrants and their family members, are slightly different and consider whether an immigration category

0: is *not permitted to work*,
1: has to apply for a *working permit*,
2: gets *unlimited working rights after a certain period* or *accelerated proce-dure* (e.g. no labour market test) and
3: has the same *full access as nationals*.

An index was created based on the average value of the four immigration categories, which was then rescaled from 0 to 3 to range between 0 and 1. The relevant immigration laws and regulations related to the entry and settlement of immigrants as well as their employment were identified using secondary sources, such as the report on immigration laws published by the International Organization for Migration (IOM 2009) and comments in the MIPEX dataset are used as sources (for an overview, see appendix table MA.3). Whenever possible, the national legislation as of 1 January 2007 was considered.

Turning to *immigrants' social rights* here understood as access to social programmes (unemployment, family-related and social assistance), the indi-cators were built as follows. Drawing on research by North, de Wenden and Taylor (1987, quoted in Brubaker 1989, 159; Soysal 1994, 123) on immi-grants' access to social programmes, two aspects are especially important: access of each immigration category and the length of residence. The for-mer considers whether a particular residence permit grants access to social programmes, while the latter accounts for whether certain countries have

implemented a waiting period or a ban of a number of years. During a specified period, immigrants are not allowed access to universal or means-tested
social programmes, that is, other than contribution-based social programmes.
This approach is often chosen in traditional immigration countries where
permanent residence permits are granted from the beginning of the stay (e.g.
Australia and the United States). However, the length of residence is also
relevant for contributory social programmes, where a specific time of previous employment is required. Five years of residence in a country has been
chosen as a threshold as in most countries this is the time immigrants have to
wait to apply for a permanent residence permit. In contrast, a lower threshold
of fifty-two weeks for contribution-based welfare programmes was applied.
For labour migrants, and immigrants with temporary residence permits in
general, permits are often issued on a yearly basis. Moreover, the renewal of
their permits depends on having a job. Consequently, a threshold of fifty-two
weeks accounts for whether immigrants might benefit from contribution-
based programmes, while holding their first residence (and work) permit.
Last but not least, a category has been included which takes into account that
merely being employed gives access to social programmes. Accordingly, this
leads to the following categories:

0: no access
1: contribution period ≥ fifty-two weeks of employment or waiting period
   ≥ five years
2: contribution period < fifty-two weeks of employment or waiting period
   < five years
3: employment
4: full access

The coding proceeded as follows: specific social programmes (e.g. unemployment insurance, unemployment assistance, programmes for lone parents
and child-raising allowances) and relevant social laws and regulations were
selected based on secondary sources such as the country notes for the MIPEX
dataset in Huddleston et al. (2011), information in the comparative tables on
social protection published by the MISSOC (2007) website for all European
countries, the country chapters of the OECD Benefits and Wages report (primarily Australia, Canada and United States, see OECD 2007b) as well as the
report 'Social Security Programs throughout the World' (SSA 2006, 2007;
see appendix table MA.3 for the full list). Then, national social security laws
for each specific social programme were collected. The data were coded first
at the most specific level, that is, for each single social programme and each
immigration category, and then aggregated to one of the four broader social
programmes, still for each immigration category separately, and as a final
step for all immigration categories together. The four social programmes

are (1) unemployment programmes, including unemployment insurance and unemployment assistance, (2a) dual-earner programmes, (2b) traditional family benefits and (3) social assistance. The indices have been rescaled from 0 to 4 to range between 0 and 1.

Data were collected for other immigration categories, namely EU citizens and recognised refugees, and other factors deemed important in former studies such as the legality of residence and work, the country of origin and physical presence in the country (see North, de Wenden and Taylor 1987, quoted in Brubaker 1989, 159; Soysal 1994). Due to the low variation across countries (e.g. EU citizens and refugees are usually granted full access to employment and social programmes; country of origin makes little difference in contrast to legal residence and physical presence), this information is not included in the index.

Control Variables

Immigrant Population and Economic Factors – Country Level

Various indicators are collected to account for the control variables at the macro-level, namely composition of the immigrant population and economic factors. One proxy for the former is the proportion of the foreign-born population from industrialised countries (including the member states of the EU and the EFTA, Australia, Canada, Japan, New Zealand and the United States, OECD 2015c). The three additional indicators relate to the share of immigration inflow via three types of permits based on work, family and humanitarian reasons. Because immigration inflows are highly dependent on the global political situation, the five-year average between 2003 and 2007 was used, where data were available. The data for these indicators are published in the international migration outlook (OECD several years, Eurostat 2013).

The indicator used to assess a country's economic situation is GDP growth, a five-year average, which is available in Comparative Political Data Set (Armingeon et al. 2015). In addition, data referring to the unemployment rate as percentage of the whole and the immigrant labour force as well as the employment differences between the foreign-born and the native-born population were also collected, all from the OECD Factbook (2013a). Finally, the data for the share of the shadow economy as percentage of official GDP in 2007 were taken from Feld and Schneider (2010, Table 13).

Structural Factors – Individual Level

Households instead of individuals were chosen as individual-level units for the analysis. As mentioned earlier, the income for the poverty measures are based on the aggregated income of all household members rather than for each member individually. The main reason for this approach is that specific social provisions and taxes are available only at the household level (e.g.

traditional family benefits, social assistance and income taxes).[15] Consequently, as discussed in chapter 2, household determinants rather than characteristics of individuals are expected to affect poverty. Rather than identifying
a head of household, usually defined as the person with the highest income,
and attributing his or her individual characteristics to the whole household
as the majority of poverty studies do, this book departs from the idea that
poverty is a 'family-level concept' (Kesler 2015, 40) and chose an alternative strategy: taking into account the socio-demographic characteristics of
all adult household members. The advantage of this approach is that it considers the existing diversity of lifestyles and household forms, for example,
households with dual-earners and atypically employed persons pursuing part-
time or fixed-term employment (Häusermann and Schwander 2012). This
mixed category approach further facilitates the decision regarding whether
a household should be considered to have an immigrant background when
adults born both abroad and in the country are present. Depending solely on
information of one household member hides the fact that native/immigrant
households face different opportunities to households where all members
were born either abroad or in the country of residence (see also Obućina
2014). The assignment of individual socio-demographic characteristics to a
household was composed of three stages, outlined next.

First, adults were identified in the respective national income surveys
based on household composition. Respondents living in one- or two-person
households without children were classified as adults, whereas in a household
with children, the oldest or the two oldest persons (lone parents and couples)
were selected. In the remaining multi-person households, the following criteria were chosen according to the definitions proposed by Eurostat. On the one
hand, all individuals above twenty-five years were coded as adults. On the
other hand, only economically active individuals aged between eighteen and
twenty-four were selected as adults based on labour force status and market
income.

In a second stage, socio-demographic characteristics were assigned to the
adults. For the *immigrant background*, the indicator refers to the place of
birth, which distinguishes two categories: non-immigrant and immigrant.[16]
The same practice of allocating adults the respective characteristic was done
to operationalise the structural factors, that is, socio-demographic characteristics such as education and skills. The indicator *education* distinguishes
three categories: (1) low: ISCED 0–2, lower secondary education or less,
(2) medium: ISCED 3–4, upper secondary and post-secondary non-tertiary
education and (3) high: ISCED 5–6, tertiary education or above. *Skills* are
measured based on the occupation (ISCO-88 code) following the procedure
proposed by Häusermann (2010) that differentiates between five categories:
(1) low-service functionaries, (2) blue-collar and lower-level white-collar

workers, (3) mixed service functionaries, (4) socio-cultural (semi-) professionals and (5) capital accumulators. Finally, the following labour market
indicators are based on information on the main activity status during the
respective fiscal year.[17] *Labour market participation* is based on whether an
adult pursued paid employment, was unemployed or inactive. In addition,
two dummy variables were created to assess employment conditions, namely
whether the adult was self-employed or employed atypically (employed
part-time, part of the year, that is, less than twelve months employed, on a
temporary contract, as a family worker or unemployed).

In a third stage, the information for adults was aggregated for each
household by combining the information of all adults. Table M.1 provides
an overview of the 'pure' categories derived in the second step as well as
the combination thereof (in italics). For instance, a household composed of
two adults, one with a primary education (ISCED = 1) and the other with an
upper secondary education (ISCED = 3), is coded as mixed (7 'Mixed low
(0–4)'). It should be noted that some possible combinations are conflated. For
example, the mixed categories of the indicator 'occupation' only distinguish
whether skill levels of all household members are equal to or greater ISCO-88
code 41 (coded as 7 'Mixed skills, low'), less or equal to ISCO-88 code 32
(coded as 9 'Mixed skills, high') or includes adults with different skill levels
(coded as 8 'Mixed skills').

The aggregation for *labour market participation* and *self-employment/
atypical employment* is slightly different. Here, the number of affected persons per household was assigned to one of three categories: (1) no earner,
(2) one earner and (3) multiple earners; and (1) no one atypically/self-
employed, (2) at least one person and (3) all atypically/self-employed. In
addition, five control variables, the *number of children aged two or below*,
aged three to five, *aged six to twelve*, *aged thirteen to seventeen* and the *number of adults sixty-five years or above*, were included.

STATISTICAL METHODS

This book estimates multilevel models with random intercepts using maximum likelihood estimations to analyse whether variations in integration
policies, as well as in the labour market and social policies, can explain cross-
national immigrants' poverty and poverty gaps between immigrants and
non-immigrants. Such models allow the consideration of context variation
and the simultaneous estimation of the effect of individual- and country-level
variables. Since the data exhibit a multilevel character, that is, the individuals
(level-1 observations, here households) are nested within a contextual unit
(level-2 units, here countries), the observations within a country are not truly

Table M.1. Operationalisation – individual- and household-level characteristics

Variable	Operationalisation by adults and households (in italics)
Place of birth Nationality	Variables measuring place of birth: 1 'Non-immigrant', 2 'Immigrant', *3 'Mixed'*
Education	Variables based on ISCED educational level: 1 'Low (ISCED 0–2)', 2 'Medium (ISCED 3–4)', 3 'High (ISCED 5–6)', *7 'Mixed low (0–4)', 8 'Mixed (0–6)', 9 Mixed high (3–6)'*
Occupation	Variables based on ISCO88 classification (or equivalent): 1 'Low service functionaries', 2 'Blue collar and lower-white collar workers', 3 'Mixed service functionaries', 4 'Socio-cultural (semi-) professionals', 5 'Capital accumulators', *7 'Mixed skills, low', 8 'Mixed skills' 9 'Mixed skills, high'* (Canada: based on the North American Industry Classification System 2007, NAICS 2007; United States: based on the Standard Occupational Classification 2000, SOC 2000)
Labour market participation	Variables measuring main activity status during fiscal year: *1 'No one employed' 2 'One person employed', 3 'Multiple earners'* (based on individual information: 1 'Employed', 2 'Unemployed' 3 'Inactive')
Atypical employment	Variable measuring atypical employment (part-time, part of the year, temporary contract, family worker and unemployed): *1 'No one employed atypically' 2 'At least one person employed atypically' 3 'All employed atypically'*
Self-employment	Variable measuring self-employment: *1 'No one self-employed' 2 'At least one person self-employed' 3 'All self-employed'*
Children per household	Variables measuring the number of children aged ≤2 years, 3–5 years, 6–12 years and 13–17 years
Elderly per household	Variable measuring the number of adults aged 65 years or above

independent. The use of standard regression analysis is problematic because it tends to underestimate the standard errors and therefore increases the potential for Type 1 errors, that is, producing significant coefficients when in fact the null hypothesis is true. In contrast, multilevel models reduce the probability of these errors by allowing the intercept and slopes of individual-level variables to vary across the contextual units. Therefore, rather than treating the dependency of the observations as a nuisance, it incorporates it into the model by extracting information in order to estimate the relationship between the variables (see Steenbergen and Jones 2002; Snijders and Bosker 2012).

In other words, multilevel models are used because social and economic policies as well as integration policies differ across countries and all households living in a specific country are exposed to the same set of policies. Therefore, it is central to consider the unobserved country-level effect. In addition, multilevel logistic regression not only allows estimating the explanatory potential of policies at the macro-level, after controlling for socio-demographic characteristics at the household level, but also assesses the relative impact of country-level variables compared to household-level characteristics.

Analytical Approach

Since the dependent variable is dichotomous, logit maximum likelihood models are used to assess the impact of social and economic policies on *immigrants' poverty* and the moderating effect of integration policies concerning the access of immigrants to the labour market and social programmes. The logit random intercept models expressed in log-odds can be decomposed into a level-1 model:

$$\log\left(\frac{\pi_{ij}}{1-\pi_{ij}}\right) = \beta_{0j} + \beta X_{ij} \tag{1}$$

At the individual level, the dependent variable is poverty, indicating whether an immigrant household i in country j is poor (= 1) or not (= 0). X represents a vector of individual-level variables (i.e. educational level and labour market participation). The model is comparable to a simple logistic model with the difference that the parameters vary across level-2 units denoted by the j subscripts. Consequently, a unit change in a variable x_1 of two households from the same country is associated with a β_1 change in their log-odds. To facilitate interpretation, all continuous variables have been centred at their means. β_{0j} refers to the intercept, which can vary across countries and therefore can be reformulated as a function of the level-2 variables:

$$\beta_{0j} = \gamma_{00} + \gamma_0 Z_j + U_{0j} \tag{2}$$

$$\beta = \gamma \tag{3}$$

In equations (2) and (3), γ denotes the fixed level-2 parameters, with γ_{00} being the individual-level intercept, that is, the population average of the transformed probabilities. Z refers to a vector of country-level variables (e.g. immigrants' social rights, minimum wage setting and unemployment programme generosity). The random effect is described by the residual term U_{0j}, which represents the country-specific intercept. The deviations U_{0j} are assumed to be independent from each other and normally distributed, with a mean of zero and a variance of τ_0^2 (Snijders and Bosker 2012). Including equations (2) and (3) into (1) yield the mixed model:

$$\log\left(\frac{\pi_{ij}}{1-\pi_{ij}}\right) = \gamma_{00} + \gamma_0 Z_j + \gamma X_{ij} + U_{0j} \tag{4}$$

The multilevel logistic analysis for immigrants' poverty is conducted in STATA using the 'xtmelogit' command.[18] Although the literature agrees that nineteen level-2 units should be sufficient to estimate meaningful and significant multilevel models (Rabe-Hesketh and Skrondal 2012), this book is aware of the relatively small number of countries included in the analysis. Therefore, the models try to minimise the number of country-level variables. In addition, the jackknife repeated replication method, a re-sampling technique, is applied. This statistical method is used to estimate robust standard errors and confidence intervals. The basic idea behind the jackknife technique is to re-compute the estimates based on a subsample of the original observation. In other words, the model is re-estimated excluding one observation, here all observations of one country, from the sample (Wolfe and Dunn 2003). This approach allows for controlling for the impact of each country on the regression coefficient.

Appendix

APPENDIX TABLES AND FIGURE FOR CHAPTER 2

Appendix Table 2A.1. Poverty rates (50 per cent of median income) and alternative measures, by country

	DK	NO	SE	FI	AT	BE	DE	CH	FR	NL	UK	AU	CA	US	IE	ES	GR	IT	PT	all
Non-migrants																				
Poverty rates (pre)	16.2	17.2	13.3	18.4	16.6	17.2	18.1	9.2	15.2	17.8	20.4	20.9	15.5	20.3	26.0	17.3	18.6	17.2	18.5	**17.6**
Poverty rates (post)	5.2	7.2	4.1	5.6	5.2	5.4	9.0	5.9	4.9	6.1	9.0	10.0	9.1	14.5	7.9	12.4	12.1	12.1	11.8	**8.3**
Poverty reduction, gross	69.2	66.7	71.6	70.9	71.8	73.6	58.7	53.6	73.0	73.0	60.6	52.5	42.9	32.6	70.9	46.7	54.1	45.4	53.4	**60.1**
Poverty increase, gross	1.1	8.2	2.6	1.2	3.1	4.8	8.4	17.9	5.6	7.5	4.7	0.5	1.9	4.1	1.3	18.3	19.1	15.8	17.6	**7.6**
Poverty reduction (PRE)	68.0	58.4	69.0	69.7	68.6	68.8	50.3	35.6	67.3	65.4	55.9	52.0	41.1	28.5	69.6	28.5	34.9	29.6	35.8	**52.5**
Income gap (pre)	0.66	0.62	0.57	0.62	0.63	0.76	0.70	0.47	0.62	0.68	0.69	0.64	0.51	0.57	0.65	0.61	0.58	0.61	0.58	**0.62**
Income gap (post)	0.35	0.44	0.30	0.28	0.32	0.27	0.32	0.32	0.25	0.40	0.32	0.29	0.32	0.36	0.22	0.37	0.38	0.37	0.28	**0.33**
Intensity (pre)	10.7	10.7	7.6	11.5	10.4	13.1	12.7	4.3	9.3	12.1	14.0	13.4	7.9	11.6	17.0	10.5	10.8	10.5	10.7	**11.0**
Intensity (post)	1.8	3.1	1.2	1.5	1.7	1.5	2.9	1.9	1.2	2.5	2.9	2.9	3.0	5.2	1.8	4.6	4.6	4.5	3.3	**2.7**
Immigrants																				
Poverty rates (pre)	52.3	41.3	46.4	50.5	26.1	44.1	40.1	18.5	43.0	50.0	42.3	26.0	31.0	33.2	36.6	21.6	21.2	19.7	22.7	**35.1**
Poverty rates (post)	23.6	21.3	18.6	21.1	15.3	27.0	19.7	15.1	20.7	9.0	23.0	15.6	19.7	29.7	13.3	25.9	23.8	23.6	21.2	**20.4**
Poverty reduction, gross	57.3	55.6	63.5	58.5	46.1	43.8	54.6	35.4	58.5	81.9	48.7	42.1	37.3	14.5	64.5	18.0	24.4	19.5	29.4	**44.9**
Poverty increase, gross	2.4	7.2	3.6	0.2	4.8	5.1	3.7	17.3	6.6	0.0	3.1	2.1	0.8	3.8	0.9	37.8	36.8	39.5	23.0	**10.5**
Poverty reduction (PRE)	54.9	48.4	60.0	58.3	41.3	38.8	50.9	18.1	51.8	81.9	45.6	40.0	36.4	10.7	63.6	-19.8	-12.4	-20.0	6.4	**34.5**

Income gap (pre)	0.78	0.72	0.70	0.74	0.68	0.78	0.73	0.51	0.67	0.75	0.70	0.61	0.48	0.44	0.75	0.53	0.37	0.51	0.56	0.63
Income gap (post)	0.48	0.34	0.36	0.19	0.32	0.29	0.27	0.31	0.24	0.43	0.31	0.29	0.28	0.32	0.50	0.42	0.33	0.40	0.33	0.34
Intensity (pre)	40.9	29.6	32.3	37.5	17.7	34.5	29.3	9.4	28.8	37.6	29.5	15.9	14.9	14.5	27.3	11.5	7.8	10.0	12.6	23.2
Intensity (post)	11.4	7.4	6.8	3.9	5.0	7.9	5.3	4.7	4.9	3.9	7.2	4.5	5.6	9.6	6.6	10.9	7.8	9.4	7.0	6.8
Mixed																				
Poverty rates (pre)	15.3	7.6	17.1	22.3	18.3	23.5	24.1	7.9	23.8	14.3	18.5	15.3	16.1	17.5	20.0	18.5	16.6	17.9	15.6	17.4
Poverty rates (post)	5.5	3.2	6.3	5.6	9.1	10.4	8.3	5.8	9.6	2.7	9.0	5.7	8.2	13.6	6.9	14.6	14.2	11.4	10.2	8.4
Poverty reduction, gross	67.7	67.9	67.3	74.7	56.9	62.4	72.7	63.4	63.7	87.6	65.3	63.5	50.4	29.6	66.2	51.0	45.7	42.6	60.5	61.0
Poverty increase, gross	3.5	9.7	3.9	0.0	6.6	6.5	7.2	37.0	3.9	6.4	13.8	0.7	1.0	7.3	0.9	30.0	30.9	6.3	26.3	10.6
Poverty reduction (PRE)	64.2	58.2	63.4	74.8	50.3	55.8	65.5	26.5	59.8	81.1	51.5	62.9	49.4	22.3	65.3	20.9	14.8	36.3	34.3	56.7
Income gap (pre)	0.59	0.64	0.52	0.63	0.64	0.63	0.64	0.43	0.64	0.61	0.60	0.60	0.40	0.43	0.60	0.46	0.55	0.53	0.43	0.56
Income gap (post)	0.42	0.29	0.36	0.24	0.20	0.21	0.45	0.25	0.28	0.24	0.35	0.21	0.20	0.29	0.17	0.40	0.33	0.39	0.25	0.29
Intensity (pre)	9.0	4.9	8.9	14.0	11.8	14.7	15.5	3.4	15.1	8.8	11.0	9.2	6.4	7.5	12.0	8.5	9.1	9.5	6.8	9.8
Intensity (post)	2.3	0.9	2.3	1.4	1.8	2.2	3.7	1.5	2.7	0.6	3.2	1.2	1.6	3.9	1.2	5.8	4.7	4.5	2.6	2.5
Poverty line (pre)*	19,051	19,710	13,677	12,701	11,619	12,171	11,969	20,375	9,917	13,180	20,669	14,723	16,299	12,633	13,214	7,345	6,643	9,311	5,042	–
Poverty line (post)*	15,172	18,614	13,017	12,476	12,099	11,646	12,127	17,331	10,896	10,821	19,865	14,074	14,768	12,480	14,669	7,911	6,791	10,023	5,742	–

Note: * based on income of all households in the sample, in US dollar.

Source: EU-SILC (European countries), HILDA (Australia), SLID (Canada) and CPS (United States).

Appendix Table 2A.2. Correlation between different measures of poverty

	Based on market income								Based on disposable income									
	Non-migrants			Migrants					Non-migrants			Migrants						
	PR	IG	INT	PR	IG	INT	AME, raw	AME, net	PR	IG	INT	PR	IG	INT	AME, raw	AME, net		
Based on market income																		
Non-immigrants Poverty rates	–																	
Income gap	**.49**	–																
Intensity	**.93**	.76	–															
Migrants Poverty rates	.09	.53	.27	–														
Income gap	.14	.71	.41	**.79**	–													
Intensity	.09	.63	.32	**.97**	.90	–												
AME, raw	-.17	.40	.03	**.96**	.73	.93	–											
AME, net	-.23	-.28	-.30	**.34**	.04	.26	.37	–										
Based on disposable income																		
Non-immigrants Poverty rates	.41	-.20	.20	-.62	-.73	-.70	-.72	-.21	–									
Income gap	-.21	-.11	-.22	-.10	-.27	-.14	-.08	.07	.29	–								
Intensity	.25	-.21	.07	-.56	-.73	-.65	-.63	-.16	.94	.57	–							
Migrants Poverty rates	.02	.06	.00	-.07	-.32	-.16	-.06	-.13	.46	.15	.49	–						
Income gap	.23	.10	.22	.00	.12	.06	-.12	.14	.07	.27	.13	-.18	–					
Intensity	.10	.07	.07	-.12	-.21	-.13	-.17	-.03	.43	.34	.51	.72	.54	–				
AME, raw	-.23	.00	-.20	.01	-.22	-.08	.10	-.11	.16	.05	.22	.91	-.29	.57	–			
AME, net	-.25	-.42	-.39	-.57	-.73	-.65	-.51	.13	.50	.19	.53	.59	-.16	.43	.56	–		
Non-imm. PRE scores	.10	.53	.30	.78	.88	.85	.74	.14	-.85	-.38	-.86	-.40	.01	-.37	-.23	.56	–	
Migrants PRE scores	.10	.39	.25	.82	.81	.84	.79	.28	-.75	-.27	-.76	-.56	-.02	-.53	-.42	-.63	.87	.91

Note: PR: poverty rates, IG: income gap, INT: intensity. Parameters mentioned in the text are highlighted in bold.

Source: EU-SILC (European countries), HILDA (Australia), SLID (Canada) and CPS (United States).

Appendix Table 2A.3. Average marginal effects (AME) coefficients, by country

	Immigrant households				Mixed households			
	AME based on market income (raw)	AME based on market income (net)	AME based on disposable income (raw)	AME based on disposable income (net)	AME based on market income (raw)	AME based on market income (net)	AME based on disposable income (raw)	AME based on disposable income (net)
DK	24.4 (2.8)***	4.3 (2.6)†	9.6 (1.7)***	2.0 (1.8)	−1.0 (3.7)	1.9 (2.4)	0.3 (2.5)	2.2 (1.9)
NO	17.5 (2.2)***	5.0 (2.5)*	8.8 (1.4)***	3.3 (1.6)*	−13.3 (3.2)***	−3.9 (2.3)†	−6.0 (2.4)*	−2.0 (1.9)
SE	22.6 (1.3)***	9.0 (1.4)***	8.7 (.9)***	4.3 (.9)***	3.9 (1.8)*	5.5 (1.5)***	2.3 (1.2)†	3.4 (1.2)**
FI	23.2 (3.6)***	4.1 (2.3)†	8.3 (1.6)***	2.5 (1.8)	3.7 (3.2)	2.0 (1.8)	0.0 (2.3)	−1.3 (1.6)
	21.9	*5.6*	*8.9*	*3.0*	*−1.7*	*1.4*	*−0.8*	*0.6*
AT	8.4 (2.0)***	0.4 (1.5)	7.6 (1.2)***	4.3 (1.1)***	1.7 (3.3)	0.4 (1.9)	3.8 (2.4)	3.5 (1.8)*
BE	2.9 (2.3)***	2.9 (1.1)**	13.1 (1.6)***	6.2 (.9)***	6.1 (2.1)**	3.4 (1.3)*	5.0 (1.3)***	4.9 (1.1)***
DE	17.0 (2.2)***	4.0 (1.4)***	7.6 (1.4)***	2.6 (1.4)†	5.5 (2.0)**	1.9 (1.5)	−0.8 (1.7)	−0.1 (1.5)
CH	7.9 (1.4)***	2.9 (1.3)*	7.5 (1.2)***	4.2 (1.1)***	−1.5 (1.8)	3.6 (1.6)*	−0.1 (1.5)	2.6 (1.4)†
FR	2.8 (1.7)***	3.2 (1.3)*	9.9 (1.2)***	4.1 (1.1)***	8.1 (2.0)***	3.1 (1.3)**	4.3 (1.3)**	2.8 (1.1)*
NL	22.7 (3.3)***	5.5 (2.2)*	2.4 (1.9)	0.1 (1.9)	−3.9 (3.0)	−0.5 (2.0)	−4.8 (2.0)*	−3.8 (1.8)*
	16.3	*3.2*	*8.0*	*3.6*	*2.7*	*2.0*	*1.2*	*1.7*
UK	17.6 (2.4)***	2.1 (1.6)	9.9 (1.7)***	3.1 (1.5)*	−2.1 (3.0)	3.1 (1.7)†	0.0 (2.0)	3.6 (1.8)*
AU	4.8 (2.3)*	0.6 (2.1)	4.8 (1.7)**	1.9 (1.8)	−6.3 (2.6)*	1.7 (1.9)	−5.8 (2.0)**	−1.6 (1.7)
CA	13.8 (1.8)***	6.6 (1.4)***	9.1 (1.5)***	5.2 (1.2)***	.7 (2.6)	1.6 (2.1)	−1.3 (2.4)	1.5 (2.1)
US	11.3 (0.6)***	3.6 (.4)***	12.4 (0.5)***	5.7 (0.4)***	−3.0 (.9)**	1.5 (0.6)*	−1.0 (0.8)	2.8 (0.6)***
IE	9.5 (4.3)*	3.5 (2.6)	4.4 (3.0)	1.3 (2.4)	−6.6 (4.1)	2.9 (2.2)	−1.1 (2.9)	2.7 (2.7)
	11.4	*2.5*	*8.1*	*3.0*	*−3.5*	*2.3*	*−1.8*	*1.9*
ES	3.9 (3.6)	3.7 (1.6)*	1.3 (2.6)***	8.3 (1.5)***	1.1 (2.7)	3.3 (1.7)†	2.2 (1.9)	2.9 (1.8)
GR	2.5 (2.7)	4.3 (2.1)*	9.2 (2.0)***	9.9 (2.0)***	−2.0 (3.4)	1.4 (2.5)	2.1 (2.8)	4.3 (2.7)
IT	2.3 (2.3)	0.9 (1.6)	8.9 (1.6)***	5.0 (1.4)***	0.6 (1.9)	3.2 (1.6)*	−.8 (1.8)	0.8 (1.6)
PT	3.9 (4.8)	2.6 (3.7)	7.4 (3.7)*	5.7 (4.5)	−3.1 (3.9)	3.7 (2.8)	−1.7 (3.2)	1.6 (2.8)
	3.2	*2.9*	*8.9*	*7.2*	*−0.8*	*2.9*	*0.4*	*2.4*

Note: Standard errors in parentheses.

† p < .10, * p < .05, ** p < .01, *** p < .001.

Source: EU-SILC (European countries), HILDA (Australia), SLID (Canada) and CPS (United States).

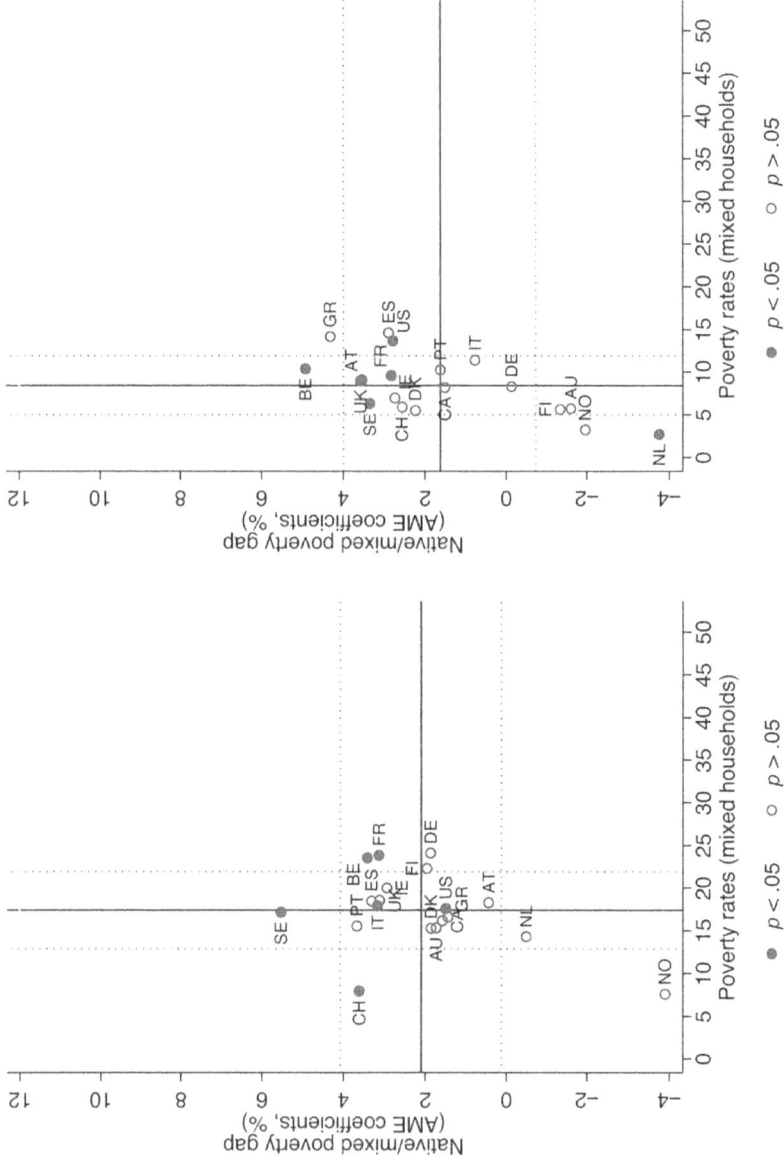

Appendix Figure 2A.1 Poverty measures based on market and disposable income (50 per cent of median income), mixed households. *Left*, based on market income; *right*, based on disposable income. *Source:* EU-SILC (European countries), HILDA (Australia), SLID (Canada) and CPS (United States).

Appendix Table 4A.1.   Determinants of immigrants' poverty based on market income (50 per cent of median income, square root scale)

	Model 1a	Model 1b	Model 2a	Model 2a (labour migrants)	Model 2b	Model 2b (labour migrants)
GDP growth (5-year average)	.210	.228	.083	.161	.153	.255[†]
	(.16)	(.16)	(.15)	(.15)	(.17)	(.14)
Industrialised countries, % foreign-born	-.002	-.014	-.003	-.010	-.012	-.019*
	(.01)	(.01)	(.01)	(.01)	(.01)	(.01)
Index labour market (paid employment)	-.384	-.903	-.213	-.923	-.880	-1.092
	(1.13)	(1.20)	(.99)	(.64)	(1.07)	(.68)
Wage bargaining coordination	-.069					
	(.11)					
Wage bargaining coordination X access (emp.)	1.351					
	(.95)					
Government intervention		-.161				
		(.12)				
Government intervention X access (emp.)		-1.160				
		(1.42)				
Minimum wage setting			.036	.029		
			(.04)	(.04)		
Minimum wage setting X access (emp.)			-.872*	-.601*		
			(.34)	(.24)		
Minimum wage (% of median)					.001	.002
					(.01)	(.00)
Minimum wage X access (emp.)					-.084[†]	-.069**

(Continued)

	Model 1a	Model 1b	Model 2a	Model 2a (labour migrants)	Model 2b	Model 2b (labour migrants)
					(.05)	(.03)
Constant	-2.162***	-2.166***	-2.187***	-2.147***	-2.149***	-2.088***
	(.14)	(.14)	(.13)	(.12)	(.14)	(.13)
Intercept	-.737***	-.722***	-.850***	-.850***	-.750***	-.750***
	(.18)	(.18)	(.19)	(.19)	(.18)	(.18)
Var (countries)	.229	.236	.183	.183	.223	.223
Intra-class correlation	.065	.067	.053	.053	.063	.063
Log-likelihood	-5,726.092	-5,726.266	-5,724.207	-5,724.207	-5,725.809	-5,725.809
N (households)	15,150	15,150	15,150	15,150	15,150	15,150
N (countries)	19	19	19	19	19	19

Note: Coefficients (log odds) of random intercept logit models, standard errors in parentheses. All models are estimated including household-level variables (not shown).

⁺ p < .10, * p < .05, ** p < .01, *** p < .001.

Appendix Table 4A.2. Determinants of immigrants' poverty reduction (50 per cent of median income, square root scale)

	Model 1	Model 2a	Model 2b	Model 2b (permanent residents)	Model 3
GDP growth (5-year average)	-.071	.338*	.202	.331*	.410⁺
	(.19)	(.17)	(.19)	(.16)	(.25)
Industrialised countries, % foreign-born	.005	.002	-.006	-.026*	-.024
	(.01)	(.01)	(.01)	(.01)	(.02)
Index access (unemployment)	3.721***				
	(1.07)				
Unemployment programmes (generosity)	1.298				
	(1.21)				

Unemployment programmes X access (progr.)	−5.350			
	(12.73)			
Index access (dual-earner)		−.379		
		(.65)		
Dual-earner programmes (generosity)		.030***		
		(.01)		
Dual-earner programmes X access (progr.)		−.008		
		(.03)		
Index access (traditional family benefits)			1.689*	3.122***
			(.76)	(.79)
Traditional family benefits (generosity)			.072*	.052†
			(.03)	(.03)
Traditional family benefits X access (progr.)			.194†	.215*
			(.11)	(.09)
Index access (social assistance)				.162
				(.53)
Social assistance (generosity)				.028
				(.02)
Social assistance X access (progr.)				−.056
				(.06)
Constant	−2.634***	−2.624***	−2.614***	−2.530***
	(.16)	(.16)	(.16)	(.19)
Intercept	−.761***	−.810***	−.635***	−.558**
	(.19)	(.20)	(.19)	(.18)
Var (countries)	.218	.198	.281	.327
Intra-class correlation	.062	.057	.079	.091
Log-likelihood	−3,661.733	−3,660.905	−3,663.710	−3,611.834
N (households)	15,150	15,150	15,150	14,891
N (countries)	19	19	19	18

Note: Coefficients (log odds) of random intercept logit models, standard errors in parentheses. All models are estimated including household-level variables (not shown).

† $p < .10$, * $p < .05$, ** $p < .01$, *** $p < .001$.

Appendix Table 4A.3. Determinants of immigrants' poverty based on market income (60 per cent of median income, OECD equivalence scale)

	Model 1a	Model 1b	Model 2a	Model 2a (labour migrants)	Model 2b	Model 2b (labour migrants)
GDP growth (5-year average)	.187	.208	.092	.179	.174	.258†
	(.14)	(.14)	(.14)	(.14)	(.16)	(.14)
Industrialised countries, % foreign-born	-.001	-.010	-.005	-.011	-.012	-.018*
	(.01)	(.01)	(.01)	(.01)	(.01)	(.01)
Index labour market (paid employment)	-.245	-.591	-.282	-.871	-.766	-.948
	(.98)	(1.07)	(.91)	(.61)	(.99)	(.66)
Wage bargaining coordination	-.045					
	(.10)					
Wage bargaining coordination X access (emp.)	1.551†					
	(.82)					
Government intervention		-.168				
		(.11)				
Government intervention X access (emp.)		-.442				
		(1.27)				
Minimum wage setting			.017	.012		
			(.04)	(.03)		
Minimum wage setting X access (emp.)			-.735*	-.449†		
			(.32)	(.23)		
Minimum wage (% of median)					-.001	-.000
					(.00)	(.00)
Minimum wage X access (emp.)					-.058	-.045†
					(.04)	(.03)
Constant	-1.872***	-1.898***	-1.901***	-1.871***	-1.876***	-1.836***
	(.12)	(.13)	(.12)	(.12)	(.13)	(.12)
Intercept	-.888***	-.846***	-.929***	-.929***	-.834***	-.834***
	(.18)	(.18)	(.19)	(.19)	(.18)	(.18)

Var (countries)	.169	.184	.156	.156	.189	.189
Intra-class correlation	.049	.053	.045	.045	.054	.054
Log-likelihood	-6,296.990	-6,297.578	-6,296.324	-6,296.324	-6,297.781	-6,297.781
N (households)	15,150	15,150	15,150	15,150	15,150	15,150
N (countries)	19	19	19	19	19	19

Note: Coefficients (log odds) of random intercept logit models, standard errors in parentheses. All models are estimated including household-level variables (not shown).

† $p < .10$, * $p < .05$, ** $p < .01$, *** $p < .001$.

Appendix Table 4A.4. Determinants of immigrants' poverty reduction (60 per cent of median income, OECD equivalence scale)

	Model 1	Model 2a	Model 2b	Model 2b (permanent residents)	Model 3
GDP growth (5-year average)	-.121	.261†	.108	.179	.196
	(.18)	(.14)	(.17)	(.16)	(.24)
Industrialised countries, % foreign-born	.009	.006	-.003	-.016	-.012
	(.01)	(.01)	(.01)	(.01)	(.02)
Index access (unemployment)	2.886**				
	(1.05)				
Unemployment programmes (generosity)	1.569				
	(1.18)				
Unemployment programmes X access (progr.)	-13.075				
	(12.36)				
Index access (dual-earner)		-.466			
		(.54)			
Dual-earner programmes (generosity)		.031***			
		(.01)			

(Continued)

Appendix Table 4A.4. Continued

	Model 1	Model 2a	Model 2b	Model 2b (permanent residents)	Model 3
Dual-earner programmes X access (progr.)		-.019			
		(.02)			
Index access (traditional family benefits)			1.736*	2.545**	
			(.68)	(.78)	
Traditional family benefits (generosity)			.066*	.041	
			(.03)	(.03)	
Traditional family benefits X access (progr.)			.148	.120	
			(.10)	(.09)	
Index access (social assistance)					.104
					(.51)
Social assistance (generosity)					.025
					(.02)
Social assistance X access (progr.)					-.059
					(.05)
Constant	-2.693***	-2.638***	-2.661***	-2.692***	-2.591***
	(.16)	(.15)	(.16)	(.15)	(.19)
Intercept	-.798***	-1.021***	-.765***	-.854***	-.613**
	(.20)	(.22)	(.20)	(.20)	(.19)
Var (countries)	.203	.130	.216	.181	.294
Intra-class correlation	.058	.038	.062	.052	.082
Log-likelihood	-3,212.717	-3,209.084	-3,213.113	-3,211.621	-3,164.547
N (households)	15,150	15,150	15,150	15,150	14,891
N (countries)	19	19	19	19	18

Note: Coefficients (log odds) of random intercept logit models, standard errors in parentheses. All models are estimated including household-level variables (not shown).

$^+ p < .10$, $^* p < .05$, $^{**} p < .01$, $^{***} p < .001$.

Appendix Table 4A.5.   Determinants of immigrants' poverty based on market income (40 per cent of median income, OECD equivalence scale)

	Model 1a	Model 1b	Model 2a	Model 2a (labour migrants)	Model 2b	Model 2b (labour migrants)
GDP growth (5-year average)	.200	.184	.058	.089	.125	.175
	(.16)	(.16)	(.16)	(.17)	(.18)	(.15)
Industrialised countries, % foreign-born	-.004	-.012	-.003	-.007	-.011	-.014
	(.01)	(.01)	(.01)	(.01)	(.01)	(.01)
Index labour market (paid employment)	.415	-.208	.462	-.329	-.104	-.406
	(1.16)	(1.21)	(1.03)	(.70)	(1.09)	(.71)
Wage bargaining coordination	.010					
	(.11)					
Wage bargaining coordination X access (emp.)	1.286					
	(.97)					
Government intervention		-.160				
		(.12)				
Government intervention X access (emp.)		-1.219				
		(1.43)				
Minimum wage setting			.027	.018		
			(.04)	(.04)		
Minimum wage setting X access (emp.)			-.800*	-.569*		
			(.36)	(.26)		
Minimum wage (% of median)					.000	-.000
					(.01)	(.00)
Minimum wage X access (emp.)					-.080	-.070**
					(.05)	(.03)
Constant	-2.904***	-2.906***	-2.929***	-2.892***	-2.892***	-2.830***
	(.15)	(.15)	(.14)	(.14)	(.15)	(.14)
Intercept	-.715***	-.722***	-.805***	-.805***	-.741***	-.741***
	(.18)	(.18)	(.19)	(.19)	(.18)	(.18)
Var (countries)	.239	.236	.200	.200	.227	.227

(Continued)

Appendix Table 4A.5. Continued

	Model 1a	Model 1b	Model 2a	Model 2a (labour migrants)	Model 2b	Model 2b (labour migrants)
Intra-class correlation	.068	.067	.057	.057	.065	.065
Log-likelihood	−4,942.649	−4,942.508	−4,941.160	−4,941.160	−4,942.169	−4,942.169
N (households)	15,150	15,150	15,150	15,150	15,150	15,150
N (countries)	19	19	19	19	19	19

Note: Coefficients (log odds) of random intercept logit models, standard errors in parentheses. All models are estimated including household-level variables (not shown).

† p < .10, * p < .05, ** p < .01, *** p < .001.

Appendix Table 4A.6. Determinants of immigrants' poverty reduction (40 per cent of median income, OECD equivalence scale)

	Model 1	Model 2a	Model 2b	Model 2b (permanent residents)	Model 3
GDP growth (5-year average)	−.021	.332+	.188	.341+	.446
	(.24)	(.19)	(.22)	(.19)	(.29)
Industrialised countries, % foreign-born	.008	.008	−.002	−.025+	−.021
	(.01)	(.01)	(.01)	(.01)	(.02)
Index access (unemployment)	3.274*				
	(1.36)				
Unemployment programmes (generosity)	1.272				
	(1.53)				
Unemployment programmes X access (progr.)	3.993				
	(16.05)				
Index access (dual-earner)		−.713			
		(.74)			

	(1)	(2)	(3)	(4)	(5)
Dual-earner programmes (generosity)		.036***			
		(.01)			
Dual-earner programmes X access (progr.)		.017			
		(.03)			
Index access (traditional family benefits)			1.605⁺	3.344***	
			(.87)	(.90)	
Traditional family benefits (generosity)			.083*	.068*	
			(.04)	(.03)	
Traditional family benefits X access (progr.)			.249*	.294**	
			(.13)	(.10)	
Index access (social assistance)					-.088
					(.62)
Social assistance (generosity)					.026
					(.02)
Social assistance X access (progr.)					-.049
					(.06)
Constant	-2.777***	-2.847***	-2.770***	-2.852***	-2.670***
	(.18)	(.18)	(.18)	(.16)	(.21)
Intercept	-.503**	-.668***	-.489**	-.690***	-.392*
	(.18)	(.19)	(.18)	(.19)	(.18)
Var (countries)	.366	.263	.376	.252	.457
Intra-class correlation	.100	.074	.103	.071	.122
Log-likelihood	-3,710.511	-3,707.524	-3,710.605	-3,707.157	-3,670.114
N (households)	15,150	15,150	15,150	15,150	14,891
N (countries)	19	19	19	19	18

Note: Coefficients (log odds) of random intercept logit models, standard errors in parentheses. All models are estimated including household-level variables (not shown).

⁺ $p < .10$, * $p < .05$, ** $p < .01$, *** $p < .001$.

Appendix Table 4A.7. Determinants of immigrants' poverty based on market income (60 per cent of median income, square root scale)

	Model 1a	Model 1b	Model 2a	Model 2a (labour migrants)	Model 2b	Model 2b (labour migrants)
GDP growth (5-year average)	.205	.228+	.107	.194	.186	.285*
	(.14)	(.14)	(.14)	(.13)	(.15)	(.13)
Industrialised countries, % foreign-born	-.001	-.011	-.005	-.012	-.012	-.019*
	(.01)	(.01)	(.01)	(.01)	(.01)	(.01)
Index labour market (paid employment)	-.596	-.977	-.580	-1.051+	-1.088	-1.152+
	(.97)	(1.06)	(.89)	(.57)	(.96)	(.61)
Wage bargaining coordination	-.053					
	(.09)					
Wage bargaining coordination X access (emp.)	1.516+					
	(.81)					
Government intervention		-.160				
		(.11)				
Government intervention X access (emp.)		-.554				
		(1.26)				
Minimum wage setting			.014	.009		
			(.03)	(.03)		
Minimum wage setting X access (emp.)			-.776*	-.534*		
			(.31)	(.22)		
Minimum wage (% of median)					-.001	-.000
					(.00)	(.00)
Minimum wage X access (emp.)					-.066	-.054*
					(.04)	(.02)
Constant	-1.720***	-1.742***	-1.748***	-1.711***	-1.719***	-1.670***
	(.12)	(.13)	(.12)	(.11)	(.13)	(.12)
Intercept	-.901***	-.854***	-.961***	-.961***	-.864***	-.864***
	(.18)	(.18)	(.19)	(.19)	(.18)	(.18)

Var (countries)	.165	.181	.146	.146	.178	.178
Intra-class correlation	.048	.052	.043	.043	.051	.051
Log-likelihood	−6,257.578	−6,258.257	−6,256.581	−6,256.581	−6,258.088	−6,258.088
N (households)	15,150	15,150	15,150	15,150	15,150	15,150
N (countries)	19	19	19	19	19	19

Note: Coefficients (log odds) of random intercept logit models, standard errors in parentheses. All models are estimated including household-level variables (not shown).

$^+ p < .10, * p < .05, ** p < .01, *** p < .001.$

Appendix Table 4A.8.   Determinants of immigrants' poverty reduction (60 per cent of median income, square root scale)

	Model 1	Model 2a	Model 2b	Model 2b (permanent residents)	Model 3
GDP growth (5-year average)	−.167	.193	.081	.140	.156
	(.18)	(.15)	(.17)	(.17)	(.24)
Industrialised countries, % foreign-born	.012	.010	.002	−.011	−.008
	(.01)	(.01)	(.01)	(.01)	(.02)
Index access (unemployment)	3.076**				
	(1.02)				
Unemployment programmes (generosity)	1.848				
	(1.15)				
Unemployment programmes X access (progr.)	−1.734				
	(12.19)				
Index access (dual-earner)		−.257			
		(.57)			
Dual-earner programmes (generosity)		.029***			
		(.01)			

(Continued)

Appendix Table 4A.8. Continued

	Model 1	Model 2a	Model 2b	Model 2b (permanent residents)	Model 3
Dual-earner programmes X access (progr.)		-.019 (.02)			
Index access (traditional family benefits)			1.948** (.67)	2.659*** (.81)	
Traditional family benefits (generosity)			.059[+] (.03)	.031 (.03)	
Traditional family benefits X access (progr.)			.169[+] (.10)	.124 (.09)	
Index access (social assistance)					.224 (.52)
Social assistance (generosity)					.021 (.02)
Social assistance X access (progr.)					-.058 (.05)
Constant	-2.761*** (.16)	-2.710*** (.16)	-2.735*** (.16)	-2.769*** (.16)	-2.662*** (.19)
Intercept	-.826*** (.20)	-.959*** (.21)	-.770*** (.20)	-.825*** (.20)	-.599** (.19)
Var (countries)	.192	.147	.214	.192	.302
Intra-class correlation	.055	.043	.061	.055	.084
Log-likelihood	-3,167.917	-3,165.502	-3,168.632	-3,167.650	-3,123.579
N (households)	15,150	15,150	15,150	15,150	14,891
N (countries)	19	19	19	19	18

Note: Coefficients (log odds) of random intercept logit models, standard errors in parentheses. All models are estimated including household-level variables (not shown).

[+] $p < .10$, * $p < .05$, ** $p < .01$, *** $p < .001$.

Appendix Table 4A.9.   Determinants of immigrants' poverty based on market income (40 per cent of median income, square root scale)

	Model 1a	Model 1b	Model 2a	Model 2a (labour migrants)	Model 2b	Model 2b (labour migrants)
GDP growth (5-year average)	.193	.187	.046	.090	.117	.185
	(.16)	(.16)	(.16)	(.16)	(.17)	(.14)
Industrialised countries, % foreign-born	-.000	-.009	.001	-.004	-.008	-.012
	(.01)	(.01)	(.01)	(.01)	(.01)	(.01)
Index labour market (paid employment)	.088	-.482	.182	-.481	-.437	-.573
	(1.15)	(1.20)	(1.00)	(.67)	(1.06)	(.68)
Wage bargaining coordination	-.008					
	(.11)					
Wage bargaining coordination X access (emp.)	1.336					
	(.96)					
Government intervention		-.160				
		(.12)				
Government intervention X access (emp.)		-1.087				
		(1.42)				
Minimum wage setting			.031	.022		
			(.04)	(.04)		
Minimum wage setting X access (emp.)			-.863*	-.613*		
			(.35)	(.25)		
Minimum wage (% of median)					.001	.000
					(.01)	(.00)
Minimum wage X access (emp.)					-.086+	-.074**
					(.05)	(.03)
Constant	-2.712***	-2.718***	-2.738***	-2.697***	-2.698***	-2.632***
	(.14)	(.15)	(.13)	(.13)	(.14)	(.14)

(Continued)

Appendix Table 4A.9. Continued

	Model 1a	Model 1b	Model 2a	Model 2a (labour migrants)	Model 2b	Model 2b (labour migrants)
Intercept	-.730***	-.728***	-.846***	-.846***	-.765***	-.765***
	(.18)	(.18)	(.19)	(.19)	(.18)	(.18)
Var (countries)	.232	.233	.184	.184	.216	.216
Intra-class correlation	.066	.066	.053	.053	.062	.062
Log-likelihood	-4,952.841	-4,952.825	-4,950.911	-4,950.911	-4,952.185	-4,952.185
N (households)	15,150	15,150	15,150	15,150	15,150	15,150
N (countries)	19	19	19	19	19	19

Note: Coefficients (log odds) of random intercept logit models, standard errors in parentheses. All models are estimated including household-level variables (not shown).

† $p < .10$, * $p < .05$, ** $p < .01$, *** $p < .001$.

Appendix Table 4A.10. Determinants of immigrants' poverty reduction (40 per cent of median income, square root scale)

	Model 1	Model 2a	Model 2b	Model 2b (permanent residents)	Model 3
GDP growth (5-year average)	-.012	.304†	.179	.298†	.395
	(.22)	(.17)	(.20)	(.18)	(.26)
Industrialised countries, % foreign-born	.006	.007	-.002	-.022†	-.019
	(.01)	(.01)	(.01)	(.01)	(.02)
Index access (unemployment)	3.078*				
	(1.24)				
Unemployment programmes (generosity)	1.427				
	(1.40)				
Unemployment programmes X access (progr.)	4.511				
	(14.68)				

	(1)	(2)	(3)	(4)	(5)
Index access (*dual-earner*)	−.601				
	(.66)				
Dual-earner programmes (generosity)	.034***				
	(.01)				
Dual-earner programmes X access (progr.)	.018				
	(.03)				
Index access (*traditional family benefits*)			1.618*	3.012***	
			(.79)	(.86)	
Traditional family benefits (generosity)			.077**	.061*	
			(.04)	(.03)	
Traditional family benefits X access (progr.)			.251*	.275**	
			(.11)	(.10)	
Index access (*social assistance*)					.016
					(.58)
Social assistance (generosity)					.025
					(.02)
Social assistance X access (progr.)					−.032
					(.06)
Constant	−2.681***	−2.755***	−2.678***	−2.755***	−2.601***
	(.17)	(.16)	(.17)	(.15)	(.20)
Intercept	−.604**	−.791***	−.592**	−.745***	−.478**
	(.19)	(.19)	(.18)	(.19)	(.18)
Var (countries)	.299	.206	.306	.225	.385
Intra-class correlation	.083	.059	.085	.064	.105
Log-likelihood	−3,774.212	−3,770.922	−3,774.257	−3,771.614	−3,733.206
N (households)	15,150	15,150	15,150	15,150	14,891
N (countries)	19	19	19	19	18

Note: Coefficients (log odds) of random intercept logit models, standard errors in parentheses. All models are estimated including household-level variables (not shown).

$^{†}\, p < .10$, $^{*}\, p < .05$, $^{**}\, p < .01$, $^{***}\, p < .001$.

Appendix Table 4A.11.   Determinants of immigrants' poverty based on market income (excluding the United States)

	Model 1a	Model 1b	Model 2a	Model 2a (labour migrants)	Model 2b	Model 2b (labour migrants)
GDP growth (5-year average)	.158 (.14)	.104 (.14)	.085 (.14)	.123 (.16)	.115 (.15)	.168 (.15)
Industrialised countries, % foreign-born	-.001 (.01)	-.005 (.01)	-.003 (.01)	-.008 (.01)	-.004 (.01)	-.011 (.01)
Index labour market (paid employment)	.685 (1.13)	.453 (1.07)	.565 (1.05)	-.378 (.75)	.616 (1.11)	-.339 (.78)
Wage bargaining coordination	-.006 (.10)					
Wage bargaining coordination X access (emp.)	.783 (.91)					
Government intervention		-.132 (.10)				
Government intervention X access (emp.)		-1.559 (1.24)				
Minimum wage setting			.016 (.04)	.013 (.04)		
Minimum wage setting X access (emp.)			-.545 (.35)	-.379 (.24)		
Minimum wage (% of median)					-.001 (.00)	-.000 (.00)
Minimum wage X access (emp.)					-.047 (.04)	-.044+ (.02)
Constant	-2.506*** (.16)	-2.512*** (.16)	-2.506*** (.16)	-2.477*** (.16)	-2.510*** (.16)	-2.447*** (.16)
Intercept	-.886*** (.19)	-.941*** (.19)	-.939*** (.19)	-.946*** (.20)	-.907*** (.19)	-.959*** (.20)

Var (countries)	.170	.152	.153	.151	.163	.147
Intra-class correlation	.049	.044	.044	.044	.047	.043
Log-likelihood	-2,621.798	-2,620.846	-2,621.007	-2,620.996	-2,621.418	-2,620.773
N (households)	7,493	7,493	7,493	7,493	7,493	7,493
N (countries)	18	18	18	18	18	18

Note: Coefficients (log odds) of random intercept logit models, standard errors in parentheses. All models are estimated including household-level variables (not shown).

$^†p < .10$, $^*p < .05$, $^{**}p < .01$, $^{***}p < .001$.

Appendix Table 4A.12.   Determinants of immigrants' poverty reduction (excluding the United States)

	Model 1	Model 2a	Model 2b	Model 2b (permanent residents)	Model 3
GDP growth (5-year average)	-.124	.255	.287	.314	.410
	(.25)	(.17)	(.22)	(.26)	(.27)
Industrialised countries, % foreign-born	.010	.008	-.011	-.027	-.026
	(.01)	(.01)	(.01)	(.02)	(.02)
Index access (unemployment)	3.567**				
	(1.35)				
Unemployment programmes (generosity)	1.561				
	(1.29)				
Unemployment programmes X access (progr.)	-6.152				
	(15.37)				
Index access (dual-earner)		-.213			
		(.70)			
Dual-earner programmes (generosity)		.030***			
		(.01)			

(Continued)

Appendix Table 4A.12. Continued

	Model 1	Model 2a	Model 2b	Model 2b (permanent residents)	Model 3
Dual-earner programmes X access (progr.)	-.004				
	(.03)				
Index access (traditional family benefits)		1.301	2.984*		
		(.87)	(1.19)		
Traditional family benefits (generosity)		.056	.055+		
		(.04)	(.03)		
Traditional family benefits X access (progr.)		.377*	.291		
		(.19)	(.35)		
Index access (social assistance)					-.013
					(.62)
Social assistance (generosity)					.026
					(.02)
Social assistance X access (progr.)					-.035
					(.08)
Constant	-2.959***	-2.961***	-2.806***	-2.962***	-2.805***
	(.19)	(.19)	(.21)	(.20)	(.22)
Intercept	-.692***	-.789***	-.700***	-.865***	-.545**
	(.19)	(.20)	(.20)	(.20)	(.19)
Var (countries)	.250	.206	.247	.177	.336
Intra-class correlation	.071	.059	.070	.051	.093
Log-likelihood	-2,230.576	-2,229.104	-2,230.455	-2,227.759	-2,181.891
N (households)	7,493	7,493	7,493	7,493	7,234
N (countries)	18	18	18	18	17

Note: Coefficients (log odds) of random intercept logit models, standard errors in parentheses. All models are estimated including household-level variables (not shown).

+ p < .10, * p < .05, ** p < .01, *** p < .001.

Appendix Table 4A.13. Determinants of immigrants' poverty based on market income (jackknife estimations)

	Model 1a	Model 1b	Model 2a	Model 2a (labour migrants)	Model 2b	Model 2b (labour migrants)
GDP growth (5-year average)	.193	.209	.074	.129	.150	.220
	(.27)	(.28)	(.27)	(.24)	(.30)	(.21)
Industrialised countries, % foreign-born	-.001	-.011	-.003	-.008	-.012	-.017
	(.02)	(.03)	(.01)	(.01)	(.01)	(.01)
Index labour market (paid employment)	.232	-.219	.299	-.589	-.299	-.706
	(1.21)	(1.77)	(1.12)	(.96)	(1.41)	(1.00)
Wage bargaining coordination	-.053					
	(.18)					
Wage bargaining coordination X access (emp.)	1.489					
	(1.63)					
Government intervention		-.179				
		(.26)				
Government intervention X access (emp.)		-.881				
		(2.20)				
Minimum wage setting			.030	.022		
			(.05)	(.05)		
Minimum wage setting X access (emp.)			-.833	-.567		
			(.50)	(.41)		
Minimum wage (% of median)					.001	.001
					(.01)	(.01)
Minimum wage X access (emp.)					-.076	-.064
					(.06)	(.05)
Constant	-2.336***	-2.350***	-2.364***	-2.327***	-2.329***	-2.274***
	(.21)	(.21)	(.19)	(.19)	(.22)	(.23)

(Continued)

	Model 1a	Model 1b	Model 2a	Model 2a (labour migrants)	Model 2b	Model 2b (labour migrants)
Intercept	-.768**	-.751*	-.852**	-.875**	-.759**	-.873***
	(.22)	(.29)	(.23)	(.23)	(.25)	(.20)
Var (countries)	.215	.223	.182	.174	.219	.174
Intra-class correlation	.061	.063	.052	.050	.063	.050
Log-likelihood	-5,764.945	-5,765.157	-5,763.534	-5,763.326	-5,765.026	-5,763.280
N (households)	15,150	15,150	15,150	15,150	15,150	15,150
N (countries)	19	19	19	19	19	19

Note: Coefficients (log odds) of random intercept logit models, standard errors in parentheses. All models are estimated including household-level variables (not shown).

$^{\dagger} p < .10$, $^{*} p < .05$, $^{**} p < .01$, $^{***} p < .001$.

Appendix Table 4A.14. Determinants of immigrants' poverty reduction (jackknife estimations)

	Model 1	Model 2a	Model 2b	Model 2b (permanent residents)	Model 3
GDP growth (5-year average)	.268	.266	.094	.079	-.014
	(.19)	(.29)	(.25)	(.26)	(.25)
Industrialised countries, % foreign-born	-.019	.006	-.008	-.004	.002
	(.01)	(.01)	(.01)	(.02)	(.02)
Index access (unemployment)	-2.056				
	(1.35)				
Unemployment programmes (generosity)	-1.035				
	(1.24)				
Unemployment programmes X access (progr.)	3.759				
	(17.96)				

Index access (dual-earner)		−.326			
		(1.08)			
Dual-earner programmes (generosity)		.029+			
		(.01)			
Dual-earner programmes X access (progr.)		−.000			
		(.04)			
Index access (traditional family benefits)			−1.212*	−1.429	
			(.53)	(1.00)	
Traditional family benefits (generosity)			−.031	−.015	
			(.07)	(.06)	
Traditional family benefits X access (progr.)			.007	.015	
			(.15)	(.21)	
Index access (social assistance)					−.304
					(.57)
Social assistance (generosity)					−.018
					(.02)
Social assistance X access (progr.)					.093
					(.06)
Constant	−2.616***	−2.608***	−2.613***	−2.624***	−2.741***
	(.15)	(.39)	(.18)	(.17)	(.21)
Intercept	−.907*	−.859**	−1.013*	−.966*	−.944*
	(.33)	(.28)	(.44)	(.39)	(.35)
Var (countries)	.163	.179	.132	.145	.151
Intra-class correlation	.047	.052	.039	.042	.044
Log-likelihood	−6,191.612	−3,711.382	−6,190.365	−6,190.785	−6,069.564
N (households)	15,150	15,150	15,150	15,150	14,891
N (countries)	19	19	19	19	18

Note: Coefficients (log odds) of random intercept logit models, standard errors in parentheses. All models are estimated including household-level variables (not shown).

$^+ p < .10$, $^* p < .05$, $^{**} p < .01$, $^{***} p < .001$.

APPENDIX TABLES FOR METHODOLOGICAL APPENDIX

Appendix Table MA.1. **Number of households, by immigrant status (2007)**

	Place of birth			Nationality			
	Non-immigrants	Mixed	Immigrants	Non-immigrants	Mixed	Immigrants	Total
AU	3,660	612	770	–	–	–	5,042
	72.6%	12.1%	15.3%	–	–	–	
AT	4,049	347	539	4,341	321	273	4,935
	82.0%	7.0%	10.9%	88.0%	6.5%	5.5%	
BE	3,804	447	471	4,102	305	315	4,722
	80.6%	9.5%	10.0%	86.9%	6.5%	6.7%	
CA	3,739	659	896	–	–	–	5,294
	70.6%	12.4%	16.9%	–	–	–	
DK	3,951	230	132	4,090	156	67	4,313
	91.6%	5.3%	3.1%	94.8%	3.6%	1.6%	
FI	7,914	272	123	8,101	136	72	8,309
	95.2%	3.3%	1.5%	97.5%	1.6%	0.9%	
FR	6,300	673	530	6,951	304	248	7,503
	84.0%	9.0%	7.1%	92.6%	4.1%	3.3%	
DE	8,665	529	332	9,126	279	121	9,526
	91.0%	5.6%	3.5%	95.8%	2.9%	1.3%	
GR	3,449	185	261	3,594	113	188	3,895
	88.5%	4.7%	6.7%	92.3%	2.9%	4.8%	
IE	2,853	371	293	3,174	154	189	3,517
	81.1%	10.5%	8.3%	90.2%	4.4%	5.4%	
IT	13,507	789	664	14,063	328	569	14,960
	90.3%	5.3%	4.4%	94.0%	2.2%	3.8%	
NL	7,209	451	221	7,700	142	39	7,881
	91.5%	5.7%	2.8%	97.7%	1.8%	0.5%	
NO	4,110	312	241	4,355	202	106	4,663
	88.1%	6.7%	5.2%	93.4%	4.3%	2.3%	
PT (2008)	2,677	206	86	2,883	43	43	2,969
	90.2%	6.9%	2.9%	97.1%	1.4%	1.4%	
ES	8,330	451	506	8,651	240	396	9,287
	89.7%	4.9%	5.4%	93.2%	2.6%	4.3%	
SE	4,281	465	499	4,878	249	118	5,245
	81.6%	8.9%	9.5%	93.0%	4.7%	2.2%	
CH	3,503	611	760	3,889	427	558	4,874
	71.9%	12.5%	15.6%	79.8%	8.8%	11.4%	
UK	5,296	495	376	5,726	236	205	6,167
	85.9%	8.0%	6.1%	92.9%	3.8%	3.3%	
US	48,276	4,430	7,659	53,075	3,123	4,167	60,365
	80.0%	7.3%	12.7%	87.9%	5.2%	6.9%	
Total	145,573	12,535	15,359	153,224	7,062	7,887	173,467
	83.9%	7.2%	8.9%	91.1%	4.2%	4.7%	

Source: EU-SILC (European countries), HILDA (Australia), SLID (Canada), CPS (United States).

Appendix Table MA.2. Operationalisation of labour market and welfare state institutions

Variable	Operationalisation
Wage bargaining coordination	Index based on Kenworthy's classification of wage-setting coordination scores (excluding government intervention): 5 = (a) centralised bargaining by peak association(s), with or without government involvement and government imposition of wage schedule/freeze, with peace obligation (e.g. Sweden prior to 1980), (b) informal centralisation of industry-level bargaining by a powerful and monopolistic union confederation (e.g. Austria prior to 1983, (c) extensive, regularised pattern setting and highly synchronised bargaining coupled with coordination of bargaining by influential large firms (Japan prior to 1998); 4 = (a) centralised bargaining by peak associations with or without government involvement and government imposition of wage schedule/freeze, without peace obligation (e.g. Ireland 1987–2009); (b) informal (intra-associational and/or inter-associational) centralisation of industry and firm-level bargaining by peak associations (both sides) (e.g. Spain 2002–8); (c) extensive, regularised pattern setting coupled with high degree of union concentration (e.g. Germany most years); 3 = (a) informal (intra-associational or inter-associational) centralisation of industry and firm-level bargaining by peak associations (one side, or only some unions) with or without government participation (Italy since 2000), (b) industry-level bargaining with irregular and uncertain pattern setting and only moderate union concentration (e.g. Denmark 1981–86), (c) government arbitration or intervention (example: UK 1966–8, 1972–4); 2 = mixed industry and firm-level bargaining, with no or little pattern bargaining and relatively weak elements of government coordination through the setting of basic pay rates (statutory minimum wage) or wage indexation (example France most years); 1 = fragmented wage bargaining, confined largely to individual firms or plants (e.g. UK since 1980). *Source:* Visser (2013) ICTWSS.
Government intervention in wage bargaining	Index measuring government intervention in wage bargaining based on Hassel (2005): 5 = the government imposes private sector wage settlements, places a ceiling on bargaining outcomes or suspends bargaining; 4 = the government participates directly in wage bargaining (tripartite bargaining, as in social pacts); 3 = the government influences wage-bargaining outcomes indirectly through price ceilings, indexation, tax measures, minimum wages and pattern setting through public sector wages; 2 = the government influences wage bargaining by providing an institutional framework of consultation and information

(Continued)

Variable	Operationalisation
	exchange, by conditional agreement to extend private sector agreements and by providing a conflict resolution mechanism which links the settlement of disputes across the economy and/ or allows the intervention of state arbitrators or Parliament; 1 = none of the above. *Source*: Visser (2013) ICTWSS.
Minimum wage setting	Index measuring minimum wage setting: 8 = minimum wage is set by government, without fixed rule; 7 = minimum wage is set by government but government is bound by fixed rule (index-based minimum wage); 6 = minimum wage set by judges or expert committee, as in award-system; 5 = national minimum wage is set by government, but after (non-binding) tripartite consultations; 4 = national minimum wage is set through tripartite negotiations; 3 = national minimum wage is set by agreement (as in 1 or 2) but extended and made binding by law or Ministerial decree; 2 = minimum wages are set by national (cross-sectoral or inter-occupational) agreement ('autonomous agreement') between unions and employers; 1 = minimum wages are set by (sectoral) collective agreement or tripartite wage boards in (some) sectors; 0 = no statutory minimum wage, no sectoral or national agreements. *Source*: Visser (2013) ICTWSS.
Minimum wage (% of median wage)	Variable measuring the minimum wage (in local currency and PPP adjusted) in percentage of the median wage (local currency and PPP adjusted). *Source*: OECD (2015c).
Unemployment programmes	Variable measuring average net replacement rates during the initial phase of unemployment of six different household types (single person, one-earner and two-earner couples without and with two children) earning 67% and 134%, respectively, of the average wage. *Source*: OECD (2015c).
Dual earner programmes	Variable measuring maternity, paternity and parental leave for the year 2007/8: full-rate equivalent of paid parental leave. *Source*: OECD (2015c).
Traditional family benefits	Variable measuring average traditional family benefits of three different household types (lone parents, one- and two-earner couples) earning 67% and 134%, respectively, in percentage of the average wage. *Source*: OECD (2007b).
Social assistance	Variable measuring average minimum income protection of three different household types (single-, lone and two-parent family), in percentage of yearly average wage. *Source*: Nelson (2007) SaMip.

Appendix Table MA.3. Selected social programmes and data sources

Australia

Unemployment assistance	Newstart allowance: Social Security Act 1991, Vol.1, Part 2.12
Social assistance	Special benefit: Social Security Act 1991, Vol.2, Part 2.15
Maternity leave	Maternity payment (lump-sum): A New Tax System (Family Assistance) Act 1999, Division 2A
Child benefit	Family Tax Benefit Part A: A New Tax System (Family Assistance) Act 1999, Division 1A
Child-raising	Family Tax Benefit Part B: A New Tax System (Family Assistance) Act 1999, Division 1A
Childcare allowances	Child Care Benefit (CCB), Child Care Tax Rebate (CCTR): A New Tax System (Family Assistance) Act 1999, Division 4A
Lone-parent benefits	Parenting payment (PP): Social Security Act 1991, Vol.2, Part 2.10
Labour market access	Migration Act 1958, Migration Regulations 1994, Australian Government Department of Immigration and Citizenship.

Austria

Unemployment insurance	Arbeitslosengeld (unemployment benefit): Unemployment Insurance Act (Arbeitslosenversicherungsgesetz, ALVG) of 14 November 1977.
Unemployment assistance	Notstandshilfe (unemployment assistance): Unemployment Insurance Act (Arbeitslosenversicherungsgesetz, ALVG) of 14 November 1977.
Social assistance	Sozialhilfe (maternity allowance): Wiener Sozialhilfegesetz (WrSHG, WrLGBl 1973/11 zuletzt idF 2000/27).
Maternity leave	Wochengeld (maternity allowance): General Social Insurance Act (Allgemeines Sozialversicherungsgesetz, ASVG) of 9 September 1955.
Child benefit	Familienbeihilfe (family allowance): Families' Compensation Act (Familienlastenausgleichsgesetz) of 24 October 1967.
Child-raising benefits	Kinderbetreuungsgeld (childcare allowance): Child-raising Allowance Act (Kinderbetreuungsgeldgesetz, KBGG) of 7 August 2001.
Lone-parent benefits	Alleinverdiener- und Alleinerzieherabsetzbetrages (single earner and single parent tax allowance): Families' Compensation Act (Familienlastenausgleichsgesetz) of 24 October 1967. Income Tax Act (Einkommensteuergesetz, EStG) of 7 Juli 1988.
Additional family benefits	Kinderabsetzungsbetrag (child tax allowance): Families' Compensation Act (Familienlastenausgleichsgesetz) of 24 October 1967. Income Tax Act (Einkommensteuergesetz, EStG) of 7 Juli 1988.
Labour market access	Aliens Employment Act (Ausländerbeschäftigungsgesetz, AuslBG) of 20 March 1975.
Other sources:	Settlement and Residence Act (Niederlassung und Aufenthaltsgesetz, NAG)

(Continued)

Belgium

Unemployment insurance	Allocations de chômage (unemployment benefits): Royal Decree of 25 November 1991 with regulations concerning unemployment (Belgian Monitor of 31 December 1991). Ministerial decree concerning the schemes of application of unemployment regulations (Belgian Monitor of 25 January 1992).
Social assistance	Revenu d'intégration (integration income): Law of 26 May 2002 on the Right to social integration (Droit à l'intégration sociale).
Maternity leave	Indemnité de maternité (maternity benefit): Health Care and Sickness Benefit Compulsory Insurance Act (Loi relative à l'assurance obligatoire soins de santé et indemnités), co-ordinated on 14 July 1994, Royal Decree of 3 July 1996 on the execution of this Act and Regulation of 16 April 1997 on the execution of Article 80, 5° of this same Act.
Child benefit	Allocations familiales (family allowance): Royal Decree of 19 December 1939 on family allowances for employed workers.
Child-raising benefits	Congé parental (parental leave): Royal Decree of 29 October 1997 on the introduction of a right to parental leave.
Additional family benefits	Prestations familiales garanties (guaranteed family benefits): Law of 20 July 1971 on guaranteed family allowances.
Labour market access	Royal Decree of 30 April 1999 on the employment of foreign workers, Royal Decree of 3 February 2003 dispensing certain categories of immigrants from the obligation to obtain a professional card to pursue an independent activity.

Canada

Unemployment insurance	Employment Insurance: Employment Insurance Act S.C. 1996, c.23.
Unemployment assistance	Employment assistance (Ontario Works): Ontario Works Act, 1997 and Ontario Regulation 134/98.
Social assistance	Basic financial assistance/Income assistance (Ontario Works): Ontario Works Act, 1997 and Ontario Regulation 134/98.
Maternity leave	Maternity benefits: Employment Insurance Act S.C. 1996, c.23.
Child benefit	Canada Child Tax Benefit: Income Tax Act R.S.C., 1985, c.1 (Section 122.6).
Child-raising benefits	Parental care: Employment Insurance Act S.C. 1996, c.23.
Childcare allowances	Universal Child Care Benefit (UCCB): Universal Child Care Benefit Act S.C. 2006, c. 4, s. 168.
Labour market access	Immigration and Refugee Protection Regulations S.C. 2001, c.27.

Denmark

Unemployment insurance	Arbejdsløshedsforsikring (unemployment insurance): Con. Act No 874 of 11 September 2005 on unemployment insurance (om arbejdsløshedsforsikring mv).
Social assistance	Kontanthjælp (Social Bistand, social assistance): Con. Act No 1009 of 24 October 2005 on Active Social Policy (om aktiv social politik).

Maternity leave	Dagpenge ved fødsel (maternity cash benefit): Act. No. 566 of 9 June 2006 on right to leave and cash benefits in the event of birth (barselsloven).
Child benefit	Børne- og ungeydelse, børnetilskud (child benefit): Con. Act No 909 of 3 September 2004 on child benefits (om Børnetilskud).
Childcare allowances	Childcare allowances: MISSOC 2007.
Labour market access	Aliens Consolidation Act No. 945 of 1 September 2006, Aliens Order Nr. 63 of 22 January 2007

Finland

Unemployment insurance	Perustoimeentuloturva (basic security), ansioperusteinen sosiaaliturva (earnings-related security): Unemployment Allowances Act (Työttömyysturvalaki) of 30 December 2002. KELA (2008).
Unemployment assistance	Työmarkkinatuki (labour market support): Unemployment Allowances Act (Työttömyysturvalaki) of 30 December 2002. KELA (2008).
Social assistance	Toimeentulotuki (living allowance): Social Assistance Act (Laki toimeentulotuesta) of 30 December 1997. KELA (2008).
Maternity leave	Äitiysraha, vanhempainraha, isyysraha (maternity, parental and paternity allowance): Maternity Grant Act (Äitiysavustuslaki) of 28 May 1993. Sickness Insurance Act (Sairausvakuutuslaki) of 21 December 2004. KELA (2008).
Child benefit	Lapsilisä (child benefit): Child Allowances Act (Lapsilisälaki) of 21 August 1992. KELA (2008).
Child-raising benefits	Lasten kotihoidon tuki (child home care allowance): Act on children's home and personal care assistance 20.12.1996/1128 (Laki lasten kotihoidon ja yksityisen hoidon tuesta 20.12.1996/1128). KELA (2008).
Childcare allowances	Lasten yksityisen hoidon tuki (private childcare allowance): Act on children's home and personal care assistance 20.12.1996/1128, §7 (Laki lasten kotihoidon ja yksityisen hoidon tuesta 20.12.1996/1128).
Additional family benefits	Osittainen hoitoraha (partial childcare allowance): Act on children's home and personal care assistance 20.12.1996/1128, §13
Labour market access	Aliens Act (301/2004, amendments up to 619/2007 included)

France

Unemployment insurance	Assurance de chômage (unemployment insurance): Articles L351-3 to L351-8 of Labour Code (Code du travail).
Unemployment assistance	Régime de solidarité (unemployment assistance): Articles L351-9 to L351-11 of Labour Code (Code du travail).
Social assistance	Droit a l'integration sociale (right to social integration, former: Revenu Minimum d'Insertion, guaranteed minimum income): Social action and Family Code (Code de l'action sociale et de la famille), articles L262-1 and following.

(Continued)

Appendix Table MA.3.   Continued

Maternity leave	Indemnités journalières de maternité et de paternité (maternity and paternity benefits): Social Security Code (Code de la sécurité sociale, CSS), articles L331-1, and following.
Child benefit	Allocations familiales (family allowance): Social Security Code (Code de la sécurité sociale, CSS), Book V. Articles L511-1, and following.
Child-raising benefits	Complément de libre choix d'activité (CLCA, complement for child education choice): Social Security Code (Code de la sécurité sociale, CSS), Book V. Articles L531-1, and following.
Childcare allowances	Complément de libre choix de mode de garde (Colca, complement for childcare choice): Social Security Code (Code de la sécurité sociale, CSS), Book V. Articles L531-1, and following.
Lone-parent benefits	Allocation de parent isolé (API, single parent allowance): Social Security Code (Code de la sécurité sociale, CSS), Book V. Articles L524-1, and following.
Labour market access	Code on the entry and stay of foreigners and on asylum rights (Code de l'entrée et du séjour des étrangers et du droit d'asile)

Germany

Unemployment Insurance	Arbeitslosenversicherung (unemployment insurance): Social Code (Sozialgesetzbuch), Book III, of 24 March 1997.
Unemployment Assistance	Arbeitslosengeld II (unemployment benefit II): Social Code (Sozialgesetzbuch), Book II, of 24 December 2003.
Social assistance	Sozialhilfe (social assistance): Social Code (Sozialgesetzbuch), Book XII, of 27 December 2003.
Maternity leave	Mutterschaftsgeld (maternity benefit): Act on the protection of working mothers (Gesetz zum Schutze der erwerbstätigen Mutter, MuSchG) in the version promulgated on 20 June 2002 (BGBl. I p. 2318); as last amended by Article 32 of the Act of 14 November 2003 (BGBl. I p. 2190).
Child benefit	Kindergeld (child benefit): Federal Child Benefit Act (Bundeskindergeldgesetz, BKKG) in the version published on 14 April 1964. Income tax law (Einkommensteuergesetz; EStG) in the version published on 19 October 2002, last amended by Article 1 of the Act of 28 April 2006 (BGBl. I p.1095).
Child-raising benefits	Elterngeld (parental allowance): Federal Act on parental allowance and parental leave (Bundeselterngeld- und Elternzeitgesetz – BEEG, 5 December 2006).
Additional family benefits	Elternzeit (child-raising leave): Federal Act on parental allowance and parental leave (Bundeselterngeld- und Elternzeitgesetz – BEEG, 5 December 2006).
Labour market access	Residence Act (Aufenthaltsgesetz, AufenthG) of 30 July 2004.

Greece

Unemployment insurance	Unemployment insurance: Statutory Order No. 2961/1954. Law No. 1545/1985. Law No. 1892/1990.
Maternity leave	Maternity benefit (ΕΠΙΔΟΜΑ ΚΥΟΦΟ-ΡΙΑΣ-ΛΟΧΕΙΑΣ): Legislative Decree 1846 of 14 June 1951 on social insurance as amended.
Child benefit	Child benefit: Royal Order No. 20 of 23 December 1959. Presidential Order No. 527/1984. Presidential Order No. 412/1985

Labour market access	Act No. 3386 on the entry, residence and social integration of third-country nationals into the Greek territory of 23 August 2005. Presidential Decree No. 131 on the harmonisation of the Hellenic Legislation with the Directive 2003/86/EC concerning the right of family reunification of 13 July 2006. Presidential Decree No. 150 of 29 July 2006 on the adaptation of the directive 2003/109/EC concerning the status of TCNs who are long-term residents.

Ireland

Unemployment insurance	Unemployment Benefits: Social Welfare Consolidation Act 2005, Part 2, Chp. 12, Sect. 62–68.
Unemployment assistance	Unemployment Assistance: Social Welfare Consolidation Act 2005, Part 3, Chp. 2, Sect. 140–148.
Social assistance	Supplementary Welfare Allowance: Social Welfare Consolidation Act 2005, Part 3, Chp. 9, Sect. 187–208.
Maternity leave	Maternity benefit: Social Welfare Consolidation Act 2005, Part 2, Chp. 9, Sect. 47–51.
Child benefit	Child Benefit: Social Welfare Consolidation Act 2005, Part 4, Sect. 219–223.
Lone-parent benefits	One Parent Family Payment: Social Welfare Consolidation Act 2005, Part 3, Chp. 9, Sect. 172–178.
Additional family benefits	Family Income Supplement: Social Welfare Consolidation Act 2005, Part 6, Sect. 227–233.
Labour market access	Employment Permit Act 2006.

Italy

Unemployment insurance	Indennità ordinaria di disoccupazione (ordinary unemployment benefit); l'assicurazione contro la disoccupazione (unemployment insurance): Law No. 427 of 6 August 1975. Law No. 160 of 20 May 1988. Law No. 223 of 23 July 1991. Law No. 80 of 14 May 2005.
Social assistance	Minimo vitale (minimum income): Regulation No. 19 of 6 February 2006 on the interventions and social services of the community of Milano.
Maternity leave	Indennità di maternità, congedo di maternità/paternità (maternity benefit, maternity/paternity leave): Law No. 1204 of 30 December 1971 on the protection of working mothers. Law No. 903 of 9 December 1977 on equal treatment between men and women. Law No. 53 of 8 March 2000 on provisions for maternity and paternity support.
Child benefit	L'assegno per il nucleo familiare (family allowance): Decree of 30 May 1955. Law of 17 October 1961. Law No. 153 of 13 May 1988 (family benefits). Decree No. 306 of 15 July 1999. Decree No. 452 of 21 December 2000. Law No. 296 of 27 December 2006.
Labour market access	Decree-Law No. 286 of 25 July 1998 concerning immigration and the condition of TCNs. Decree of the President of the Republic No. 394 of 31 August 1999.

(*Continued*)

Netherlands

Unemployment insurance	Unemployment Insurance (WW): Unemployment Benefit Act (Werkloosheidswet, WW).
Social assistance	Algemene Bijstand (general assistance): Work and Social Assistance Act (Wet Werk en Bijstand, WWB).
Maternity leave	Zwangerschaps- en bevallingsverlof (pregnancy and maternity leave): Work and Care Act (Wet arbeid en zorg, WAZO).
Child benefit	Algemene Kinderbijslag (general child benefit): General Child Benefit Act (Algemene Kinderbijslagwet, AKW).
Labour market access	Aliens employment Act of 21 December 1994 (Wet arbeid vreemdelingen). Aliens employment order of 23 August 1995 (Besluit uitvoering Wet arbeid vreemdelingen 1994).

Norway

Unemployment insurance	Dagpenger (unemployment benefit): National Insurance Act (folketrygdloven) of 28 February 1997, Chapter 4.
Social assistance	Stønad til livsopphold (sosialhjelp, subsistence allowance): Act on Social Services of 13 December 1991, Rundskriv I-34/2001.
Maternity leave	Foreldrepenger (parental benefit): National Insurance Act (folketrygdloven) of 28 February 1997, Chapter 14.
Child benefit	Barnetrygd (child benefit): Child Benefit Act (barnetrygdloven) of 8 March 2002.
Child-raising benefits	Engangsstønad ved fødsel (lump-sum maternity grant): National Insurance Act (folketrygdloven) of 28 February 1997, Chapter 14.
Childcare allowances	Kontantstøtte (Monthly Cash Benefit for Parents with Small Children): Act on Cash Benefit for Parents with Small Children (kontantstøtteloven) of 26 June 1998.
Lone-parent benefits	Stønad til enslig mor eller far (benefit for single mother or father): National Insurance Act (folketrygdloven) of 28 February 1997, Chapter 15.
Additional family benefits	Stønad til barnetilsyn (childcare benefit): National Insurance Act (folketrygdloven) of 28 February 1997, Chapter 15.
Labour market access	Immigration Act No. 64. of 24 June 1988. Immigration Regulations No.1028 of 21 December 1990.

Portugal

Unemployment insurance	Subsídio de desemprego (unemployment benefit): Statutory Decree 220/2006 of 3 November 2006.
Unemployment assistance	Subsídio social de desemprego (unemployment assistance): Statutory Decree 220/2006 of 3 November 2006.
Social assistance	Rendimento social de inserção/rendimento minimo garantido (Social insertion income/guaranteed minimum income): Law 13/03 of 21 May 2003. Statutory Decree 283/03 of 8 November 2003. Statutory Decree 45/05 of 29 August 2005.
Maternity leave	Protecção da maternidade (e da paternidade, maternity/paternity protection): Law 99/2003 of 27 August 2003. Law 35/2004 of 29 July 2004. Statutory Decree 154/88 of 29 April 1988 modified by Statutory Decree 333/95 of 23 December 1995. Statutory Decree 347/98 of 9 November 1998. Statutory Decree 77/2000 of 9 May 2000. Statutory Decree 77/2005 of 13 April 2005

Child benefit	Prestações familiares (family benefits): Law 32/02 of 20 December 2002. Statutory Decree 176/03 of 02 August 2003.
Labour market access	Decree-Law No. 34 concerning the conditions and procedures on the entry, permanence, exit and removal of foreign citizens from Portuguese territory, as well as the status of long-term residents of 25 February 2003. Enabling Decree No. 6 of 26 April 2004.

Spain

Unemployment insurance	Protección por desempleo (prestación), unemployment protection (benefits): Royal Decree No. 625/85 of 2 April 1985; Social Security General Act (Ley General de la Seguridad Social) approved by Legislative Royal Decree No. 1/94 of 20 June 1994; Law No. 45/2002 of 12 December 2002; Law No. 52/2003 on Employment of 16 December 2003; Royal Decree No. 3/2004 of 25 June 2004; Royal Decree No. 200/2006 of 17 February 2006; Royal Decree No. 1369/2006 of 24 November 2006.
Unemployment assistance	Protección por desempleo (subsidio), unemployment protection (subsidy): see 'unemployment insurance' above
Social assistance	Renta mínima de inserción (integration minimum income): Law No. 15/2001 on the minimum income in the community of Madrid (Ley de renta mínima de inserción en la comunidad de Madrid).
Maternity leave	Prestación por maternidad (maternity benefit): Social Security General Act (Ley General de la Seguridad Social) approved by Legislative Royal Decree No. 1/94 of 20 June 1994. Legislative Decree No. 1/95 of 24 March 1995. Law No. 39/99 of 5 November 1999 on conciliation of Labour and Family Life for workers (Ley sobre conciliación de la vida familiar y laboral de las personas trabajadoras). Royal Decree No. 1252/2001 of 16 November 2001.
Child benefit	Prestaciones por hijo a cargo (child benefit): Social Security General Act (Ley General de la Seguridad Social) approved by Legislative Royal Decree No. 1/94 of 20 June 1994. Royal Decree No. 1335/2005 of 11 November 2005.
Labour market access	Organic Law No. 4 on the Rights and Freedoms of Aliens in Spain and their Social Integration of 11 January 2000, amended by Organic Law 8/2000, Organic Law 11/2003 and Organic Law 14/2003. Implementing Regulation of Organic Law 4/2000, Official State Bulletin No. 174. 21 July 2001, amended by Royal Decree 864/2001 and 2393/2004.

Sweden

Unemployment insurance	Inkomstbortfallsförsäkring (earnings-related benefit): Unemployment Insurance Act (Lag om arbetslöshetsförsäkring) of 29 May 1997 and Regulation of 13 November 1997.
Unemployment assistance	Grundförsäkring (basic allowance): Unemployment Insurance Act (Lag om arbetslöshetsförsäkring) of 29 May 1997 and Regulation of 13 November 1997.
Social assistance	Ekonomiskt bistånd (socialbidrag), financial assistance (social assistance): Social Services Act No. 453 of 7 June 2001. Law of January 2002.

(Continued)

Appendix Table MA.3. Continued

Maternity leave	Föräldrapenning (parental benefits): National Insurance Act (Lag om allmän försäkring) No. 381 of 25 May 1962. Law on parental insurance (föräldraförsäkring) of January 1974. Law on Parental Leave (föräldraledighetslag) No. 584 of 24 May 1995.
Child benefit	Barnbidrag (child benefit): General Child Benefit Act (Lag om allmänna barnbidrag) No. 529 of 26 June 1947.
Labour market access	Aliens Act No. 716 of 29 March 2005. Aliens Ordinance No. 97 of 23 February 2006.

Switzerland

Unemployment insurance	Arbeitslosenversicherung (unemployment insurace): Federal Law on compulsory unemployment insurance and allowances in case of insolvency of 25 June 1982 (Bundesgesetz über die obligatorische Arbeitslosenversicherung und die Insolvenzentschädigung). Federal law on general provisions concerning legislation on social insurances of 6 October 2000 (Bundesgesetz über den Allgemeinen Teil des Sozialversicherungsrechts).
Social assistance	Sozialhilfe (social assistance): Canton Zurich: Social Assistance Law (Zürcher Sozialhilfegesetz) of 14 June 1981.
Maternity leave	Mutterschaftsentschädigung (maternity allowance): Federal law on income compensation allowances in case of service and in case of maternity of 25 September 1952 (Bundesgesetz über den Erwerbsersatz für Dienstleistende und bei Mutterschaft). Federal law on general provisions concerning legislation on social insurances of 6 October 2000 (Bundesgesetz über den Allgemeinen Teil des Sozialversicherungsrechts).
Child benefit	Kinderzulage (child allowance): Canton Zurich: Law on the child allowance for employees (Zürcher Gesetz über Kinderzulagen für Arbeitnehmer) of 8 June 1958.
Labour market access	Federal law and regulations on the temporary and permanent residence of foreign nationals (Bundesgesetz und Verordnung über den Aufenthalt und Niederlassung der Ausländer, ANAG/ANAV). Regulations on the numerical limitation of foreigners (Verordnung über die Begrenzung der Zahl der Ausländer, BVO).

United Kingdom

Unemployment insurance	Contribution-based jobseeker's allowance: Jobseekers Act 1995. CPAG (2008).
Unemployment assistance	Income-based jobseeker's allowance: Jobseekers Act 1995. CPAG (2008).
Social assistance	Income support: Income Support (General) Regulations 1987. Social Security Administration Act 1992. CPAG (2008).
Maternity leave	Statutory maternity pay and maternity allowance: Social Security Contributions and Benefits Act 1992. Social Security Administration Act 1992. The Welfare Reform and Pension Act 1999. Employment Act 2002. CPAG (2008).

Child benefit	Child benefit: Social Security Contributions and Benefits Act 1992. CPAG (2008).			
Childcare allowances	Working tax credit: The Tax Credits Act 2002. CPAG (2008).			
Additional family benefits	Child tax credit: The Tax Credits Act 2002. CPAG (2008).			
Labour market access	Immigration Act of 28 October 1971, Immigration rules.			
United States				
Unemployment insurance	Unemployment Insurance: Michigan Employment Security Act 1 of 1936 (Ex. Sess.). Country chapter benefits and wages (OECD 2007b).			
Social assistance	Supplemental Security Income (SSI), Food Stamps: Code of Federal Regulations, Title 8 – Aliens and Nationality.			
Child benefit	Temporary Assistance for Needy Families (TANF): Code of Federal Regulations, Title 8 – Aliens and Nationality.			
Labour market access	Immigration and Nationality Act of 1952. Code of Federal Regulations – Aliens and Nationality.			

Appendix Table MA.4.   Descriptive statistics – country-level variables

	Mean	*SD*	*Min.*	*Max.*
Dependent variables				
Poverty rates (MI, migrants)	35.1	11.5	18.5	52.3
Poverty rates based on market income (non-migrants)	17.6	3.4	9.2	26.0
Poverty rates based on market income (mixed)	17.4	4.5	7.6	24.1
Poverty rates based on disposable income (migrants)	20.4	5.1	9.0	29.7
Poverty rates based on disposable income (non-migrants)	8.3	3.1	4.1	14.5
Poverty rates based on disposable income (mixed)	8.4	3.4	2.7	14.6
Poverty reduction (migrants)	34.5	29.3	−20.0	81.9
Poverty reduction (non-migrants)	52.5	16.2	28.5	69.7
Poverty reduction (mixed)	50.4	19.2	14.8	81.1
AME coefficients based on market income (raw, migrants)	13.4	7.9	2.3	24.4
AME coefficients based on market income (raw, mixed)	−0.6	5.1	−13.3	8.1
AME coefficients based on market income (net, migrants)	4.3	2.2	0.8	9.9
AME coefficients based on market income (net, mixed)	2.3	2.2	−3.3	6.3
AME coefficients based on disposable income (raw, migrants)	8.4	2.6	2.4	13.1
AME coefficients based on disposable income (raw, mixed)	−0.2	3.1	−6.0	5.0
AME coefficients based on disposable income (net, migrants)	4.3	2.5	0.4	9.8
AME coefficients based on disposable income (net, mixed)	1.8	2.2	−3.6	4.3
Independent variables				
Index labour market (paid employment)	.71	.11	.50	.87
Index labour market (paid employment, permanent residents)	1.00	.00	1.00	1.00

(Continued)

Appendix Table MA.4.   Continued

	Mean	SD	Min.	Max.
Index labour market (paid employment, permanent residents, family members)	.93	.14	.67	1.00
Index labour market (paid employment, labour migrants)	.47	.18	.17	.67
Index labour market (paid employment, labour migrants, family members)	.68	.32	.00	1.00
Index access (unemployment)	.39	.12	.25	.63
Index access (unemployment, permanent residents)	.46	.17	.25	.75
Index access (unemployment, permanent residents, family members)	.42	.16	.25	.75
Index access (unemployment, labour migrants)	.34	.16	.00	.50
Index access (unemployment, labour migrants, family members)	.34	.16	.00	.50
Index access (parental leave)	.51	.24	.00	1.00
Index access (parental benefits, permanent residents)	.54	.26	.00	1.00
Index access (parental benefits, permanent residents, family members)	.53	.26	.00	1.00
Index access (parental benefits, labour migrants)	.51	.24	.00	1.00
Index access (parental benefits, labour migrants, family members)	.48	.22	.00	1.00
Index access (traditional family benefits)	.75	.24	.13	1.00
Index access (traditional family benefits, permanent residents)	.89	.20	.25	1.00
Index access (traditional family benefits, permanent residents, family members)	.86	.20	.25	1.00
Index access (traditional family benefits, labour migrants)	.63	.35	.00	1.00
Index access (traditional family benefits, labour migrants, family members)	.63	.35	.00	1.00
Index access (social assistance)	.55	.33	.00	1.00
Index access (social assistance, permanent residents)	.84	.33	.00	1.00
Index access (social assistance, permanent residents, family members)	.58	.36	.00	1.00
Index access (social assistance, labour migrants)	.38	.42	.00	1.00
Index access (social assistance, labour migrants, family members)	.38	.42	.00	1.00
Wage bargaining coordination	2.9	1.2	1.0	5.0
Government intervention	2.6	1.1	1.0	5.0
Minimum wage setting	4.0	3.0	1.0	8.0
Minimum wage (% of median wage)	27.9	25.2	0.0	63.3
Unemployment programmes (generosity)	.72	.11	.44	.88
Dual-earner programmes (generosity)	26.4	17.8	0.0	66.2
Traditional family benefits (generosity)	9.0	5.0	0.0	18.5
Social assistance (generosity)[a]	40.6	11.0	18.9	65.8
Industrialised countries, % foreign-born	38.9	14.5	13.1	79.3
Permit based statistics, work (%), 2003–2007[a]	13.7	10.6	0.6	36.4
Permit based statistics, family (incl. accompanying family) (%), 2003–2007[a]	39.4	15.1	15.9	71.7
Permit based statistics, humanitarian (%), 2003–2007[a]	9.1	6.5	0.1	21.9
GDP growth (5-year average)	2.8	0.9	1.2	4.7

	Mean	SD	Min.	Max.
Unemployment rate (%)	5.8	2.0	2.5	8.7
Unemployment rate (migrants)	9.1	3.6	3.3	16.3
Employment rates (diff. btw. foreign and native-born)	0.8	9.0	−10.8	17.8
Size of the shadow economy (in % of official GDP, 2007)	14.3	4.8	7.2	25.1

Note: All variables are uncentred and N = 19 if not mentioned otherwise, except missing data for Greecedata missing for Greece.

[a] Data missing for Greece.

Source: EU-SILC (European countries), HILDA (Australia), SLID (Canada) and CPS (United States).

Appendix Table MA.5. Descriptive statistics – household-level variables (immigrant and full sample)

	Migrant households				All households			
	Mean	SD	Min./Max.	N	Mean	SD	Min./Max.	N
Dependent variables:								
Poverty rates (MI)	.30	.46	0/1	15,359	.19	.40	0/1	173,467
Poverty rates (DPI)	.23	.42	0/1	15,359	.11	.32	0/1	173,467
Poverty reduction								
Ref. not poor (both MI and DPI)	.68	.47	0/1	15,359	.79	.41	0/1	173,467
Poor (only MI)	.10	.30	0/1	15,359	.09	.29	0/1	173,467
Poor (only DPI)	.02	.15	0/1	15,359	.01	.11	0/1	173,467
Poor (MI and DPI)	.20	.40	0/1	15,359	.10	.30	0/1	173,467
Independent variables (household):								173,467
Ref. non-immigrant	–	–	–	–	.84	.37	–	173,467
Immigrant	–	–	–	–	.09	.28	–	173,467
Mixed	–	–	–	–	.07	.26	–	173,467
Ref. low education	.23	.42	0/1	15,162	.13	.34	0/1	172,938
Medium	.24	.43	0/1	15,162	.29	.46	0/1	172,938
High	.27	.44	0/1	15,162	.24	.43	0/1	172,938
Mixed, low	.12	.32	0/1	15,162	.13	.33	0/1	172,938
Mixed	.05	.22	0/1	15,162	.05	.22	0/1	172,938
Mixed, high	.10	.30	0/1	15,162	.16	.36	0/1	172,938
Ref. low-service functionaries	.16	.36	0/1	15,345	.09	.28	0/1	173,382
Blue-collar workers	.21	.41	0/1	15,345	.13	.34	0/1	173,382
Mixed service functionaries	.06	.24	0/1	15,345	.07	.26	0/1	173,382
Socio-cultural professionals	.11	.32	0/1	15,345	.13	.34	0/1	173,382
Capital accumulators	.11	.31	0/1	15,345	.09	.29	0/1	173,382
Mixed skills, low	.11	.31	0/1	15,345	.12	.33	0/1	173,382
Mixed skills	.15	.36	0/1	15,345	.25	.43	0/1	173,382

(Continued)

Appendix Table MA.5. Continued

	Migrant households				All households			
	Mean	SD	Min./Max.	N	Mean	SD	Min./Max.	N
Mixed skills, high	.03	.17	0/1	15,345	.07	.25	0/1	173,382
Other	.06	.24	0/1	15,345	.05	.21	0/1	173,382
Ref. no one employed	.11	.31	0/1	15,350	.10	.30	0/1	173,427
One person	.50	.50	0/1	15,350	.40	.49	0/1	173,427
Multiple earners	.39	.49	0/1	15,350	.50	.50	0/1	173,427
Ref. no one employed atypically	.58	.49	0/1	15,350	.56	.50	0/1	173,427
At least one person	.22	.41	0/1	15,350	.28	.45	0/1	173,427
All	.20	.40	0/1	15,350	.17	.37	0/1	173,427
Ref. no one self-employed	.88	.33	0/1	15,350	.83	.37	0/1	173,427
At least one person	.06	.23	0/1	15,350	.10	.30	0/1	173,427
All	.07	.25	0/1	15,350	.07	.25	0/1	173,427
Number of children, aged ≤2	.17	.43	0/4	15,359	.13	.38	0/4	173,467
Number of children, aged 3–5	.18	.44	0/4	15,359	.13	.38	0/4	173,467
Number of children, aged 6–12	.42	.72	0/5	15,359	.33	.66	0/5	173,467
Number of children, aged 13–17	.30	.61	0/6	15,359	.26	.56	0/6	173,467
Number of persons, aged ≥65	.07	.31	0/4	15,359	.08	.33	0/4	173,467

Note: Ref. = used as reference category for the analysis in chapter 4.

Source: EU-SILC (European countries), HILDA (Australia), SLID (Canada) and CPS (United States).

Appendix Table MA.6. Descriptive statistics – household-level variables, by country (immigrant sample)

Migrant households	DK	NO	SE	FI	AT	BE	DE	CH	FR	NL
Dependent variables										
Poverty rates (MI)	.37	.37	.44	.46	.24	.43	.40	.19	.38	.29
Poverty rates (DPI)	.16	.22	.19	.20	.15	.26	.21	.15	.15	.07
Poverty reduction										
Ref. not poor (both MI and DPI)	.61	.59	.55	.53	.75	.55	.58	.78	.60	.71
Poor (only MI)	.23	.19	.26	.28	.11	.20	.21	.08	.25	.22
Poor (only DPI)	.02	.04	.01	.01	.02	.02	.02	.03	.02	.00
Poor (MI and DPI)	.14	.18	.17	.19	.13	.23	.19	.11	.14	.07
Independent variables (household)										

Migrant households	DK	NO	SE	FI	AT	BE	DE	CH	FR	NL
Ref. low education	.21	.32	.15	.12	.20	.20	.11	.16	.41	.18
Medium	.27	.23	.32	.38	.37	.29	.29	.27	.19	.34
High	.23	.28	.18	.26	.14	.32	.32	.25	.19	.24
Mixed, low	.13	.09	.15	.09	.20	.07	.07	.17	.12	.10
Mixed	.05	.05	.05	.05	.02	.03	.05	.04	.04	.04
Mixed, high	.12	.03	.14	.10	.07	.09	.16	.11	.05	.10
Ref. low-service functionaries	.16	.24	.20	.19	.24	.23	.10	.18	.16	.14
Blue-collar workers	.22	.14	.21	.19	.25	.20	.15	.17	.22	.14
Mixed service functionaries	.05	.04	.04	.02	.04	.11	.09	.06	.08	.13
Socio-cultural professionals	.21	.17	.14	.18	.07	.09	.18	.21	.10	.25
Capital accumulators	.03	.10	.04	.13	.04	.07	.03	.09	.06	.07
Mixed skills, low	.08	.07	.15	.04	.23	.11	.19	.10	.21	.03
Mixed skills	.11	.08	.09	.05	.09	.09	.17	.12	.09	.13
Mixed skills, high	.03	.03	.02	.04	.01	.03	.05	.05	.03	.04
Other	.12	.13	.10	.16	.03	.07	.05	.02	.05	.08
Ref. no one employed	.23	.22	.19	.25	.13	.32	.28	.14	.25	.19
One person	.52	.50	.45	.53	.51	.50	.49	.59	.52	.56
Multiple earners	.26	.28	.36	.22	.36	.18	.23	.27	.23	.25
Ref. no one employed atypically	.71	.68	.54	.42	.51	.49	.44	.58	.50	.39
At least one person	.19	.17	.25	.30	.26	.28	.37	.18	.27	.25
All	.10	.15	.21	.28	.24	.23	.19	.24	.23	.35
Ref. no one self-employed	.90	.88	.88	.78	.93	.91	.93	.92	.93	.93
At least one person	.03	.06	.06	.11	.02	.04	.03	.03	.03	.03
All	.07	.06	.06	.11	.05	.05	.04	.05	.05	.05
Number of children, aged ≤2	.17	.16	.15	.21	.17	.19	.14	.12	.16	.12
Number of children, aged 3–5	.20	.18	.14	.16	.16	.16	.13	.13	.19	.14
Number of children, aged 6–12	.41	.37	.36	.40	.36	.37	.32	.39	.45	.34
Number of children, aged 13–17	.42	.28	.46	.45	.28	.24	.21	.24	.36	.21
Number of persons, aged ≥65	.04	.01	.05	.02	.03	.02	.04	.04	.06	.00
N	132	241	499	123	539	471	332	760	530	221

(Continued)

Migrant households	UK	AU	CA	US	IE	ES	GR	IT	PT
Dependent variables									
Poverty rates (MI)	.34	.26	.26	.31	.36	.25	.25	.19	.22
Poverty rates (DPI)	.19	.17	.16	.27	.14	.26	.25	.23	.17
Poverty reduction									
Ref. not poor (both MI and DPI)	.64	.74	.73	.68	.63	.68	.68	.73	.74
Poor (only MI)	.16	.09	.10	.05	.22	.06	.07	.04	.08
Poor (only DPI)	.02	.00	.00	.02	.00	.08	.07	.08	.03
Poor (MI and DPI)	.17	.17	.16	.25	.14	.19	.17	.15	.14
Independent variables (household)									
Ref. low education	.15	.29	.09	.23	.16	.32	.28	.38	.45
Medium	.33	.13	.05	.23	.23	.23	.33	.37	.17
High	.30	.40	.54	.27	.40	.13	.10	.06	.19
Mixed, low	.09	.08	.04	.12	.06	.18	.13	.13	.08
Mixed	.02	.08	.15	.04	.03	.06	.03	.02	.05
Mixed, high	.10	.03	.13	.10	.12	.08	.12	.04	.06
Ref. low-service functionaries	.20	.09	.12	.14	.20	.24	.14	.25	.20
Blue-collar workers	.15	.11	.13	.22	.11	.20	.32	.35	.16
Mixed service functionaries	.07	.12	.14	.05	.06	.02	.03	.04	.05
Socio-cultural professionals	.16	.21	.10	.09	.13	.05	.03	.07	.14
Capital accumulators	.10	.10	.08	.15	.10	.03	.02	.03	.05
Mixed skills, low	.08	.05	.05	.08	.16	.37	.30	.14	.30
Mixed skills	.13	.09	.24	.19	.14	.06	.11	.08	.08
Mixed skills, high	.06	.04	.02	.03	.03	.01	.00	.00	.01
Other	.05	.18	.12	.05	.05	.02	.04	.03	.01
Ref. no one employed	.16	.17	.09	.05	.22	.10	.08	.09	.07
One person	.49	.55	.44	.49	.43	.36	.51	.66	.53
Multiple earners	.34	.29	.47	.46	.35	.54	.41	.25	.40
Ref. no one employed atypically	.63	.53	.60	.63	.49	.29	.47	.55	.55
At least one person	.19	.19	.23	.20	.26	.35	.18	.17	.19
All	.18	.28	.16	.16	.25	.36	.35	.28	.27
Ref. no one self-employed	.90	.82	.80	.88	.90	.87	.83	.84	.87
At least one person	.05	.07	.11	.06	.04	.07	.07	.05	.07
All	.05	.12	.09	.06	.05	.06	.10	.10	.06
Number of children, aged ≤2	.16	.09	.08	.19	.14	.22	.16	.19	.14
Number of children, aged 3–5	.15	.10	.12	.22	.18	.20	.17	.13	.10

Migrant households	UK	AU	CA	US	IE	ES	GR	IT	PT
Number of children, aged 6–12	.42	.27	.38	.49	.34	.42	.25	.26	.27
Number of children, aged 13–17	.24	.27	.30	.32	.23	.28	.25	.17	.31
Number of persons, aged ≥65	.07	.05	.18	.09	.01	.05	.06	.02	.06
N	376	770	896	7,659	293	506	261	664	86

Note: Ref. = reference category used for the analysis in chapter 4.

Source: EU-SILC (European countries), HILDA (Australia), SLID (Canada) and CPS (United States).

Appendix Table MA.7. Descriptive statistics – household-level variables, by country (full sample)

Migrant households	DK	NO	SE	FI	AT	BE	DE	CH	FR	NL
Dependent variables										
Poverty rates (MI)	.12	.17	.16	.19	.19	.24	.22	.11	.18	.14
Poverty rates (DPI)	.04	.08	.06	.07	.07	.09	.10	.07	.06	.03
Poverty reduction										
Ref. not poor (both MI and DPI)	.88	.81	.83	.81	.80	.75	.77	.87	.81	.85
Poor (only MI)	.08	.10	.11	.12	.13	.16	.13	.06	.13	.12
Poor (only DPI)	.00	.02	.00	.00	.01	.01	.02	.02	.01	.01
Poor (MI and DPI)	.03	.07	.05	.07	.06	.08	.09	.05	.05	.02
Independent variables (household)										
Ref. non-immigrant	.92	.88	.82	.95	.82	.81	.91	.72	.84	.91
Migrant	.03	.05	.10	.01	.11	.10	.03	.16	.07	.03
Mixed	.05	.07	.09	.03	.07	.09	.06	.13	.09	.06
Ref. low education	.10	.10	.06	.08	.07	.14	.04	.05	.15	.11
Medium	.29	.31	.38	.29	.49	.27	.37	.36	.30	.25
High	.21	.25	.21	.23	.11	.29	.28	.20	.21	.24
Mixed, low	.16	.15	.13	.15	.16	.11	.06	.13	.17	.17
Mixed	.06	.05	.03	.06	.03	.05	.04	.05	.04	.06
Mixed, high	.17	.15	.20	.18	.14	.14	.22	.21	.13	.17
Ref. low-service functionaries	.09	.12	.12	.09	.15	.11	.06	.10	.10	.06

(Continued)

Appendix Table MA.7.   Continued

Migrant households	DK	NO	SE	FI	AT	BE	DE	CH	FR	NL
Blue-collar workers	.12	.11	.13	.20	.13	.13	.08	.10	.13	.09
Mixed service functionaries	.06	.05	.06	.04	.13	.11	.10	.08	.08	.09
Socio-cultural professionals	.18	.18	.18	.12	.09	.12	.23	.21	.14	.20
Capital accumulators	.04	.07	.05	.09	.03	.06	.03	.08	.05	.07
Mixed skills, low	.15	.11	.17	.11	.22	.16	.14	.11	.22	.11
Mixed skills	.24	.20	.20	.21	.20	.22	.25	.23	.19	.23
Mixed skills, high	.10	.10	.08	.09	.04	.06	.09	.09	.07	.10
Other	.02	.05	.02	.04	.01	.02	.02	.01	.02	.04
Ref. no one employed	.08	.09	.06	.09	.11	.19	.15	.08	.12	.09
One person	.28	.37	.32	.32	.44	.37	.44	.52	.41	.35
Multiple earners	.65	.54	.62	.59	.45	.44	.41	.40	.47	.57
Ref. no one employed atypically	.71	.64	.51	.55	.55	.46	.46	.51	.52	.31
At least one person	.22	.24	.32	.28	.29	.37	.36	.27	.31	.42
All	.07	.12	.17	.16	.16	.17	.18	.22	.18	.27
Ref. no one self-employed	.88	.88	.86	.67	.86	.88	.90	.85	.90	.87
At least one person	.09	.07	.10	.20	.09	.08	.06	.07	.06	.09
All	.03	.04	.04	.12	.06	.04	.04	.08	.04	.05
Number of children, aged ≤2	.12	.13	.16	.11	.12	.13	.08	.10	.13	.15
Number of children, aged 3–5	.13	.12	.12	.11	.12	.12	.10	.10	.14	.15
Number of children, aged 6–12	.35	.34	.29	.30	.29	.28	.26	.29	.33	.34
Number of children, aged 13–17	.30	.28	.34	.30	.22	.23	.21	.23	.24	.23
Number of persons, aged ≥65	.03	.02	.03	.06	.09	.06	.05	.05	.05	.02
N	4,313	4,663	5,245	8,309	4,935	4,722	9,526	4,874	7,503	7,881

Migrant households	UK	AU	CA	US	IE	ES	GR	IT	PT
Dependent variables									
Poverty rates (MI)	.22	.20	.16	.21	.29	.21	.22	.18	.22
Poverty rates (DPI)	.10	.11	.10	.16	.10	.15	.13	.11	.12
Poverty reduction									
Ref. not poor (both MI and DPI)	.77	.80	.84	.78	.71	.76	.74	.80	.75
Poor (only MI)	.13	.09	.06	.06	.19	.09	.13	.09	.13
Poor (only DPI)	.01	.00	.00	.01	.01	.03	.04	.02	.03
Poor (MI and DPI)	.08	.11	.10	.14	.10	.11	.10	.09	.09
Independent variables (household)									
Ref. non-immigrant	.86	.73	.71	.80	.81	.90	.89	.90	.90
Migrant	.06	.15	.17	.13	.08	.05	.07	.04	.03
Mixed	.08	.12	.12	.07	.11	.05	.05	.05	.07
Ref. low education	.09	.29	.05	.07	.27	.32	.26	.27	.61
Medium	.46	.12	.05	.34	.16	.09	.20	.25	.04
High	.21	.28	.64	.29	.20	.16	.14	.07	.06
Mixed, low	.09	.13	.03	.08	.16	.17	.22	.27	.16
Mixed	.02	.10	.11	.03	.09	.16	.07	.06	.10
Mixed, high	.13	.07	.13	.19	.13	.10	.11	.08	.04
Ref. low-service functionaries	.11	.08	.09	.08	.10	.12	.09	.08	.10
Blue-collar workers	.08	.13	.08	.12	.12	.19	.25	.20	.22
Mixed service functionaries	.07	.09	.17	.06	.05	.05	.05	.06	.04
Socio-cultural professionals	.11	.19	.13	.11	.08	.08	.09	.13	.06
Capital accumulators	.08	.09	.09	.16	.09	.03	.04	.04	.02
Mixed skills, low	.19	.08	.03	.04	.19	.28	.21	.16	.32
Mixed skills	.25	.15	.29	.29	.27	.21	.20	.25	.20
Mixed skills, high	.08	.07	.04	.07	.06	.04	.03	.05	.03
Other	.02	.12	.09	.07	.02	.01	.03	.02	.00
Ref. no one employed	.11	.11	.06	.07	.17	.10	.13	.14	.10
One person	.35	.45	.40	.41	.38	.41	.43	.48	.34
Multiple earners	.54	.44	.54	.52	.45	.50	.44	.38	.56

(*Continued*)

Appendix Table MA.7. Continued

Migrant households	UK	AU	CA	US	IE	ES	GR	IT	PT
Ref. no one employed atypically	.60	.46	.59	.60	.54	.49	.59	.62	.55
At least one person	.29	.27	.25	.25	.30	.30	.24	.23	.29
All	.11	.27	.16	.15	.16	.20	.17	.15	.16
Ref. no one self-employed	.85	.82	.83	.86	.80	.80	.63	.73	.75
At least one person	.10	.09	.11	.09	.12	.12	.20	.13	.16
All	.05	.09	.07	.05	.08	.09	.17	.14	.08
Number of children, aged ≤2	.10	.15	.10	.15	.11	.11	.11	.11	.07
Number of children, aged 3–5	.12	.13	.09	.16	.14	.11	.11	.09	.08
Number of children, aged 6–12	.32	.34	.27	.39	.37	.27	.26	.23	.25
Number of children, aged 13–17	.24	.27	.21	.29	.28	.21	.21	.18	.23
Number of persons, aged ≥65	.07	.02	.10	.08	.10	.17	.19	.17	.24
N	6,167	5,042	5,294	60,365	3,517	9,287	3,895	14,960	2,969

Note: Ref. = reference category used for the analysis in chapter 4.

Source: EU-SILC (European countries), HILDA (Australia), SLID (Canada) and CPS (United States).

Notes

Introduction

1 In this book, 'immigrant' and 'non-immigrant' refers to a person's place of birth of persons, e.g., non-immigrants include second-generation foreigners that do not have the nationality of their country of residence. By contrast, 'citizen' is used for persons who are nationals of the residence country and thus entitled to all citizenship rights, including civil, social and political rights.

2 Permanent residents can also be considered as an immigration category. As Hammar (1985) argues, immigration policies affect foreigners until they become naturalised citizens and thus include those policies regulating permanent residence. Moreover, traditional immigration countries such as the United States, Canada and Australia grant permanent residence permits from the beginning of the stay in the receiving country.

3 For instance, immigrants can be irregular residents because they crossed the border without having a visa permit. The capacity of nation states to reduce immigrant inflows is limited further by international agreements regarding human rights, e.g., the right to family reunification (see Morris 2003).

4 The terms 'incorporation' and 'integration' are used interchangeable in this book.

Chapter 1

1 For the attitudinal strand of welfare chauvinism, see, for example, van der Waal et al. (2010); Mewes and Mau (2012); van der Waal, de Koster and van Oorschot (2013).

2 Alternative responses, such as incorporating immigrants into the existing system without closing the borders, on the one hand, or a neo-liberal attack on the welfare state, on the other hand, seem less viable because fiscal capacities of nation states constrain the extent of redistribution and the welfare state itself creates its own

constituencies and thus political support for its maintenance (Banting 2000, 21–22). Emmenegger and Careja (2011, 186–88), however, find support for the retrenchment of social programmes where immigrants tend to be overrepresented among the beneficiaries, such as social assistance.

3 In addition, researchers not primarily concerned with welfare regimes point to the overlap of immigration and integration policies. Helbling et al. (2013, 10) argue that 'integration policies (settlement) might attract or deter immigrants and compensate for restrictive or liberal access regulation (entry)'. At the same time, immigration laws could be an efficient means of integration as they allow the selection of immigrants upon entry.

4 However, many authors criticised this historical argument. Kymlicka (1995, 180), for example, points out that certain social groups such as women, children and native minorities have been historically granted first social rights and then political rights. In addition, he argues that Marshall's conceptualisation neglects that 'they might feel excluded despite the possession of citizenship'. Associated with this is the critique that Marshall does not appreciate cultural rights as a precondition for participation (Bauböck 2001; see Bloemraad, Korteweg and Yurdakul 2008, 157).

5 Moreover, Marshall treats these rights 'equally' and puts social rights on the same level as civil and political rights, endowed in the status of being a citizen. But this interpretation is problematic. As Emmenegger and Careja (2011, 167) argue, social rights have a different quality. While civil and political rights are non-transferable and granted automatically, social rights are redistributive and depend on the fiscal capacity of the state and political mobilisation of certain groups. The conflict bearing potential inherent in this qualitative difference of social rights is also evident in the public and scholarly 'welfare chauvinism' debate.

6 Stratification refers to the extent to which welfare states intervene in the structure of inequality and change social relations. With regard to social rights, it can also be understood as a consequence thereof for the society.

7 For the sake of completeness, Esping-Andersen's alternative definition of de-commodification should be mentioned, namely 'as [the] degree to which individuals, or families, can uphold a socially acceptable standard of living independent of market participation' (Esping-Andersen 1990, 37). This definition does not assume that an individual is already employed and thus entails a rights-based interpretation of social rights; that is, that all individuals are entitled equally to social benefits on the basis of citizenship (see also Stephens 2010, 513–14).

8 The fact that an individual is young, low-skilled and/or female does not mean that he/she is automatically an outsider. However, these characteristics increase the probability that these individuals will be exposed to new social risks such as atypical employment, unemployment and insufficient social coverage (see also Häusermann and Schwander 2012).

9 A nation can be broadly defined as a group of people who perceive themselves as belonging to a certain state. This means that a nation is an 'imagined community' (Anderson 1983) because it is the result of subjective self-identification and, in contrast to other 'imagined communities', imagines its community in relation to a state regardless of whether the state actually exists or is a political goal the community strives for (e.g. Miller 1995). National identity refers to the salience and content of nations.

10 The cultural-ethnic model, with Germany as a prime example, rests upon exclusive markers such as ethnicity and a community of descent, reflected in the 'ius sanguinis' principle of the naturalisation process. The civic-territorial model, prevalent in France, on the other hand, builds on a civic culture and political institutions, and naturalisation is politically supported based on the place of birth, the 'ius solis' principle.

11 For example, several scholars proposed to add a cultural dimension to account for the extent to which naturalised immigrants can maintain their native traditions and customs (see Safran 1997; Koopmans and Statham 2000; Koopmans et al. 2005; Castles and Miller 2009; Howard 2009).

12 Interestingly, one of the prevailing citizenship approaches predicting continuing diverging trajectories due to path dependencies and different traditions of nationhood has not yet been related to welfare state regimes and their principles of entitlement based on need, work and residence (but see Faist 1995; Brochmann and Hammar 1999; Banting 2000).

13 Helbling et al. (2013, 9) propose to define immigration more broadly as 'people moving from one nation state to another and thereby take up residence in the destination country'. Nevertheless, they also exclude commuting and tourism from their definition.

14 Examples of co-ethnics are groups that share the same language and country of destination (German 'Aussiedler'), religion (Jews) or former colonial ties (e.g. British Commonwealth citizens).

15 However, European countries have started to introduce permanent residence schemes for newcomers. For example, Germany grants permanent residence permits to high-skilled immigrants, in this case scientists (see Residence Act, Aufenthaltsgesetz §19).

16 Although illegal and irregular migration are commonly used synonymously, the former is more narrowly defined and refers to crossing borders illegally, while the latter also includes irregularities resulting from visa overstaying or illegal employment of immigrants with legal residence permits (see Jandl and Kraler 2006, 339–41).

17 Hammar (1990, 14–18) identifies three entrance gates immigrants have to pass through in order to become full citizens.

18 It should be noted that the terms used in this book do not coincide with Hammar (1985, 7), who uses 'immigration policies' as an umbrella term encompassing immigration policy ('regulation of immigration flows and control of aliens') and integration policies ('immigrant policy').

19 Another example is self-sufficiency. While, for the purpose of family reunification, all advanced industrialised countries require that the eligible sponsor has sufficient financial means to maintain their families, albeit at different financial levels, in a number of countries, labour migrants also have to prove that they can maintain themselves (see IOM 2009; Huddleston et al. 2011). Skilled immigrants seeking work in the United Kingdom must prove that they have £800 in available funds in their bank account three months prior to applying for a work permit (Ruhs 2011).

20 Note that 'immigrant policies', termed by Hammar (1985), and integration policies, more widely used in the migration literature, are used synonymously.

21 de Giorgi and Pellizzari's (2006) results at the macro-level show that more generous welfare states are related to higher migration inflows, particularly low-skilled foreign workers. Menz (2004), on the other hand, claims that colonial legacies

and cultural similarities between the home and the host country of newcomers are better predictors for the number and composition of migrants across countries than the generosity of their social systems.

22 Different scholars argue that ethnic and racial fractionalisation, under specific conditions, prevent the emergence of expansive welfare states (Alesina and Glaeser 2004), for example, by constraining the organisation of labour (Stephens 1979). The empirical evidence so far is mixed. Alesina and Glaeser (2004, 140–48), for instance, found a strong correlation between social welfare spending and racial/linguistic fractionalisation. By contrast, Soroka, Banting and Johnston (2006) found that increased immigration did not lead to shrinking welfare states between 1970 and 1998, though the growth rate of social welfare spending was smaller in countries more open to migration.

23 Crepaz (2008, 158–59) and Crepaz and Damron (2009) arrive at similar conclusions, namely that higher de-commodification goes with lower levels of welfare chauvinism, despite relying on a different measure of welfare chauvinism not directly related to social rights (e.g. whether immigrants take jobs away from people who were born in the country, bring down average wages and take more out than they put in).

24 For a critical discussion on the tensions between the right to freely migrate within the EU and the right to full access to welfare benefits of EU citizens, see Ruhs (2015).

25 In October 2015, for instance, Germany introduced accelerated procedures to handle and repatriate rejected asylum seekers. But at the same time, the German asylum seekers bill relaxed requirements for family reunification of persons with subsidiary protection and other temporary residence permits issued for humanitarian reasons, including well-integrated adolescents (Deutsches Rotes Kreuz 2015). Around the same time, the Swedish parliament passed new rules tightening the conditions for asylum seekers to stay in the country by introducing temporary residence permits for adults migrating without children. Extension of this permit was made dependent on whether the applicant still needed protection or had found employment (Jacobsen 2015).

26 Comparably, the unemployment security system in Italy is less developed in terms of replacement rates compared to other countries. This is due to highly protective employment laws, which make it very difficult to fire workers, and thus render unemployment protection obsolete (see Esping-Andersen 1999). Estevez-Abe, Iversen and Soskice (2001, 169), however, point to the undervaluation of Italian unemployment protection by semi-public insurance arrangements such as the Cassa Integrazione and regional associations.

27 Two broader explanations exist to explain why different actors are interested in reducing earnings differentials (see Wallerstein 1999, 674–76; Rueda and Pontusson 2000, 360–61). The first refers to the political mechanism of centralisation, which changes the power distribution of actors in favour of low-wage unions. Based on the logic of the median voter model, low-wage unions support redistributive wage demands only if the average wage surpasses the median wage. The second ideological

explanation refers to the characteristic of centralisation, which renders wage differentials more transparent and therefore more politicised.

28 Usually, relative poverty (or head counts) is calculated based on the share of households with a disposable income below 50 per cent of a country's median income (e.g. Korpi and Palme 1998; Brady 2003; Moller et al. 2003; Misra, Moller and Budig 2007; Bäckman 2009). In contrast, absolute poverty is defined as the share with income below a certain level held constant across countries and timespan, for example, 50 per cent of the median income of the United States in a particular year (e.g. Kenworthy 1999; Scruggs and Allan 2006).

29 The reasons put forward by Nelson (2012, 150) for the differences are that savings and support from relatives along with public in-kind benefits and income from informal work allow individuals to make use of basic goods, while personal preferences in lifestyles explain why the materially deprived do not have to be income poor.

30 The results further show that the length of parental leave has a curvilinear effect on poverty, which is explained by the fact that long family leave reduces a mother's labour market attachment and opportunities (see also Lalive and Zweimüller 2009).

31 Nonetheless, descriptive research on poverty rates among the unemployed shows a steady increase in EU27 countries from 40 per cent in 2004 to around 45 per cent in 2008 (based on the EU official poverty threshold of 60 per cent of the median income), which is explained by a policy shift towards more conditionality and means testing (see Cantillon 2011, 443–44).

32 In contrast to France, Germany and Switzerland, the UK and the Netherlands have made a great effort by including special antidiscrimination laws in civil code and establishing state offices dealing with discrimination complaints (see Mahnig and Wimmer 2000, 194–95; Koopmans et al. 2005, 45–51).

33 This is also the case for immigrants during their first years in Austria (five years), Denmark (seven years) and Germany (eight years).

Chapter 2

1 The countries included in the analysis are Australia (AU), Austria (AT), Belgium (BE), Canada (CA), Denmark (DK), Finland (FI), France (FR), Germany (DE), Greece (GR), Ireland (IE), Italy (IT), Netherlands (NL), Norway (NO), Portugal (PT, data for 2008), Spain (ES), Sweden (SE), Switzerland (CH), the United Kingdom (UK) and the United States (US).

2 Poverty rates have been calculated using alternative poverty thresholds, that is, 40 per cent and 60 per cent of the median income, and alternative equivalence scales such as the square root scale, commonly used by the Luxembourg Income Study (LIS). The correlation for poverty measures based on market income is quite high, regardless of whether all households considered or differentiated by the migrant background (correlation coefficients above .89). These correlations can also be found for various poverty measures of non-immigrants based on disposable income (for mixed households the correlation coefficients above .81). However, discrepancies are higher for immigrants' poverty measures, in general correlation coefficients above .73,

except correlating 40 per cent and 60 per cent adjusted for OECD equivalence scale ($r = .59$, $p < .01$), 40 per cent and 60 per cent adjusted by square root scale ($r = .58$, $p < .01$), 60 per cent (OECD) and 40 per cent (square root; $r = .43$, $p < .1$) and 40 per cent (OECD) and 60 per cent (square root; $r = .68$, $p < .01$).

3 This finding is also supported by a t-test, while the means of immigrants' and non-immigrants' poverty rates are significantly different at the 1 per cent level (results not shown).

4 This pattern is consistent when using alternative poverty thresholds (40 per cent and 60 per cent) or equivalence scale (square root).

5 Irregular migration can include different facets such as no regular/legal status (irregular), no appropriate papers (undocumented) and no legal permit for entry stay or work (unauthorized, see Vogel 2009).

6 The respective Swiss and US-American estimates are considerably lower. The reasons put forward by Feld and Schneider (2010) are fewer regulations and a lower indirect tax burden.

7 Overall 71 per cent of variance in non-immigrants' poverty rates can be explained by a regime dummy (results not shown.)

8 Regardless of which poverty threshold (40 per cent or 60 per cent) or equivalence scale (square root) is chosen, Belgium, Denmark and Sweden rank as the top three countries with the highest differences in poverty rates between immigrants and non-immigrants. The picture is less consistent when looking at those countries with the smallest differences, with only Australia consistently scoring in the top three. Moreover, these changes in ranking suggest that the disposable income of immigrants in the Netherlands is very close to the poverty threshold. This will be discussed in more detail later in the chapter.

9 The basic assumption behind this approach of calculating poverty reduction scores is that the market income distribution would remain unchanged even if no social transfers existed. However, this approach has been criticised for different reasons, such as the endogenous effect of the tax system and generosity of welfare programmes on the incentives of the working-age population to pursue paid employment or the fact that welfare states not only redistribute income between individuals but also over the life cycle (for a critical review, see Kim 2000; Bergh 2005). This book tries to circumvent these criticisms by focusing on the working-age population and the impact of individual social programmes that aim to redistribute income within the population, such as family benefits or social assistance.

10 A country's poverty threshold increases when taking taxes and transfers into account compared to the poverty threshold based on market income. PRE scores are negative for immigrant households if their net social benefits (i.e. the difference between taxes and transfers) do not change to same extent as those for non-immigrant households. Consequently, even if immigrant households are net receivers of social benefits due to the higher poverty threshold, the relative share of poor households increases (see poor immigrants' mean income before and after taxes and transfers in appendix table 2A.1).

11 Moreover, income gaps and poverty based on market income are more strongly correlated in immigrant households than in non-immigrant households ($rs = .79$ and $.49$, $p < .05$; see appendix table 2A.2).

12   This finding is also supported by the non-significant correlation between poverty rates and income gaps based on disposable income, which is, however, not solely driven by these two outliers.

13   The cross-country average is 3.1 (SD = 1.2), for non-immigrant households 2.7 (SD = 1.2) and for immigrant households 6.8 (SD = 2.3).

14   The correlation coefficients between poverty rates and the intensity measure, both based on disposable income, are still relatively high for non-immigrant and mixed households (both coefficients are around .9) and .73 for migrant households.

15   Also migration literature questions whether ethnic origin is adequate for classifying immigrants and comparing different ethnic groups to native citizens. According to Glick Schiller and Çağlar (2008, 42), the assumption that members of the same country of origin share the same set of values and national identities masks not only variation between immigrants coming from the same country but also differences within the receiving society, and neglects that some features might be shared between immigrants and native citizens. In addition, the focus on ethnic groups does not consider that ethnic bounds are only one form in class or religious communities where incorporation can occur.

16   This result refers to the full sample, including all countries. The logistic regressions have been weighted using the household survey weight combined with the number of household members.

17   In addition, variables measuring the number of persons in a household employed atypically and in self-employment, number of persons aged up to two years, up to five years, up to twelve years and up to seventeen years and number of persons aged sixty-five and above living in a household were included in the regression models (for more details, see methodological appendix).

18   Comparing immigrants' poverty rates based on market income with raw and net AME coefficients further supports the importance of socio-demographic factors. While the correlation for the former is relatively high and positive (r = .96, see appendix table 2A.2), the respective correspondence with net average marginal effects coefficients, after controlling for socio-demographic factors, is considerably lower (r = .34).

19   For mixed households, the coefficients are even lower and in the majority of countries not significant. The major exceptions are the United States, Sweden, Belgium, Switzerland, France and Italy, where they are exposed to 3 percentage points higher poverty risk as compared to non-immigrant households.

20   It is important to mention that the classification of the countries just described remains robust, even if alternative poverty thresholds (40 per cent and 60 per cent) and equivalence scales (squared root) are used.

21   This is also evident when looking at the correlation coefficient (r = .59, p < .01).

22   The case of the Netherlands is not as robust as Ireland's. Although the post-tax and transfer income gaps were relatively high in both countries, varying the poverty threshold only affects the Dutch results, namely poverty gaps become significant when using 60 per cent of the median income and either the modified OECD or the square root equivalence scale.

Chapter 3

1   Figures regarding the numbers for the foreign population (based on nationality) between 1985 and 2007 provide further support for this trend, although the share
with around 7.5 per cent in 2007 is somewhat lower (data for Australia and Canada
not available).

2   Germany, along with France, was also among the first nation states that
actively restricted workers' rights. In Germany, specific contract clauses implemented around 1890 prohibited Poles from leaving their jobs for better employment
opportunities and forced them to return to their employers under the threat of incar-
ceration or deportation (Castles and Miller 2009, 87–90).

3   However, labour migration to Sweden, mostly from Finland and Southern
Europe, mainly took place between 1949 and 1971 (Ruhs 2009, 22). Nowadays, it
consists of asylum seekers and family members, while permanent-type labour migration of third-country nationals in 2005 and 2006 was less than 400 persons per year
(ibid.).

4   This 'Italians agreement' of 1963, which was accompanied by a social security
agreement, gradually granted seasonal workers certain rights, such as the right to family reunification after eighteen months or the right to pursue any paid employment
after five years through an annual permit (see Wimmer 1998, 213–16).

5   Both exceptions, Denmark (35 per cent) and Germany (25 per cent), can be
explained by the data sources which are not detailed enough for the year 2007, that is,
listing of countries of origin, as the comparison between 2007, 2009 and 2010 shows,
Denmark's share of foreign residents in 2009 is around 40 per cent and Germany's in
2010 around 35 per cent.

6   As of 1 January 2012, the percentage of individuals born in other EU27 member states made up 3.4 per cent (17.2 millions) of the total population compared to the
6.5 per cent of those born in non-EU countries (33 million, Eurostat 2013).

7   Examples are not only Chinese immigrants in Canada and Australia, who
replaced Italians among the top three countries of origin in the 1990s, but also an
increase in the Turkish population in European countries. They represent the largest immigrant group not only in Germany and the Netherlands but also in Denmark
(OECD 2016).

8   Since most countries have more than one programme for labour migrants (see
also Ruhs 2011, 2013), the data have been collected for those specific programmes
(for an overview see appendix table MA.3).

9   In addition, an analysis of immigrants' poverty in times of crisis needs to take
into account further alternative explanations such as the extent of exposure to the
crisis and the resulting extent of retrenchment.

10   Depending on the country, the legislation also includes civil partners, direct
relatives in the ascending line of both spouses and adult children.

11   With the Council Directive 2003/109/EC of 25 November 2003, the EU has
aimed for a long-term resident status for third-country nationals to standardise the
practices of their member states. As of 1 January 2007, this directive had not yet been
implemented in the majority of countries, which requires five years of legal residence
in the territory of a member state among other conditions. Denmark, Ireland and the
United Kingdom are not bound by this directive (see EC 2011).

12 Finland can also be mentioned among those countries. According to Section 77 of the Aliens Act, the residence permit for an employed person entitles the holder to work in one or several professional fields. Work permits can be restricted to a specific employer for special reasons, but this is not the main practice (see country notes of MIPEX questionnaire 2007, Niessen et al. 2007).

13 Moreover, high-skilled immigrants are granted accelerated and facilitated access to residence permits, which includes separate application counters (Bloemraad 2014, 278).

14 In Switzerland, some immigration categories, including family members of Swiss citizens and permanent residents, EU15 citizens and nationals from countries with bilateral agreements, such as the United States, Canada, Ireland, Monaco and San Marino, enjoy privileged access to permanent residence permits after five years.

15 Irish immigrants are allowed to change their employer after an initial period of twelve months (IOM 2009, 331).

16 For newly formed relationships, German residents with temporary residence permits have to wait five years for family reunification (Residence Act, 30 July 2002 Art. 30(1)).

17 In Canada, the law requires that the sponsor is either a Canadian citizen or a permanent resident. The case mentioned earlier refers to family members who are allowed to enter the country together with the migrant worker (see Immigration and Refugee Act, Art. 13(1)).

18 The correlation coefficients are as follows: coordination of wage setting: $r = -.18$, $p = .46$, government intervention in wage bargaining: $r = .17$, $p = .47$, minimum wage setting: $r = .02$, $p = .95$ and excluding countries without minimum wages: $r = -.07$, $p = .83$, minimum wage (percentage of median wage): $r = .17$, $p = .50$, excluding countries without minimum wage: $r = .63$, $p < .05$, $n = 11$.

19 The major exception concerning physical presence relates to whether children have to reside in the country of residence. This is often clarified by bilateral social security agreements, which regulate not only whether entitlements are paid abroad but also whether the social insurance contributions made abroad are considered as a contribution period.

20 North, de Wenden and Taylor (1987, quoted in Soysal 1994, 123) further consider factors such as the 'zeal with which eligibility rules are enforced', 'state or province of residence (in federal states)' and 'nature of the program'. The information on the latter has been collected but not included in the index, while zeal of enforcement has been excluded as it focuses on implementation rather than the social policy itself. Concerning the second factor, the primary focus of this study is cross-national comparisons and thus national laws and regulations. Thus, policy variations at the state, province or municipal level have not been taken into account (for a discussion, see methodological appendix).

21 US immigrants also get credit for the forty quarters of work requirement for work performed not only by his/her parents when the immigrant was under eighteen but also by the spouse during marriage (National Immigration Law Center 2002, table 1, updated March 2005).

22 The United Kingdom of Great Britain and Northern Ireland, the Channel Islands and the Isle of Man.

23   The right of residence can also be prolonged for more than three months if the inactive EU citizen has sufficient means for himself or herself and his or her family as well as health insurance. Moreover, EU citizens are allowed to seek employment for up to six months under the condition of not becoming a burden on the social assistance system (see Directive 2004/38/EC on the right of citizens of the EU and their family members to move and reside freely within the territory of the member states).

24   Countries that do not explicitly refer to the legal status of immigrants are Germany, Ireland and Sweden, though the latter requires residence and a work permit in order to register in Försäkringskassan.

25   See Regulation (EU) No. 1231/2010 of 24 November 2010 extending Regulation (EC) No 883/2004 and Regulation (EC) No 987/2009 to nationals of third countries who are not already covered on the grounds of their nationality.

26   In cases where several subprogrammes – for example, unemployment insurance and unemployment assistance – are provided, the average of these social programmes is calculated weighting them equally.

27   The correlation coefficient is $-.19$ ($p = .43$).

28   A national paid parental leave was introduced on 1 January 2011 that covers working parents. It covers not only parents in full-time and part-time employment but also seasonal workers and self-employed persons (Baird and Williamson 2011).

29   The correlation coefficient is $.59$ ($p < .01$).

30   Furthermore, single parents are exempted from the qualifying waiting period if they became a lone parent during their stay in Australia (Social Security Act 1991, section 500(1)(d)(i)).

31   In contrast to the universal childcare arrangements mentioned earlier in the text, these programmes limit the maximum number of hours (up to thirty hours a week in Germany) or income of the working parent (€14,600 in Austria, around 40 per cent of the AW; see MISSOC 2007, Comparative Tables Part 2).

32   It should be mentioned that although Spain ranks among the most inclusive countries towards immigrants, family benefits are granted based on a means test which is set relatively low, that is, a yearly income of €9,328.39 (about 42 per cent of the average wage, see MISSOC comparative country tables [2007]).

33   The correlation coefficient is $-.12$ ($p = .61$, excluding the United States: $r = -.59$, $p < .01$).

34   Recent immigrants and refugees living in Denmark, including Danish citizens who have stayed abroad for more than seven out of the past eight years, are instead entitled to an introductory benefit (starthjælp), which is less generous than regular social assistance (Sainsbury 2012, 110).

35   According to the regulations of the community of Milano, only permanent residents, that is, the *titolari di carta di soggiorno*, are granted access to social assistance, which however was declared to be not in accord with national legislation by the administrative tribunal of the Lombardia on September 2010 (Sentenza N.6353 del 21/09/2010 – Tar Lombardia Milano).

36   The correlation coefficient is $.29$ ($p = .25$).

37   The same argument, that is, the non-universal character of social programmes, can also explain why, despite the efficiency of special social programmes targeting immigrants' needs, they are difficult to introduce (see Brubaker 1989, 180n22; Mahnig 2001).

38 But also organised labour might play a role in the internal social inclusion argument as economic competition from immigrants who would otherwise work for any remuneration and labour conditions is reduced (Faist 1995; Banting 2000; Römer 2017).

39 Mahnig and Wimmer (2000) explain the efforts of the Dutch state to provide culturally defined social groups with equal rights with its historically emerged conceptions as to how the state and society should relate (e.g. the idea to empower immigrant minorities reflects how the Dutch nation state coped with the Catholic minority; Mahnig and Wimmer 2000, 190–92).

40 The countries include Australia, Canada, Japan, New Zealand, Switzerland, United States and the Vatican City (Maas 2014, 271).

Chapter 4

1 Parts of the findings have been published in Eugster (2018) and reprinted by permission of SAGE Publications.

2 Poverty reduction considers whether a household defined as poor based on market income moves out of poverty when taking the welfare and tax system into account. Thus, in contrast to poverty based on disposable income, the poverty situation before taxes and transfers is included.

3 Occupation is based on ISCO-88 classification or equivalent (for details, see methodological appendix).

4 An extended model controlling for 'age' and 'household composition' neither significantly improves the model fit nor considerably changes the direction and significance level of the coefficients. Therefore, the more concise models including the share of children and elderly persons are presented.

5 This proverb mistakenly attributed to John F. Kennedy in 1963 originates, according to his speechwriter Ted Sorensen (2008, 227), from a slogan used by New England's regional chamber of commerce.

6 The only exception at the 10 per cent significance level are differences in employment rates of foreign- and native-born residents, with higher employment rates of immigrants corresponding with lower poverty.

7 Other migration-related indicators include the share of permits issued for work or free movement and share of top three immigrant groups in percentage of foreign and foreign-born population.

8 However, interpreting the effects through differentiation and differences in predicted values, as the literature suggests, does not yield different results (not shown; see Braumoeller 2004; Kam and Franzese 2007). A likelihood ratio (LR) test further shows that the complex model including the interaction term does not improve the model fit of the simple model with the two lower-order terms.

9 The square root scale, in contrast to the OECD scale, assigns the same weight to each household member regardless of whether that member is a child or an adult.

10 Even if alternative indicators for labour market discrimination are used as controls, no significant effects can be found (results not shown). The indicators include measures for prejudice against migrants, based on the percentage of respondents who

do not want to have migrants or foreign workers as neighbours (data from WVS 2014), over qualification rates of higher-educated foreign-born workers aged fifteen to sixty-four (data from OECD 2015c, 117), but also the proportion of foreign-born employment and share of immigrant employment in low-skilled occupations (data from OECD 2009, 88).

11 Alesina and Glaeser (2004) argue that the American exceptionalism concerning welfare distribution and poverty reduction can be traced back to racial and ethnic heterogeneity as well as historical, cultural and political differences.

12 The reason is that global (or country-specific) coefficients and standard errors are estimated based on the observed deviations within each country, which vary depending on sample size and the variance within the country. Here, I thank Peter Selb, Isabelle Stadelmann-Steffen and Ben Jann for their helpful support.

13 However, regarding the traditional family benefits model, at least when estimating the results only for immigrant families with children below seventeen, the coefficient resulting from the jackknife estimation is positive and significant at the 5 per cent level.

14 An additional problem is that existing multilevel estimation techniques, at least to my knowledge, do not allow weighting the observations using survey-specific weights. This is problematic due to a potential selection bias of immigrants participating in income surveys.

15 At least for the data used here, when looking at the income distribution, it can be said that immigrants are represented in all income deciles, but they tend to be concentrated in the lower deciles across countries, regardless of whether income is measured before or after taxes and transfers.

16 To my knowledge, national income surveys and the EU-SILC survey do not provide detailed information on the type of residence permit of the respondents. Thus, alternative sources should be considered for more detailed analysis.

17 For example, in Switzerland, the share of immigrants from the EU15 countries is above 50 per cent compared to around 14 per cent in Germany and Greece (see chapter 3).

18 But the shape of income distribution matters too (Gundersen and Ziliak 2004, 61). Even if inequality remains stable, the poor living in a highly unequal society gain proportionally less from growth than those living in a more equal society (Ravallion 2001).

19 Here, integration is understood more broadly on a general level as a central feature of societies that indicates how closely their members are related to each other or, in other terms, whether the society as a whole is more or less integrated (Esser 2001, 98; Entzinger and Biezeveld 2003, 6).

20 An example is the reform of the starthjælp (for immigrants and citizens who have not lived for the past seven years in the country), where the social benefits of long-term recipients were cut by replacing one's partner's benefit with a partner's supplement (see Brochmann and Hagelund 2011, 18–19).

21 Indeed the estimations show that the generosity of unemployment compensation as well as traditional family benefits reduces material deprivation, at least when European countries are considered and a seven-point index as proposed by Whelan

and Maitre is used (2007; see also Corrigan 2014). Unfortunately, comparable data are not available for Australia, Canada and the United States, three countries that not only stand out regarding their immigration history but also partly share a common entitlement practice of social rights for immigrants.

22 Other explanations could be discretionary practices by bureaucracies and administrative entities or immigrants' lack of awareness regarding their social rights. Borjas and Hilton (1996, 596–97) show for the United States that immigrant nationalities differ in relation to the social benefits they receive. The role of ethnic network communities, who pass the information about particular social programmes to newly arrived immigrants, is used to explain this.

23 Further consequences would be welfare dependency as an obstacle to obtaining a permanent residence status or citizenship (see Koopmans, Michalowski and Waibel 2012).

24 For example, before the German immigration reform in 2004, relying on social assistance was a reason for expulsion, even if an individual fulfilled the eligibility criteria for social assistance (Davy and Çınar 2001, 387n214).

25 The introduction of language and civic requirements, especially those before arrival (immigration policies), also more or less explicitly aim to limit the immigration of family members (see Groenendijk 2011, 14).

26 Differences are whether point systems (alongside educational qualifications and language proficiency) also award previous experience in a professional field with occupations in demand (Hawthorne 2008).

27 Different employment trajectories can also be found within the refugee class. Bevelander and Pendakur (2012) find that government-assisted refugees are often settled where housing exist but only few employment opportunities, while landed (or asylum) refugees who have their own resources often settle in places with better employment opportunities. Consequently, they point to variations in access to social capital and mobility choice.

28 For example, the Dutch government in a cabinet policy paper in 2006 aimed to shift immigration policies towards attracting highly qualified immigrants. Comparably, German legislation has implemented regulations that facilitate the immigration of high-skilled persons (OECD 2008).

Methodological Appendix

1 Due to missing data, New Zealand and Japan are excluded from the analysis.

2 For the robustness tests in chapter 4, not only alternative poverty lines (40 per cent and 60 per cent of median income) but also an alternative equivalence scale, based on the square root of the number of persons living in the same household, were calculated.

3 The income definition of the Luxembourg Income Study has been applied to the Australian, Canadian and American household income survey. This definition excludes property taxes on wealth and the value of the company car as income but includes alimonies (paid and received), interest repayments on mortgage and pensions from individual private plans.

4   PRE scores $= \dfrac{\text{poverty}_{pre} - \text{poverty}_{post}}{\text{poverty}_{post}}$ (see Mitchell 1991, 65).

5   The three alternative situations are households moving into poverty (incl. in the net poverty reduction) and households that remain poor/non-poor after taking social transfer and taxes into account.

6   This approach of comparing poverty rates based on market and disposable income rests on the counterfactual assumption that market incomes would be the same if no social programmes existed (but see critique by Kim 2000 and Bergh 2005, for example, the endogenous effect of the tax system and generosity of the welfare state on labour supply).

7   On the benefits of absolute poverty, that is, an income threshold that is constant across countries and times, see Kenworthy (1999, 1120–22), Brady (2009, 31–33) and Scruggs and Allan (2006, 883).

8   EU-SILC Version 6 from 01-08-11. The responsibility for all conclusions drawn from the data lies entirely with the author. The data for Switzerland have been provided by the Bundesamt für Statistik (2007).

9   The HILDA survey even provides further immigration-related indicators such as years since arrival or language spoken at home but unfortunately not on residence permits.

10   In principle, immigrants and non-immigrants might be denied formal rights in law, for example, the legal right to a minimum wage, because there is no effective state protection or enforcement of this law. On the other hand, individuals might enjoy rights that are not formulated in law, such as access to medical treatment with a legal right to health care (see Ruhs 2011, 14).

11   The combination of net replacement rates for different households is problematic per se (e.g. high variation between single person households and one-earner households with children as in Australia, 36 per cent versus 72 per cent). The principal component analysis resulting in one factor shows that the indicators are highly and positively correlated with factor loadings above .84 (81.7 per cent of variance explained).

12   The factor loadings of the resulting single component are above .89 (83.9 per cent of variance explained).

13   An alternative could be the use of a child benefit package for a couple with two children but one earner based on level of earnings (50 per cent, 100 per cent and 150 per cent of AW) relative to a childless couple on the same earning level (see Bradshaw and Finch 2010).

14   The single factor using principal component analysis shows that the indicators are positively correlated with factor loadings above .90 (88.8 per cent of variance explained).

15   However, the use of equivalised incomes allows the selection of individuals or households as units of analysis as the same income value is assigned to each household member.

16   For the EU-SILC countries, the immigrant category includes those from EU and non-EU countries. This distinction is not available for the Canadian dataset, which contains only an indicator of whether the respondent is born in Canada. Australia and

the United States provide information on the place of birth at the country level, which allows identification of respondents from industrialised countries, that is, EU-25 and EFTA, Australia, Canada, Japan, New Zealand and the United States.

17 Three employment statuses are distinguished: employed, unemployed and inactive. Note that being employed and unemployed is considered more relevant than the inactive status, for example, if a person is employed for at least one month and the rest inactive he/she is coded as employed. For ambiguous situations, the employment status was first considered, followed by the unemployment and inactive status (e.g. if a person was employed, unemployed and inactive for three months of the year, this person has been coded as employed).

18 'Xtmelogit' is based on a maximum likelihood estimation procedure using adaptive quadrature with seven integration points.

References

Addison, John T. and McKinley L. Blackburn. 1999. 'Minimum Wages and Poverty'. *Industrial and Labor Relations Review* 52 (3): 393–409.

Adsera, Alicia and Barry R. Chiswick. 2007. 'Are There Gender and Country of Origin Differences in Immigrant Labor Market Outcomes across European Destinations?' *Journal of Population Economics* 20 (3): 495–526.

Alderson, Arthur S. and François Nielsen. 2002. 'Globalization and the Great U-Turn: Income Inequality Trends in 16 OECD Countries'. *Journal of Sociology* 107 (5): 1244–99.

Aleinikoff, T. Alexander and Douglas Klusmeyer. 2002. *Citizenship Policies for an Age of Migration*. Washington, DC: Carnegie Endowment for International Peace.

Alesina, Alberto and Edward L. Glaeser. 2004. *Fighting Poverty in the US and Europe: A World of Difference*. Oxford: Oxford University Press.

Andersen, Jørgen Goul and Tor Bjørklund. 1990. 'Structural Changes and New Cleavages: The Progress Parties in Denmark and Norway'. *Acta Sociologica* 33 (3): 195–217.

Anderson, Benedict. 1983. *Imagined Communities. Reflections on the Origin and Spread of Nationalism*. London: Verso.

Andress, Hans-Jürgen and Henning Lohmann. 2008. *The Working Poor in Europe: Employment, Poverty and Globalization*. Cheltenham, UK: Edward Elgar.

Armingeon, Klaus. 2012. 'The Politics of Fiscal Responses to the Crisis of 2008–2009'. *Governance* 25 (4): 543–65.

Armingeon, Klaus, Christian Isler, Laura Knöpfel, David Weisstanner and Sarah Engler. 2015. *Comparative Political Data Set 1960–2013*. Bern: Institute of Political Science, University of Berne.

Arts, Wil A. and John Gelissen. 2010. 'Models of the Welfare State'. In *The Oxford Handbook of the Welfare State*, edited by Francis G. Castles, Stephan Leibfried, Jane Lewis, Herbert Obinger and Christopher Pierson, 569–83. Oxford: Oxford University Press.

Atkinson, Anthony B. 2015. *Inequality*. Cambridge, MA: Harvard University Press.

Aumüller, Jutta. 2016. *Arbeitsmarktintegration von Flüchtlingen: Bestehende Prax-isansätze und weiterführende Empfehlungen.* Gütersloh: Bertelsmann Stiftung.

Bäckman, Olof. 2005. 'Welfare States, Social Structure and the Dynamics of Poverty Rates: A Comparative Study of 16 Countries, 1980–2000'. Working Paper Series No. 7, Institute for Futures Studies.

———. 2009. 'Institutions, Structures and Poverty: A Comparative Study of 16 Countries, 1980–2000'. *European Sociological Review* 25 (2): 251–64.

Bäckman, Olof and Tommy Ferrarini. 2010. 'Combating Child Poverty? A Multilevel Assessment of Family Policy Institutions and Child Poverty in 21 Old and New Welfare States'. *Journal of Social Policy* 39 (2): 275–96.

Bahle, Thomas, Michaela Pfeifer and Claus Wendt. 2010. 'Social Assistance'. In *The Oxford Handbook of the Welfare State*, edited by Francis G. Castles, Stephan Leibfried, Jane Lewis, Herbert Obinger and Christopher Pierson, 448–61. Oxford: Oxford University Press.

Baird, Marian and Sue Williamson. 2011. 'Women, Work and Policy Settings in Australia in 2010'. *Journal of Industrial Relations* 53 (3): 337–52.

Bale, Tim. 2003. 'Cinderella and Her Ugly Sisters: The Mainstream and Extreme Right in Europe's Bipolarising Party Systems'. *West European Politics* 26 (3): 67–90.

Banting, Keith G. 2000. 'Looking in Three Directions: Migration and the European Welfare State in Comparative Perspective'. In *Immigration and Welfare: Challenging the Borders of the Welfare State*, edited by Michael Bommes and Andrew Geddes, 13–33. London: Routledge.

Banting, Keith G. and Will Kymlicka. 2006. *Multiculturalism and the Welfare State: Recognition and Redistribution in Contemporary Democracies.* Oxford: Oxford University Press.

Barrett, Alan and Yvonne McCarthy. 2008. 'Immigrants and Welfare Programmes: Exploring the Interactions between Immigrant Characteristics, Immigrant Welfare Dependence, and Welfare Policy'. *Oxford Review of Economic Policy* 24 (3): 542–59.

Bassanini, Andrea and Anne Saint-Martin. 2008. 'The Price of Prejudice: Labour Market Discrimination on the Grounds of Gender and Ethnicity'. In *OECD Employment Outlook*, edited by OECD, 139–202. Paris: OECD Publishing.

Bauböck, Rainer. 1994. *Transnational Citizenship: Membership and Rights in International Migration.* Aldershot, UK: Edward Elgar.

———. 2001. 'Cultural Citizenship, Minority Rights, and Self-Government'. In *Citizenship Today: Global Perspectives and Practices*, edited by T. Alexander Aleinikoff and Douglas Klusmeyer, 319–48. Washington, DC: Carnegie Endowment for International Peace.

———. 2006. *Migration and Citizenship: Legal Status, Rights and Political Participation.* Amsterdam: Amsterdam University Press.

Bauer, Thomas K., Magnus Lofstrom and Klaus F. Zimmermann. 2000. 'Immigration Policy, Assimilation of Immigrants and Natives' Sentiments towards Immigrants: Evidence from 12 OECD-Countries'. *Swedish Economic Policy Review* 7 (2): 11–53.

Bay, A.-H. Ann-Helén and Axel West Pedersen. 2006. 'The Limits of Social Solidarity: Basic Income, Immigration and the Legitimacy of the Universal Welfare State'. *Acta Sociologica* 49 (4): 419–36.

Bergh, Andreas. 2005. 'On the Counterfactual Problem of Welfare State Research: How Can We Measure Redistribution?' *European Sociological Review* 21 (4): 345–57.

Betcherman, Gordon. 2012. 'Labor Market Institutions: A Review of the Literature'. Policy Research Working Paper 6276, the World Bank.

Bevelander, Pieter and Ravi Pendakur. 2012. 'Citizenship, Co-Ethnic Populations, and Employment Probabilities of Immigrants in Sweden'. *Journal of International Migration and Integration* 13 (2): 203–22.

Blank, Rebecca. 1993. 'Why Were Poverty Rates So High in the 1980s?' In *Poverty and Prosperity in the Late Twentieth Century*, edited by Dimitri B. Papadimitriou and Edward N. Wolff, 21–55. London: Macmillan Press.

Blau, Francine D. and Lawrence M. Kahn. 2002. *At Home and Abroad: U.S. Labor Market Performance in International Perspective*. New York: Russell Sage Foundation.

Bloemraad, Irene. 2014. 'Commentary: A Restrictionist Shift That Matters'. In *Controlling Immigration: A Global Perspective*, edited by James F. Hollifield, Philip L. Martin and Pia M. Orrenius, 276–80. Stanford: Stanford University Press.

Bloemraad, Irene, Anna Korteweg and Gökçe Yurdakul. 2008. 'Citizenship and Immigration: Multiculturalism, Assimilation, and Challenges to the Nation-State'. *Annual Review of Sociology* 34 (1): 153–79.

Blume, Kræn, Björn Gustafsson, Peder J. Pedersen and Mette Verner. 2007. 'At the Lower End of the Table: Determinants of Poverty among Immigrants to Denmark and Sweden'. *Journal of Ethnic and Migration Studies* 33 (3): 373–96.

Boeri, Tito. 2009. 'Immigration to the Land of Redistribution'. IZA Discussion Paper No. 4273, Institute for the Study of Labor (IZA), Bonn.

Bommes, Michael and Andrew Geddes. 2000. *Immigration and the Welfare State: Challenging the Borders of the Welfare State*. London: Routledge.

Bonoli, Giuliano. 2005. 'The Politics of the New Social Policies: Providing Coverage against New Social Risks in Mature Welfare States'. *Policy & Politics* 33 (3): 431–49.

———. 2007. 'Time Matters: Postindustrialization, New Social Risks, and Welfare State Adaptation in Advanced Industrial Democracies'. *Comparative Political Studies* 40 (5): 495–520.

———. 2009. 'Varieties of Social Investment in Labour Market Policy'. In *What Future for Social Investment?*, edited by Nathalie Morel, Bruno Palier and Joakim Palme, 55–66. Stockholm: The Institute for Futures Studies.

Boräng, Frida. 2015. 'Large-Scale Solidarity? Effects of Welfare State Institutions on the Admission of Forced Migrants'. *European Journal of Political Research* 54 (2): 216–31.

Borjas, George J. 1989. 'Economic Theory and International Migration'. *International Migration Review* 23 (3): 457–85.

———. 1994. 'The Economics of Immigration'. *Journal of Economic Literature* 32 (4): 1667–717.

———. 1999. 'Immigration and Welfare Magnets'. *Journal of Labour Economics* 17 (4): 607–37.

Borjas, George J. and Lynette Hilton. 1996. 'Immigration and the Welfare State: Immigrant Participation in Means-Tested Entitlement Programs'. *The Quarterly Journal of Economics* 111 (2): 575–604.

Bradley, David, Evelyne Huber, Stephanie Moller, François Nielsen and John D. Stephens. 2003. 'Distribution and Redistribution in Postindustrial Democracies'. *World Politics*, Luxembourg Income Study Working Paper, 55 (2). Cambridge University Press: 193–228.

Bradshaw, Jonathan and Naomi Finch. 2010. 'Family Benefits and Services'. In *The Oxford Handbook of the Welfare State*, edited by Francis G. Castles, Stephan Leibfried, Jane Lewis, Herbert Obinger and Christopher Pierson, 462–78. Oxford: Oxford University Press.

Brady, David. 2003. 'The Politics of Poverty: Left Political Institutions, the Welfare State, and Poverty'. *Social Forces* 82 (2): 557–88.

———. 2009. *Rich Democracies, Poor People: How Politics Explain Poverty*. Oxford: Oxford University Press.

Brady, David and Ryan Finnigan. 2014. 'Does Immigration Undermine Public Support for Social Policy?' *American Sociological Review* 79 (1): 17–42.

Brady, David, Andrew S. Fullerton and Jennifer Moren Cross. 2009. 'Putting Poverty in Political Context: A Multi-Level Analysis of Adult Poverty across 18 Affluent Democracies'. *Social Forces* 88 (1): 271–99.

Braumoeller, Bear F. 2004. 'Hypothesis Testing and Multiplicative Interaction Terms'. *International Organization* 58 (4): 807–20.

Brochmann, Grete. 1999. 'The Mechanisms of Control'. In *Mechanisms of Immigration Control: A Comparative Analysis of European Regulation Policies*, edited by Grete Brochmann and Tomas Hammar, 1–27. Oxford: Berg.

———. 2014. 'Scandinavia. Governing Immigration in Advanced Welfare States'. In *Controlling Immigration: A Global Perspective*, edited by James F. Hollifield, Philip L. Martin and Pia M. Orrenius, 281–301. Stanford: Stanford University Press.

Brochmann, Grete and Anniken Hagelund. 2011. 'Migrants in the Scandinavian Welfare State'. *Nordic Journal of Migration Research* 1 (1): 13–24.

Brochmann, Grete and Tomas Hammar, eds. 1999. *Mechanisms of Immigration Control: A Comparative Analysis of European Regulation Policies*. Oxford: Berg.

Brubaker, Rogers. 1989. 'Membership without Citizenship: The Economic and Social Rights of Noncitizens'. In *Immigration and the Politics of Citizenship in Europe and North America*, edited by Rogers Brubaker, 145–62. Lanham, MD: University Press of America.

———. 1992. *Citizenship and Nationhood in France and Germany*. Cambridge, MA: Harvard University Press.

Brückner, Herbert, Gil S. Epstein, Barry McCormick, Gilles Saint-Paul, Alessandra Venturini and Klaus Zimmermann. 2002. 'Managing Migration in the European Welfare State'. In *Immigration Policy and the Welfare System*, edited by Tito

Boeri, Gordon Hanson and Barry McCormick, 1–167. Oxford: Oxford University Press.

Buhmann, Brigitte, Lee Rainwater, Guenther Schmaus and Timothy M. Smeeding. 1988. 'Equivalence Scales, Well-Being, Inequality, and Poverty: Sensitivity Estimates across Ten Countries Using the Luxembourg Income Study (LIS) Database'. *The Review of Income and Wealth* 34 (2): 115–42.

Bundesamt für Statistik. 2007. *Erhebung über die Einkommen und Lebensbedingungen (SILC) 2007.*

———. 2016. 'Ständige und Nichtständige Wohnbevölkerung nach Jahr, Kanton, Bevölkerungstyp, Geschlecht, Anwesenheitsbewilligung, Geburtsort und Alter'. Accessed 10 August 2016. https://www.bfs.admin.ch/bfs/de/home/statistiken/bevoelkerung/migration-integration.html.

Bundesregierung. 2016. 'Integrationsgesetz setzt auf Fördern und Fordern'. Accessed 8 August 2016. https://www.bundesregierung.de/Content/DE/Artikel/2016/08/2016-08-05-integrationsgesetz.html.

Burgoon, Brian. 2014. 'Immigration, Integration, and Support for Redistribution in Europe'. *World Politics* 66 (3): 365–405.

Butterwegge, Christoph and Caroline Reißlandt. 2005. 'Folgen der Hartz-Gesetze für Migrant(inn)en'. *Gesundheits- und Sozialpolitik* 59 (1): 20–24.

Cantillon, Bea. 2011. 'The Paradox of the Social Investment State: Growth, Employment and Poverty in the Lisbon Era'. *Journal of European Social Policy* 21 (5): 432–49.

Castles, Francis G. and Deborah Mitchell. 1993. 'Worlds of Welfare and Families of Nations'. In *Families of Nations: Patterns of Public Policy in Western Democracies*, edited by Francis G. Castles, 93–128. Aldershot, UK: Dartmouth.

Castles, Stephen and Mark J. Miller. 2009. *The Age of Migration: International Population Movements in the Modern World.* Basingstoke, UK: Palgrave Macmillan.

Causa, Orsetta and Sébastien Jean. 2007. 'Immigrants' Integration in OECD Countries: Do Policies Matter?' OECD Economics Department Working Papers, No. 564, OECD Publishing, Paris.

Cerna, Lucie. 2008. 'Towards an EU Blue Card? The Delegation of National High Skilled Immigration Policies to the EU Level'. COMPAS Working Paper No. 65, ESRC Centre on Migration, Policy and Society, University of Oxford.

Child Poverty Action Group. 2008. *Welfare Benefits and Tax Credits Handbook 2007/2008.* London: Child Poverty Action Group.

Chiswick, Barry R., Anh T. Le and Paul W. Miller. 2008. 'How Immigrants Fare across the Earnings Distribution in Australia and the United States'. *Industrial and Labor Relations Review* 61 (3): 353–73.

Chiswick, Barry R. and Paul W. Miller. 2015. 'International Migration and the Economics of Language'. In *Handbook of the Economics of International Migration* 1, edited by Barry R. Chiswick and Paul W. Miller, 211–69. Amsterdam: Elsevier.

Corrigan, Owen. 2014. 'Migrant Deprivation, Conditionality of Legal Status and the Welfare State'. *Journal of European Social Policy* 24 (3): 223–39.

Crepaz, Markus M. L. 2006. "If You Are My Brother, I May Give You a Dime!" Public Opinion on Multiculturalism, Trust, and the Welfare State'. In *Multiculturalism* and the Welfare State: Recognition and Redistribution in Contemporary Democracies, edited by Keith Banting and Will Kymlicka, 92–117. Oxford: Oxford University Press.

———. 2008. *Trust beyond Borders: Immigration, the Welfare State, and Identity in Modern Societies*. Ann Arbor: The University of Michigan Press.

Crepaz, Markus M. L. and Regan Damron. 2009. 'Constructing Tolerance. How the Welfare State Shapes Attitudes About Immigrants'. *Comparative Political Studies* 42 (3): 437–63.

Crettaz, Eric and Giuliano Bonoli. 2010. 'Why Are Some Workers Poor? The Mechanisms That Produce Working Poverty in a Comparative Perspective'. RECWOWE Working Paper, No. 12/2010, Reconciling Work and Welfare in Europe (REC-WOWE), Edinburgh.

Da Lomba, Sylvie. 2010. 'Legal Status and Refugee Integration: A UK Perspective'. *Journal of Refugee Studies* 23 (4): 415–36.

Damon, Arwa and Tim Hume. 2016. 'Denmark Adopts Controversial Law to Seize Asylum Seekers' Valuables'. *CNN*, 26 January.

Dancygier, Rafaela M. and David D. Laitin. 2014. 'Immigration into Europe: Economic Discrimination, Violence, and Public Policy'. *Annual Review of Political Science* 17 (1): 43–64. doi:10.1146/annurev-polisci-082012–115925.

Danziger, Sheldon H., Robert H. Haveman and Robert Plotnik. 1981. 'How Income Transfer Programs Affect Work, Savings and the Income Distribution: A Critical Review'. *Journal of Economic Literature* 19 (3): 975–1028.

Davidsson, Johan and Marek Naczyk. 2009. 'The Ins and Outs of Dualisation: A Literature Review'. RECWOWE Working Paper, No. 02/2009, Reconciling Work and Welfare in Europe (RECWOWE), Edinburgh.

Davy, Ulrike and Dilek Çınar. 2001. 'Deutschland'. In *Die Integration von Einwanderern. Rechtliche Regelungen im europäischen Vergleich*, 277–423. Frankfurt am Main: Campus Verlag.

Deutsches Rotes Kreuz. 2015. 'Änderungen im Familiennachzug nach dem AufenthG ab dem 01.08.2015'. Accessed July 29 2016. http://koelner-fluechtlingsrat.de/neu/userfiles/pdfs/2015-08-01Familiennachzug.pdf.

Dolado, Juan, Francis Kramarz, Stephen Machin, Alan Manning, David Margolis and Coen Teulings. 1996. 'The Economic Impact of Minimum Wages in Europe'. *Economic Policy* 11 (23): 317–72.

Donner, Piet Hein, Johan Remkes and Rita Verdonk. 2004. 'Justice and Home Affairs: Press Release 2618th Council Meeting', 19 November.

Dustmann, Christian and Arthur Van Soest. 2002. 'Language and the Earnings of Immigrants'. *Industrial and Labor Relations Review* 55 (3): 473–92.

Düvell, Franck. 2008. 'Clandestine Migration in Europe'. *Social Science Information* 47 (4): 479–97.

EC (European Commission). 2011. *Report from the Commission to the European Parliament and the Council on the Application of Directive 2003/109/EC Concerning the Status of Third-Country Nationals Who Are Long-Term Residents*. Brussels: European Commission.

Eger, Maureen A. 2010. 'Even in Sweden: The Effect of Immigration on Support for Welfare State Spending'. *European Sociological Review* 26 (2): 203–17.

Eichhorst, Werner and Paul Marx. 2012. 'Whatever Works: Dualization and the Service Economy in Bismarckian Welfare States'. In *The Age of Dualization*, edited by Patrick Emmenegger, Silja Häusermann, Bruno Palier and Martin Seeleib-Kaiser, 73–99. Oxford: Oxford University Press.

Emmenegger, Patrick and Romana Careja. 2011. 'The Politics of Inclusion and Exclusion: Social Policy, Migration Politics and Welfare State Nationalism'. In *Welfare Citizenship and Welfare Nationalism*, edited by Andrzej M. Suszycki, 155–90. Helsinki: Nordic Centre of Excellence NordWel.

———. 2012. 'From Dilemma to Dualization: Social and Migration Policies in the 'Reluctant Countries of Immigration'. In *The Age of Dualization*, edited by Patrick Emmenegger, Silja Häusermann, Bruno Palier and Martin Seeleib-Kaiser, 124–48. Oxford: Oxford University Press.

Emmenegger, Patrick, Silja Häusermann, Bruno Palier and Martin Seeleib-Kaiser, eds. 2012. *The Age of Dualization*. Oxford: Oxford University Press.

Emmenegger, Patrick and Robert Klemmensen. 2013. 'Immigration and Redistribution Revisited: How Different Motivations Can Offset Each Other'. *Journal of European Social Policy* 23 (4): 406–22.

Entzinger, Han and Renske Biezeveld. 2003. *Benchmarking in Immigrant Integration*. Rotterdam: European Research Centre on Migration and Ethnic Relations (ERCOMER).

Epstein, Gil S. 2009. 'Locational Choice, Ethnicity and Assimilation'. In *Handbook of Social Capital: The Troika of Sociology, Political Science and Economics*, edited by Gert Tingaard Svendsen and Gunnar Lind Haase Svendsen, 289–302. Cheltenham, UK: Edward Elgar.

EQUAL. 2007. 'Minimum Standards – and Beyond: The Contribution EQUAL to a Dignified Standard of Living for Asylum Seekers'. Background Paper for The European Policy Forum on Asylum, Malmö, Sweden, May 2007.

Esping-Andersen, Gøsta. 1990. *Three Worlds of Welfare Capitalism*. Cambridge, UK: Polity Press.

———. 1999. *Social Foundations of Postindustrial Economies*. Oxford: Oxford University Press.

Esping-Andersen, Gøsta and Jon Eivind Kolberg. 1992. 'Welfare States and Employment Regimes'. In *The Study of Welfare State Regimes*, edited by Jon Eivind Kolberg, 3–36. Armonk, NY: M. E. Sharpe.

Esser, Hartmut. 2001. 'Kulturelle Pluralisierung Und Strukturelle Assimilation: Das Problem Der Ethnischen Schichtung'. *Swiss Political Science Review* 7 (2): 97–108.

Esser, Hartmut. 2006. *Migration, Sprache und Integration*. Berlin: Arbeitsstelle Interkulturelle Konflikte und gesellschaftliche Integration (AKI), Wissenschaftszentrum Berlin für Sozialforschung (WZB).

Estevez-Abe, Margarita, Torben Iversen and David Soskice. 2001. 'Social Protection and the Formation of Skills: A Reinterpretation of the Welfare State'. In *Varieties of Capitalism: The Institutional Foundations of Comparative Advantage*, edited by Peter Hall and David Soskice, 145–83. Oxford: Oxford University Press.

Eugster, Beatrice. 2018. 'Immigrants and Poverty, and Conditionality of Immigrants' Social Rights'. *Journal of European Social Policy*. Advanced online publication. doi: 10.1177/0958928717753580.

Eurostat. 2013. 'EU Citizenship – Statistics on Cross-Border Activities'. Accessed 5 May 2017. http://ec.europa.eu/eurostat/statistics-explained/index.php/EU_citizenship_-_statistics_on_cross-border_activities.

Faist, Thomas. 1995. 'Ethnicization and Racialization of Welfare-State Politics in Germany and the USA'. *Ethnic and Racial Studies* 18 (2): 219–50.

Feld, Lars P. and Friedrich Schneider. 2010. 'Survey on the Shadow Economy and Undeclared Work in OECD Countries'. *German Economic Review* 11 (2): 109–49.

Fennema, Meindert. 2004. 'The Concept and Measurement of Ethnic Community'. *Journal of Ethnic and Migration Studies* 30 (3): 429–47.

Ferrera, Maurizio. 1996. 'The "Southern" Model of Welfare in Social Europe'. *Journal of European Public Policy* 6 (1): 17–37.

Flora, Peter and Jens Alber. 1981. 'Modernization, Democratization, and the Development of Welfare States in Western Europe'. In *The Development of Welfare States in Europe and America*, edited by Peter Flora and Arnold J. Heidenheimer, 37–80. New Brunswick, NJ: Transaction Books.

Fortin, Nicole M. and Thomas Lemieux. 1997. 'Institutional Changes and Rising Wage Inequality: Is There a Linkage?' *The Journal of Economic Perspectives* 11 (2): 75–96.

FRA (European Union Agency for Fundamental Rights). 2011. *Fundamental Rights of Migrants in an Irregular Situation in the European Union*. Luxembourg: Publications Office of the European Union.

Freeman, Gary P. 1986. 'Migration and the Political Economy of the Welfare State'. *Annals of the American Academy of Political and Social Science* 485 (1): 51–63.

———. 2004. 'Immigrant Incorporation in Western Democracies'. *International Migration Review* 38 (3): 945–69.

Freeman, Richard B. 2001. 'The Rising Tide Lifts . . .?' In *Understanding Poverty*, edited by Sheldon H. Danziger and Robert H. Haveman, 97–126. New York: Russell Sage Foundation.

Fritzell, Johan and Veli-Matti Ritakallio. 2010. 'Societal Shifts and Changed Patterns of Poverty'. *International Journal of Social Welfare* 19 (s1): 25–41.

Geddes, Andrew. 2003. 'Migration and the Welfare State in Europe'. *The Political Quarterly* 74 (s1): 150–62.

Geddes, Andrew and Daniel Wunderlich. 2009. 'Policies and "Outcomes" for Third-Country Nationals in Europe's Labour Market'. In *Legal Frameworks for the Integration of Third-Country Nationals*, edited by Jan Niessen and Thomas Huddleston, 195–218. Leiden: Martinus Nijhoff.

de Giorgi, Giacomo and Michele Pellizzari. 2006. 'Welfare Migration in Europe and the Cost of a Harmonised Social Assistance'. IZA Discussion Paper No. 2094, Institute for the Study of Labor (IZA), Bonn.

Glick Schiller, Nina and Ayse Çağlar. 2008. 'Beyond Methodological Ethnicity and towards City Scale: An Alternative Approach to Local and Transnational Pathways of Migrant Incorporation'. In *Rethinking Transnationalism: The Meso-Link of Organisations*, edited by Ludger Pries, 40–61. London: Routledge.

Goodman, Sara Wallace. 2010. 'Integration Requirements for Integration's Sake? Identifying, Categorising and Comparing Civic Integration Policies'. *Journal of Ethnic and Migration Studies* 36 (5): 753–72.

———. 2012. 'Measurement and Interpretation Issues in Civic Integration Studies: A Rejoinder'. *Journal of Ethnic and Migration Studies* 38 (1): 173–86.

Gornick, Janet C. and Markus Jäntti. 2012. 'Child Poverty in Cross-National Perspective: Lessons from the Luxembourg Income Study'. *Children and Youth Services Review* 34 (3): 558–68.

Gornick, Janet C., Marcia K. Meyers and Katherin E. Ross. 1997. 'Supporting the Employment of Mothers: Policy Variation across Fourteen Welfare States'. *Journal of European Social Policy* 7 (1): 45–70.

de Graaf-Zijl, Marloes and Brian Nolan. 2011. 'Household Joblessness and Its Impact on Poverty and Deprivation in Europe'. *Journal of European Social Policy* 21 (5): 413–31.

Gran, Brian K. and Elizabeth J. Clifford. 2000. 'Rights and Ratios? Evaluating the Relationship between Social Rights and Immigration'. *Journal of Ethnic and Migration Studies* 26 (3): 417–47.

Groenendijk, Kees. 2006. 'The Legal Integration of Potential Citizens: Denizens in the EU in the Final Years before the Implementation of the 2003 Directive on Long-Term Resident Third Country Nationals'. In *Acquisition and Loss of Nationality Policies and Trends in 15 European States. Volume 1: Comparative Analyses*, edited by Rainer Bauböck, Eva Ersbøll, Kees Groenendijk and Harald Waldrauch, 385–410. Amsterdam: Amsterdam University Press.

———. 2011. 'Pre-Departure Integration Strategies in the European Union: Integration or Immigration Policy?' *European Journal of Migration and Law* 13 (1): 1–30.

Guiraudon, Virginie. 1998. 'Citizenship Rights for Non-Citizens: France, Germany, and the Netherlands'. In *Challenge to the Nation-State: Immigration in Western Europe and the United States*, edited by Christian Joppke, 272–318. Oxford: Oxford University Press.

Gundersen, Craig and James P. Ziliak. 2004. 'Poverty and Macroeconomic Performance across Space, Race, and Family Structure'. *Demography* 41 (1): 61–86.

Hammar, Tomas. 1985. *European Immigration Policy: A Comparative Study*. Cambridge: Cambridge University Press.

———. 1990. *Democracy and the Nation State. Aliens, Denizens and Citizens in a World of International Migration*. Aldershot: Avebury.

Handlos, Line Neerup, Maria Kristiansen and Marie Norredam. 2016. 'Wellbeing or Welfare Benefits – what Are the Drivers for Migration?' *Scandinavian Journal of Public Health* 44 (2): 117–19.

Häusermann, Silja. 2010. *The Politics of Welfare State Reform in Continental Europe: Modernization in Hard Times*. Cambridge: Cambridge University Press.

Häusermann, Silja and Hanna Schwander. 2009. 'Identifying Outsiders across Countries: Similarities and Differences in the Patterns of Dualisation'. RECWOWE Working Paper, No. 09/2009, Reconciling Work and Welfare in Europe (RECWOWE), Edinburgh.

————. 2012. 'Varieties of Dualization. Labor Market Segmentation and Insider-Outsider Divides Across Regimes'. In *The Age of Dualization*, edited by Patrick Emmenegger, Silja Häusermann, Bruno Palier and Martin Seeleib-Kaiser, 27–51. Oxford: Oxford University Press.

Hawthorne, Lesleyanne. 2008. 'The Impact of Economic Selection Policy on Labour Market Outcomes for Degree-Qualified Migrants in Canada and Australia'. *IRPP Choices* 14 (5): 1–50.

Heckmann, Friedrich and Dominique Schnapper. 2003. *The Integration of Immigrants in European Societies: National Differences and Trends of Convergence*. Stuttgart: Lucius & Lucius.

Helbling, Marc. 2012. 'Public Debates, Integration Models, and Transnationalism in Western Europe'. *Journal of Immigrant & Refugee Studies* 10 (3): 241–59.

————. 2013. 'Validating Integration and Citizenship Policy Indices'. *Comparative European Politics* 11 (5): 555–76.

Helbling, Marc, Liv Bjerre, Friederike Römer and Malisa Zobel. 2013. 'The Immigration Policies in Comparison (IMPIC) Index: The Importance of a Sound Conceptualization'. *Migration and Citizenship* (Newsletter of the American Political Science Association. Organized Section on Migration and Citizenship) 1 (2): 8–14.

————. 2017. 'Measuring Immigration Policies: The IMPIC Database'. *European Political Science* 16 (1): 79–98.

Hicks, Alexander and Lane Kenworthy. 2003. 'Varieties of Welfare Capitalism'. *Socio-Economic Review* 1 (1): 27–61.

Hicks, Alexander and Duane Swank. 1984. 'On the Political Economy of Welfare Expansion. A Comparative Analysis of 18 Advanced Capitalist Democracies, 1960–1971'. *Comparative Political Studies* 17 (1): 81–119.

Hollifield, James F. 2004. 'The Emerging Migration State'. *International Migration Review* 38 (3): 885–912.

Hollifield, James F., Philip L. Martin and Pia M. Orrenius. 2014. 'The Dilemmas of Immigration Control'. In *Controlling Immigration: A Global Perspective*, edited by James F. Hollifield, Philip L. Martin and Pia M. Orrenius, 3–34. Stanford: Stanford University Press.

Hooijer, Gerda and Georg Picot. 2015. 'European Welfare States and Migrant Poverty: The Institutional Determinants of Disadvantage'. *Comparative Political Studies* 48 (14): 1879–1904.

Howard, Marc Morjé. 2009. *The Politics of Citizenship in Europe*. Cambridge: Cambridge University Press.

Huber, Evelyne and John D. Stephens. 2001. *Development and Crisis of the Welfare State: Parties and Policies in Global Markets*. Chicago: The University of Chicago Press.

Huddleston, Thomas, Jan Niessen, Eadaoin Ni Chaoimh and Emilie White. 2011. *Migrant Integration Policy Index III*. Brussels: British Council and Migration Policy Group.

IOM (International Organization for Migration). 2009. *International Migration Law N°16: Laws in the 27 EU Member States for Legal Immigration*. Geneva: International Organization for Migration.

Ireland, Patrick. 1994. *Becoming Europe: Immigration, Integration and the Welfare State*. Pittsburgh: University of Pittsburgh Press.

Iversen, Torben and Anne Wren. 1998. 'Equality, Employment, and Budgetary Restraint: The Trilemma of the Service Economy'. *World Politics* 50 (4): 507–46.

Jacobsen, Henriette. 2015. 'Sweden's New Migrant Restrictions Will Not Be in Place before 2016'. *EurActiv.com*, 28 October.

Jandl, Michael and Albert Kraler. 2006. 'Links Between Legal and Illegal Migration'. In *THESIM – Towards Harmonized European Statistics on International Migration*, edited by Michel Poulain, Nicolas Perrin, and Ann Singleton, 337–71. Louvain-la-Neuve: UCL Presses.

Joppke, Christian. 1999. 'How Immigration Is Changing Citizenship: A Comparative View'. *Ethnic Racial Studies* 22 (4): 629–52.

———. 2007a. 'Beyond National Models: Civic Integration Policies for Immigrants in Western Europe'. *West European Politics* 30 (1): 1–22.

———. 2007b. 'Transformation of Immigrant Integration: Civic Integration and Antidiscrimination in the Netherlands, France, and Germany'. *World Politics* 59 (2007): 243–73.

Kahanec, Martin and Anzelika Zaiceva. 2009. 'Labor Market Outcomes of Immigrants and Non-Citizens in the EU: An East-West Comparison'. *International Journal of Manpower* 30 (1/2): 97–115.

Kalter, Frank and Irena Kogan. 2014. 'Migrant Networks and Labor Market Integration of Immigrants from the Former Soviet Union in Germany'. *Social Forces* 92 (4): 1435–56. doi:10.1093/sf/sot155.

Kam, Cindy D. and Robert J. Franzese. 2007. *Modeling and Interpreting Interactive Hypotheses in Regression Analysis*. Ann Arbor: The University of Michigan Press.

Kenworthy, Lane. 1999. 'Do Social-Welfare Policies Reduce Poverty? A Cross-National Assessment'. *Social Forces* 77 (3): 1119–39.

———. 2001. 'Wage-Setting Measures: A Survey and Assessment'. *World Politics* 54 (1): 57–98.

———. 2011. *Progress for the Poor*. Oxford: Oxford University Press.

Kesler, Christel. 2006. 'Social Policy and Immigrant Joblessness in Britain, Germany, and Sweden'. *Social Forces* 85 (2): 743–70.

———. 2015. 'Welfare States and Immigrant Poverty: Germany, Sweden, and the United Kingdom in Comparative Perspective'. *Acta Sociologica* 58 (1): 39–61.

Kim, Hwanjoon. 2000. 'Anti-Poverty Effectiveness of Taxes and Income Transfers in Welfare States'. *International Social Security Review* 53 (4): 105–29.

King, Desmond and David Rueda. 2008. 'Cheap and Labor: The New Politics of 'Bread and Roses' in Industrial Democracies'. *Perspectives on Politics* 6 (2): 279–97.

Kingreen, Thorsten. 2010. *Soziale Rechte und Migration*. Baden-Baden: Nomos.

Kitschelt, Herbert and Anthony J. McGann. 1997. *The Radical Right in Western Europe: A Comparative Analysis*. Ann Arbor: University of Michigan Press.

Kogan, Irena. 2004. 'Last Hired, First Fired? The Unemployment Dynamics of Male Immigrants in Germany'. *European Sociological Review* 20 (5): 445–61.

———. 2006. 'Labor Markets and Economic Incorporation among Recent Immigrants in Europe'. *Social Forces* 85 (2): 697–721.

Koopmans, Ruud. 2010. 'Trade-Offs between Equality and Difference: Immigrant Integration, Multiculturalism and the Welfare State in Cross-National Perspective'. *Journal of Ethnic and Migration Studies* 36 (1): 1–26.

Koopmans, Ruud, Ines Michalowski and Stine Waibel. 2012. 'Citizenship Rights for Immigrants: National Political Processes and Cross-National Convergence in Western Europe, 1980–2008'. *American Journal of Sociology* 117 (4): 1202–45.

Koopmans, Ruud and Paul Statham. 2000. 'Migration and Ethnic Relations as a Field of Political Contention: An Opportunity Structure Approach'. In *Challenging Immigration and Ethnic Relations Politics: Comparative European Perspectives*, edited by Ruud Koopmans and Paul Statham, 13–56. Oxford: Oxford University Press.

Koopmans, Ruud, Paul Statham, Marco Giugni and Florence Passy. 2005. *Contested Citizenship: Immigration and Cultural Diversity in Europe*. Minneapolis: University of Minnesota Press.

Korpi, Walter. 1983. *The Democratic Class Struggle: Swedish Politics in a Comparative Perspective*. London: Routledge and Kegan Paul.

———. 2000. 'Faces of Inequality: Gender, Class, and Patterns of Inequalities in Different Types of Welfare States'. *Social Politics* 7 (2): 127–91.

Korpi, Walter and Joakim Palme. 1998. 'The Paradox of Redistribution and Strategies of Equality: Welfare State Institutions, Inequality, and Poverty in the Western Countries'. *American Sociological Review* 63 (5): 661–87.

Kovacheva, Vesela and Dita Vogel. 2009. 'The Size of the Irregular Foreign Resident Population in the European Union in 2002, 2005 and 2008: Aggregated Estimates'. Working Paper No.4, Hamburg Institute of International Economics. Database on Irregular Migration.

Kriesi, Hanspeter, Edgar Grande, Romain Lachat, Martin Dolezal, Simon Bornschier and Timotheos Frey. 2006. 'Globalization and the Transformation of the National Political Space: Six European Countries Compared'. *European Journal of Political Research* 45 (6): 921–56.

Kumlin, Staffan and Bo Rothstein. 2005. 'Making and Breaking Social Capital: The Impact of Welfare-State Institutions'. *Comparative Political Studies* 38 (4): 339–65.

Kymlicka, Will. 1995. *Multicultural Citizenship*. Oxford, UK: Clarendon Press.

Kyntäjä, Eve. 2003. 'Towards the Development of an Integration Policy in Finland'. In *The Integration of Immigrants in European Societies: National Differences and Trends of Convergence*, edited by Friedrich Heckmann and Dominique Schnapper, 185–211. Stuttgart: Lucius & Lucius.

Lalive, Rafael and Josef Zweimüller. 2009. 'How Does Parental Leave Affect Fertility and Return to Work? Evidence from Two Natural Experiments'. *The Quarterly Journal of Economics* 124 (3): 1363–1402.

Larsen, Christian Albrekt. 2008. 'The Institutional Logic of Welfare Attitudes: How Welfare Regimes Influence Public Support'. *Comparative Political Studies* 41 (2): 145–68.

Layton-Henry, Zig, ed. 1990. *The Political Rights of Migrant Workers in Western Europe*. London: SAGE.

Leibfried, Stephan. 1992. 'Towards a European Welfare State? On Integrating Poverty Regimes into the European Community'. In *Social Policy in a Changing Europe*, edited by Zsuzsa Ferge and Jon Eivind Kolberg, 245–79. Frankfurt am Main: Campus Verlag.

Leigh, Andrew. 2007. 'Does Raising the Minimum Wage Help the Poor?' *The Economic Record* 83 (263): 432–45.

Lewin-Epstein, Noah, Moshe Semyonov, Irena Kogan and Richard A. Wanner. 2003. 'Institutional Structure and Immigrant Integration: A Comparative Study of Immigrants' Labor Market Attainment in Canada and Israel'. *International Migration Review* 37 (2): 389–420.

Lewis, Jane. 1992. 'Gender and the Development of Welfare Regimes'. *Journal of European Social Policy* 2 (3): 159–73.

———. 1997. 'Gender and Welfare Regimes: Further Thoughts'. *Social Politics: International Studies in Gender, State & Society* 4 (2): 160–77.

Liebig, Thomas. 2009. 'Jobs for Immigrants: Labour Market Integration in Norway'. OECD Social, Employment and Migration Working Papers, No. 94, OECD Publishing, Paris.

Lohmann, Henning. 2009. 'Welfare States, Labour Market Institutions and the Working Poor: A Comparative Analysis of 20 European Countries'. *European Sociological Review* 25 (4): 489–504.

Lucassen, Leo. 2006. 'Poles and Turks in the German Ruhr Area: Similarities and Differences'. In *Paths of Integration: Migrants in Western Europe (1880–2004)*, edited by Leo Lucassen, David Feldman and Jochen Oltmer, 27–45. Amsterdam: Amsterdam University Press.

Maas, Cora J. and Joop J. Hox. 2005. 'Sufficient Sample Sizes for Multilevel Modeling'. *Methodology* 1 (3): 86–92.

Maas, Willem. 2014. 'The Netherlands. Consensus and Contention in a Migration State'. In *Controlling Immigration: A Global Perspective*, edited by James F. Hollifield, Philip L. Martin and Pia M. Orrenius, 257–75. Stanford: Stanford University Press.

Machin, Stephen, Alan Manning and Lupin Rahman. 2003. 'Where the Minimum Wage Bites Hard: Introduction of Minimum Wages to a Low Wage Sector'. *Journal of European Economic Association* 1 (1): 154–80.

Mahnig, Hans. 2001. 'Die Debatte um die Eingliederung von Migranten oder: was ist das Ziel von "Integrationspolitik" in liberalen Demokratien?' *Swiss Political Science Review* 7 (2): 124–30.

Mahnig, Hans and Andreas Wimmer. 2000. 'Country-Specific or Convergent? A Typology of Immigrant Policies in Western Europe'. *Journal of International Migration and Integration* 1 (2): 177–204.

———. 2003. 'Integration without Immigrant Policy: The Case of Switzerland'. In *The Integration of Immigrants in European Societies: National Differences and Trends of Convergence*, edited by Friedrich Heckmann and Dominique Schnapper, 135–64. Stuttgart: Lucius & Lucius.

Mandel, Hadas and Moshe Semyonov. 2005. 'Family Policies, Wage Structures, and Gender Gaps: Sources of Earnings Inequality in 20 Countries'. *American Sociological Review* 70 (6): 949–67.

Manning, Patrick. 2005. *Migration in World History*. New York: Routledge.

Manow, Philip, Bruno Palier and Hanna Schwander. 2018. *Worlds of Welfare Capitalism and Electoral Politics*. Oxford: Oxford University Press.

Marchal, Sarah, Ive Marx and Natascha Van Mechelen. 2014. 'The Great Wake-Up Call? Social Citizenship and Minimum Income Provisions in Europe in Times of Crisis'. *Journal of Social Policy* 43 (2): 247–67.

Marshall, Thomas H. 1950. *Citizenship and Social Class and Other Essays*. Cambridge: Cambridge University Press.

Martin, John P. and David Grubb. 2001. 'What Works and for Whom: A Review of OECD Countries' Experiences with Active Labour Market Policies'. *Swedish Economic Policy Review* 8 (2): 9–56.

Marx, Ive, Lina Salanauskaite and Gerlinde Verbist. 2013. 'The Paradox of Redistribution Revisited: And That It May Rest in Peace?' IZA Discussion Paper No. 7414, Institute for the Study of Labor (IZA), Bonn.

Mau, Steffen and Christoph Burkhardt. 2009. 'Migration and Welfare State Solidarity in Western Europe'. *Journal of European Social Policy* 19 (3): 213–29.

Menz, Georg. 2004. 'Migration and the European Social Model'. Maxwell European Union Center/Luxembourg Income Study Working Conference, Luxembourg, July 2004.

Mewes, Jan and Steffen Mau. 2012. 'Unraveling Working-Class Welfare Chauvinism'. In *Contested Welfare States. Welfare Attitudes in Europe and Beyond*, edited by Stefan Svallfors, 119–57. Stanford: Stanford University Press.

Meyer, Bruce D. and James X. Sullivan. 2013. 'Winning the War: Poverty from the Great Society to the Great Recession'. NBER Working Paper No. 18718, National Bureau of Economic Research, Massachusetts, MA.

Miller, David. 1995. *On Nationality*. Oxford, UK: Clarendon Press.

Misra, Joya, Stephanie Moller and Michelle J. Budig. 2007. 'Work – Family Policies and Poverty for Partnered and Single Women in Europe and North America'. *Gender & Society* 21 (6): 804–27.

Misra, Joya, Stephanie Moller, Eiko Strader and Elizabeth Wemlinger. 2012. 'Family Policies, Employment and Poverty among Partnered and Single Mothers'. *Research in Social Stratification and Mobility* 30 (1). Elsevier Ltd: 113–28.

MISSOC (Mutual Information System on Social Protection). 2007. 'MISSOC Comparative Tables Database'. Accessed 25 May 2012. http://www.missoc.org/MISSOC/INFORMATIONBASE/COMPARATIVETABLES/MISSOCDATABASE/comparativeTableSearch.jsp.

Mitchell, Deborah. 1991. *Income Transfer in Ten Welfare States*. Aldershot, UK: Avebury.

Moller, Stephanie, Evelyne Huber, John D. Stephens, David Bradley and François Nielsen. 2003. 'Determinants of Relative Poverty in Advanced Capitalist Democracies'. *American Journal of Sociology* 68 (1): 22–51.

Morel, Nathalie, Bruno Palier and Joakim Palme, eds. 2012. *Towards a Social Investment Welfare State? Ideas, Policies and Challenges*. Bristol, UK: Policy Press.

Morissens, Ann and Diane Sainsbury. 2005. 'Migrants' Social Rights, Ethnicity and Welfare Regimes'. *Journal of Social Policy* 34 (4): 637–60.

Morris, Lydia. 2002. *Managing Migration: Civic Stratification and Migrants' Rights*. New York: Routledge.

———. 2003. 'Managing Contradiction: Civic Stratification and Migrants' Rights'. *International Migration Review* 37 (1): 74–100.

Müller, Kai-Uwe and Viktor Steiner. 2008. 'Would a Legal Minimum Wage Reduce Poverty? A Microsimulation Study for Germany'. IZA Discussion Paper No. 3491, Institute for the Study of Labor (IZA), Bonn.

Multiculturalism Policy Index. 2011. Accessed July 4, 2014. http://www.queensu.ca/mcp/home.

Myles, John. 1984. *Old Age and the Welfare State: The Political Economy of Public Pensions*. Boston: Little Brown.

Myles, John and Sébastien St-Arnaud. 2006. 'Population Diversity, Multiculturalism, and the Welfare State: Should the Welfare State Theory Be Revised?' In *Multiculturalism and the Welfare State: Recognition and Redistribution in Contemporary Democracies*, edited by Keith Banting and Will Kymlicka, 339–54. Oxford: Oxford University Press.

Nannestad, Peter. 2007. 'Immigration and Welfare States: A Survey of 15 Years of Research'. *Journal of Political Economy* 23 (2): 512–32.

National Immigration Law Center. 2002. *Guide to Immigrant Eligibility for Federal Programs*. Los Angeles: National Immigration Law Center.

Nelson, Kenneth. 2004. 'Mechanisms of Poverty Alleviation: Anti-Poverty Effects of Non-Means-Tested and Means-Tested Benefits in Five Welfare States'. *Journal of European Social Policy* 14 (4): 371–90.

———. 2007. *Introducing SaMip: The Social Assistance and Minimum Income Protection Interim Dataset*. Version 2.5 Beta. October 2010. S-WoPEc No. 11/2007. Swedish Institute for Social Research.

———. 2010. 'Social Assistance and Minimum Income Benefits in Old and New EU Democracies'. *International Journal of Social Welfare* 19 (4): 367–78.

———. 2011. 'Social Assistance and EU Poverty Thresholds 1990–2008: Are European Welfare Systems Providing Just and Fair Protection against Low Income?' *European Sociological Review* 29 (2): 386–401.

———. 2012. 'Counteracting Material Deprivation: The Role of Social Assistance in Europe'. *Journal of European Social Policy* 22 (2): 148–63.

Neumark, David and William Wascher. 2002. 'Do Minimum Wages Fight Poverty?' *Economic Inquiry* 40 (3): 315–33.

———. 2007. 'Minimum Wages and Employment'. IZA Discussion Paper No. 2570, Institute for the Study of Labor (IZA), Bonn.

Niessen, Jan, Thomas Huddleston, Laura Citron, Andrew Geddes and Dirk Jacobs. 2007. *Migrant Integration Policy Index*. Brussels: British Council and Migration Policy Group.

Nolan, Brian and Christopher T. Whelan. 2010. 'Using Non-Monetary Deprivation Indicators to Analyze Poverty and Social Exclusion: Lessons from Europe?' *Journal of Policy Analysis and Management* 29 (2): 305–25.

Obućina, Ognjen. 2014. 'Paths Into and Out of Poverty among Immigrants in Sweden'. *Acta Sociologica* 57 (1): 5–23.

Ochel, Wolfgang. 2008. 'The Political Economy of Two-Tier Reforms of Employment Protection in Europe'. CESifo Working Paper No. 2461, CESifo Group, München.

O'Connor, Julia S. 1993. 'Gender, Class and Citizenship in the Analysis of Welfare State Regimes: Theoretical and Methodological Issues'. *The British Journal of Sociology* 44 (3): 501–18.

OECD. 1998. 'Making the Most of the Minimum: Statutory Minimum Wages, Employment and Poverty'. In *Employment Outlook 1998*, 31–79. Paris: OECD Publishing.

———. 2006. *International Migration Outlook*. Paris: OECD Publishing.

———. 2007a. *Babies and Bosses. Reconciling Work and Family Life. A Synthesis of Findings for OECD Countries*. Paris: OECD Publishing.

———. 2007b. 'Benefits and Wages: Country Specific Information'. Paris: OECD Publishing. Accessed February 24, 2012. http://www.oecd.org/els/soc/benefits-and-wages-country-specific-information.htm.

———. 2007c. *International Migration Outlook*. Paris: OECD Publishing.

———. 2008. *International Migration Outlook*. Paris: OECD Publishing.

———. 2009. *International Migration Outlook. SOPEMI 2009. Special Focus: Managing Labour Migration Beyond the Crisis*. Paris: OECD Publishing.

———. 2010. *International Migration Outlook*. Paris: OECD Publishing.

———. 2011. *Doing Better for Families*. Paris: OECD Publishing.

———. 2012a. *Economic Policy Growth 2012. Going for Growth*. Paris: OECD Publishing.

———. 2012b. *Settling In. OECD Indicators of Immigrant Integration 2012*. Paris: OECD Publishing.

———. 2013a. 'Factbook 2013. Economic, Environmental and Social Statistics'. Accessed October 1, 2015, http://dx.doi.org/10.1787/factbook-2013-en.

———. 2013b. *International Migration Outlook*. Paris: OECD Publishing.

———. 2015a. *In It Together. Why Less Inequality Benefits All*. Paris: OECD Publishing.

———. 2015b. *International Migration Outlook*. Paris: OECD Publishing.

———. 2015c. 'OECD.Stat'. Accessed 29 September 2015. http://stats.oecd.org/.

———. 2016. *International Migration Outlook*. Paris: OECD Publishing.

Orloff, Ann. 1993. 'Gender and the Social Rights of Citizenship: The Comparative Analysis of Gender Relations and Welfare States'. *American Sociological Review* 58 (2): 303–28.

Orrenius, Pia M. and Madeline Zavodny. 2008. 'The Effect of Minimum Wages on Immigrants' Employment and Earnings'. *Industrial and Labor Relations Review* 61 (4): 544–63.

Pager, Devah and Hana Shepherd. 2008. 'The Sociology of Discrimination: Racial Discrimination in Employment, Housing, Credit, and Consumer Markets'. *Annual Review of Sociology* 34: 181–209.

Pennings, Frans. 2003. *Introduction to European Social Security Law*. Antwerp: Intersentia.

Perrin, Guy. 1969. 'Reflections on Fifty Years of Social Security'. *International Labour Review* 99 (3): 249–92.

Peters, Margaret E. 2015. 'Open Trade, Closed Borders: Immigration Policy in the Era of Globalization'. *World Politics* 67 (1): 114–54.

Pfeifer, Michaela. 2012. 'Comparing Unemployment Protection and Social Assistance in 14 European Countries: Four Worlds of Protection for People of Working Age'. *International Journal of Social Welfare* 21 (1): 13–25.

Pierson, Paul. 2001. 'Coping with Permanent Austerity: Welfare State Restructuring in Affluent Democracies'. In *The New Politics of Welfare State*, edited by Paul Pierson, 410–56. Oxford: Oxford University Press.

Pontusson, Jonas, David Rueda and Christopher R. Way. 2002. 'Comparative Political Economy of Wage Distribution: The Role of Partisanship and Labour Market Institutions'. *British Journal of Political Science* 32 (2): 281–308.

Poptcheva, Eva-Maria and Andrej Stuchlik. 2015. *Work and Social Welfare for Asylum-Seekers and Refugees: Selected EU Member States*. European Union: EPRS | European Parliamentary Research Service.

Portes, Alejandro. 1998. 'Social Capital: Its Origins and Applications in Modern Sociology'. *Annual Review of Sociology* 24 (1): 1–24.

Poulain, Michel and Anne Herm. 2010. 'Population Stocks Relevant to International Migration'. Working Paper No. 11, Promoting Comparative Quantitative Research in the Field of Migration and Integration in Europe (PROMINSTAT).

Quintini, Glenda and Anne Saint-Martin. 2004. 'Employment Protection Regulation and Labour Market Performance'. In *OECD Employment Outlook*, edited by OECD, 61–125. Paris: OECD Publishing.

Rabe-Hesketh, Sophia and Anders Skrondal. 2012. *Multilevel and Longitudinal Modeling Using Stata*, 3rd Edition. College Station, TX: Stata Press.

Ravallion, Martin. 2001. 'Growth, Inequality and Poverty: Looking Beyond Averages'. *World Development* 29 (11): 1803–15.

Razin, Assaf and Jackline Wahba. 2015. 'Welfare Magnet Hypothesis, Fiscal Burden, and Immigration Skill Selectivity'. *Scandinavian Journal of Economics* 117 (2): 369–402.

Reeskens, Tim and Wim Van Oorschot. 2012. 'Disentangling the "New Liberal Dilemma": On the Relation between General Welfare Redistribution Preferences and Welfare Chauvinism'. *International Journal of Comparative Sociology* 53 (2): 120–39.

Römer, Friederike. 2017. 'Generous to All or "Insiders Only"? The Relationship between Welfare State Generosity and Immigrant Welfare Rights'. *Journal of European Social Policy* 27 (2): 173–96.

Romero-Ortuño, Román. 2004. 'Access to Health Care for Illegal Immigrants in the EU: Should We Be Concerned?' *European Journal of Health Law* 11: 245–72.

Rothstein, Bo. 1998. *Just Institutions Matter*. New York: Cambridge University Press.

Rueda, David and Jonas Pontusson. 2000. 'Wage Inequality and Varieties of Capitalism'. *World Politics* 52 (3): 350–83.

Ruhs, Martin. 2009. 'Migrant Rights, Immigration Policy and Human Development'. MPRA Paper No. 19206, Munich Personal RePEc Archive.

———. 2011. 'Openness, Skills and Rights: An Empirical Analysis of Labour High- and Middle-Income Countries'. COMPAS Working Paper No. 88, ESRC Centre on Migration, Policy and Society, University of Oxford.

———. 2013. *The Price of Rights: Regulating International Labor Migration*. Princeton, NJ: Princeton University Press.

———. 2015. 'Is Unrestricted Immigration Compatible with Inclusive Welfare States? The (Un)sustainability of EU Exceptionalism'. COMPAS Working Paper No. 125, ESRC Centre on Migration, Policy and Society, University of Oxford.

Rycx, François and Stephan Kampelmann. 2012. *Who Earns Minimum Wages in Europe? New Evidence Based on Household Surveys*. Brussels: ETUI aisbl.

Ryner, Magnus. 2000. 'European Welfare State Transformation and Migration'. In *Immigration and Welfare: Challenging the Borders of the Welfare State*, edited by Michael Bommes and Andrew Geddes, 51–71. London: Routledge.

Safran, William. 1997. 'Citizenship and Nationality in Democratic Systems: Approaches to Defining and Acquiring Membership in the Political Community'. *International Political Science Review* 18 (3): 313–35.

Sainsbury, Diane. 1994. *Gendering Welfare States*. London: SAGE.

———. 1996. *Gender, Equality, and Welfare States*. Cambridge: Cambridge University Press.

———. 1999. 'Gender, Policy Regimes, and Politics'. In *Gender and Welfare State Regimes*, edited by Diane Sainsbury, 245–75. Oxford: Oxford University Press.

———. 2006. 'Immigrants' Social Rights in Comparative Perspective: Welfare Regimes, Forms of Immigration and Immigration Policy Regimes'. *Journal of European Social Policy* 16 (3): 229–44.

———. 2012. *Welfare States and Immigrant Rights: The Politics of Inclusion and Exclusion*. Oxford: Oxford University Press.

Sainsbury, Diane and Ann Morissens. 2002. 'Poverty in Europe in the Mid-1990s: The Effectiveness of Means-Tested Benefits'. *Journal of European Social Policy* 12 (4): 307–27.

Scholten, Peter W. A., Han Entzinger, Eleonore Kofman, Elena Vacchelli, Albert Kraler, Christina Hollomey and Claudia Brechner. 2011. *Integration from Abroad? Perception and Impacts of Pre-Entry Tests for Third Country Nationals*. Final report of PROSINT Workpackage 4.

Schröder, Lena. 2010. 'Labour Market Characteristics and Their Impact on the Integration of Immigrants' Offspring'. In *Equal Opportunities? The Labour Market Integration of the Children of Immigrants*, edited by OECD, 129–60. Paris: OECD Publishing.

Scruggs, Lyle. 2004. *Welfare Entitlements Data Set: A Comparative Institutional Analysis of Eighteen Welfare States*. Version 1.2. Accessed 25 December 2011. http://sp.uconn.edu/~scruggs/ wp.htm.

———. 2006. 'The Generosity of Social Insurance, 1971–2002'. *Oxford Review of Economic Policy* 22 (3): 349–64.

Scruggs, Lyle and James P. Allan. 2006. 'The Material Consequences of Welfare States: Benefit Generosity and Absolute Poverty in 16 OECD Countries'. *Comparative Political Studies* 39 (7): 800–904.

Sides, John and Jack Citrin. 2007. 'European Opinion About Immigration: The Role of Identities, Interests and Information'. *British Journal of Political Science* 37 (3): 477–504.

Sjöberg, Ola. 2000. 'Unemployment and Unemployment Benefits in the OECD 1960–1990: An Empirical Test of Neo-Classical Economic Theory'. *Work, Employment & Society* 14 (1): 51–76.

Sjöberg, Ola, Joakim Palme and Eero Caroll. 2010. 'Unemployment Insurance'. In *The Oxford Handbook of the Welfare State*, edited by Francis G. Castles, Stephan Leibfried, Jane Lewis, Herbert Obinger and Christopher Pierson, 420–34. Oxford: Oxford University Press.

Snijders, Tom A. and Roel J. Bosker. 2012. *Multilevel Analysis*, 2nd Edition. London: SAGE.

Sorensen, Ted. 2008. *Counselor: A Life at the Edge of History*. New York: Harper.

Soroka, Stuart, Keith Banting and Richard Johnston. 2006. 'Immigration and Redistribution in a Global Era'. In *Globalization and Egalitarian Redistribution*, edited by Sam Bowles, Pranab Bardhan and Michael Wallerstein, 261–88. Princeton, NJ: Princeton University Press.

Soysal, Yasemin Nuhoğlu. 1994. *Limits of Citizenship. Migrants and Postnational Membership in Europe*. Chicago and London: The University of Chicago Press.

———. 2012. 'Citizenship, Immigration, and the European Social Project: Rights and Obligations of Individuality'. *British Journal of Sociology* 63 (1): 1–21.

SSA (Social Security Administration). 2006. *Social Security Programs throughout the World: Europe, 2006*. Washington, DC: Government Printing Office.

———. 2007. *Social Security Programs Throughout the World: The Americas, 2007*. Washington, DC: Government Printing Office.

Starke, Peter. 2006. 'The Politics of Welfare State Retrenchment: A Literature Review'. *Social Policy & Administration* 40 (1): 104–20.

Steenbergen, Marco R. and Bradford S. Jones. 2002. 'Modeling Multilevel Data Structures'. *American Journal of Political Science* 46 (1): 218–37.

Stephens, John D. 1979. *The Transition from Capitalism to Socialism*. London: Macmillan Press.

———. 2010. 'The Social Rights of Citizenship'. In *The Oxford Handbook of the Welfare State*, edited by Francis G. Castles, Stephan Leibfried, Jane Lewis, Herbert Obinger and Christopher Pierson, 511–25. Oxford: Oxford University Press.

Svallfors, Stefan. 2012. 'Welfare States and Welfare Attitudes'. In *Contested Welfare States: Welfare Attitudes in Europe and Beyond*, edited by Stefan Svallfors, 1–24. Stanford: Stanford University Press.

Taylor-Gooby, Peter. 2005. 'Is the Future American? Or, Can Left Politics Preserve European Welfare States from Erosion through Growing Diversity?' *Journal of Social Policy* 34 (4): 661.

Thévenon, Olivier. 2011. 'Family Policies in OECD Countries: A Comparative Analysis'. *Population and Development Review* 37 (1): 57–87.

Titmus, Richard M. 1974. *Social Policy*. London: Allen & Unwin.

Travis, Alan. 2015. 'Asylum Seekers with Children to Have Support Payments Cut'. *The Guardian*, July 16.

Van der Waal, Jeroen, Peter Achterberg, Dick Houtman, Willem de Koster and Katerina Manevska. 2010. ' "Some Are More Equal Than Others": Economic Egalitarianism and Welfare Chauvinism in the Netherlands'. *Journal of European Social Policy* 20 (4): 350–63.

Van der Waal, Jeroen, Willem De Koster and Wim Van Oorschot. 2013. 'Three Worlds of Welfare Chauvinism? How Welfare Regimes Affect Support for Distributing Welfare to Immigrants in Europe'. *Journal of Comparative Policy Analysis* 15 (2): 164–81.

Van Hook, Jennifer, Susan K. Brown and Frank D. Bean. 2006. 'For Love or Money? Welfare Reform and Immigrant Naturalisation'. *Social Forces* 85 (2): 643–66.

Van Kersbergen, Kees, Barbara Vis and Anton Hemerijck. 2014. 'The Great Recession and Welfare State Reform: Is Retrenchment Really the Only Game Left in Town?' *Social Policy & Administration* 48 (7): 883–904.

Van Lancker, Wim. 2014. *To Whose Benefit? An Empirical and Comparative Investigation into the (Un)intended Consequences of Family Policy in the Social Investment State*. Brussels: University Press Antwerp.

Van Oorschot, Wim. 2006. 'Making the Difference in Social Europe: Deservingness Perceptions among Citizens of European Welfare States'. *Journal of European Social Policy* 16 (1): 23–42.

———. 2008. 'Solidarity towards Immigrants in European Welfare States'. *International Journal of Social Welfare* 17 (1): 3–14.

Van Oorschot, Wim and Wilfred Uunk. 2007. 'Welfare Spending and the Public's Concern for Immigrants. Multilevel Evidence for Eighteen European Countries'. *Comparative Politics* 40 (1): 63–82.

Van Tubergen, Frank, Ineke Maas and Henk Flap. 2004. 'The Economic Incorporation of Immigrants in 18 Western Societies: Origin, Destination, and Community Effects'. *American Sociological Review* 69 (5): 704–27.

Vis, Barbara, Kees van Kersbergen and Tom Hylands. 2011. 'To What Extent Did the Financial Crisis Intensify the Pressure to Reform the Welfare State?' *Social Policy & Administration* 45 (4): 338–53.

Visser, Jelle. 2013. *ICTWSS Database, Database on Institutional Characteristics of Trade Unions, Wage Setting, State Intervention and Social Pacts in 34 Countries between 1960 and 2010*. Version 4.1. Amsterdam: Institute for Advanced Labour Studies, AIAS, University of Amsterdam.

Vogel, Dita. 2009. 'Comparative Policy Brief – Size of Irregular Migration'. *Size and Development of Irregular Migration to the EU – CLANDESTIO Research Project – Counting the Uncountable: Data and Trends across Europe.*

Vollmer, Bastian. 2009. 'Comparative Policy Brief – Political Discourses'. *Political Discourses on Irregular Migration in the EU – CLANDESTIO Research Project – Counting the Uncountable: Data and Trends across Europe.*

Wallerstein, Michael. 1999. 'Wage-Setting Institutions and Pay Inequality in Advanced Industrial Societies'. *American Journal of Political Science* 43 (3): 649–80.

Whelan, Christopher T. and Bertrand Maître. 2007. 'Measuring Material Deprivation with EU-SILC: Lessons from the Irish Survey'. *European Societies* 9 (2): 147–73.

————. 2010. 'Welfare Regime and Social Class Variation in Poverty and Economic Vulnerability in Europe: An Analysis of EU-SILC'. *Journal of European Social Policy* 20 (4): 316–32.

Wilensky, Harold L. 1975. *The Welfare State and Equality: Structural and Ideological Roots of Public Expenditures*. Berkeley: University of California Press.

Wimmer, Andreas. 1998. 'Binnenintegration und Aussenabschliessung. Zur Beziehung zwischen Wohlfahrtsstaat und Migrationssteuerung in der Schweiz des 20. Jahrhunderts'. In *Migration in Nationalen Wohlfahrtsstaaten. Theoretische und Vergleichende Untersuchungen*, edited by Michael Bommes and Jost Halfmann, 199–221. Osnabrück: Universitätsverlag Rasch.

Wimmer, Andreas and Nina Glick Schiller. 2003. 'Methodological Nationalism, the Social Sciences, and the Study of Migration: An Essay in Historical Epistemology'. *International Migration Review* 37 (3): 576–610.

Wolfe, Richard G and Jennifer L Dunn. 2003. 'The Jackknife and Multilevel Modeling: A New Application of an Old Trick'. *The Alberta Journal of Educational Research* XLIX (3): 252–63.

WVS (World Values Survey). 2014. 'World Values Survey 2005–2008 OFFICIAL AGGREGATE v.20140429'. Accessed 25 May 2017. www.worldvaluessurvey. org.

Yao, Yuxin and Jan C. Van Ours. 2015. 'Language Skills and Labor Market Performance of Immigrants in the Netherlands'. *Labour Economics* 34: 76–85.

Zweimüller, Josef. 2000. 'Inequality, Redistribution, and Economic Growth'. *Empirica* 27 (1): 1–20.

Index

Page references for figures are italicized

About the Author

Beatrice Eugster is Post-Doctoral Researcher at the Department of Social Science, University of Bern, Switzerland.

www.ingramcontent.com/pod-product-compliance
Lightning Source LLC
Chambersburg PA
CBHW021812270326
41932CB00007B/150